Oskar von Miller Forum
Thomas Herzog Ed.

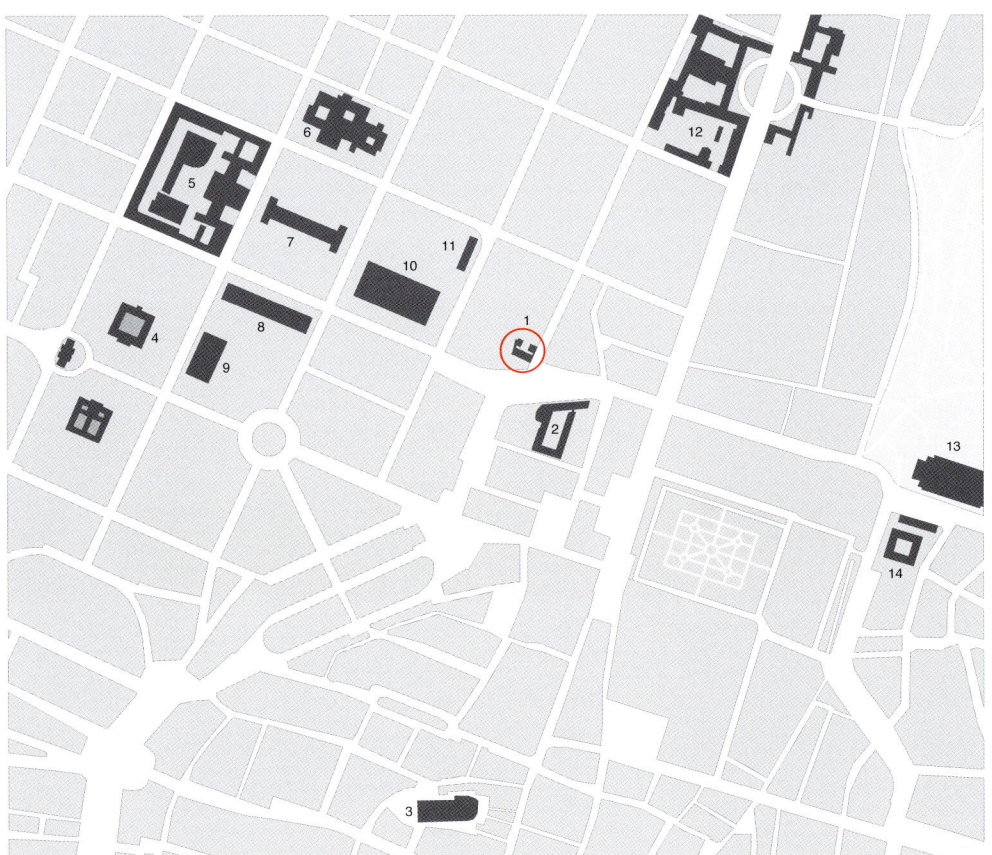

1. Oskar von Miller Forum
2. Siemens Forum
3. Dom
4. Glyptothek
5. Technische Universität
6. Neue Pinakothek
7. Alte Pinakothek
8. Museum ägyptischer Kunst und Hochschule für Film und Fernsehen
9. Musikhochschule
10. Pinakothek der Moderne
11. Museum Brandhorst
12. Ludwig-Maximilians-Universität
13. Haus der Kunst
14. Oberste Baubehörde

1. Oskar von Miller Forum
2. Siemens Forum
3. Cathedral
4. Glyptothek
5. Technische Universität München
6. Neue Pinakothek
7. Alte Pinakothek
8. Museum of Egyptian Art and University for Film and Television
9. University College of Music
10. Pinakothek der Moderne
11. Museum Brandhorst
12. Ludwig-Maximilian University
13. Haus der Kunst
14. Chief Building Authority

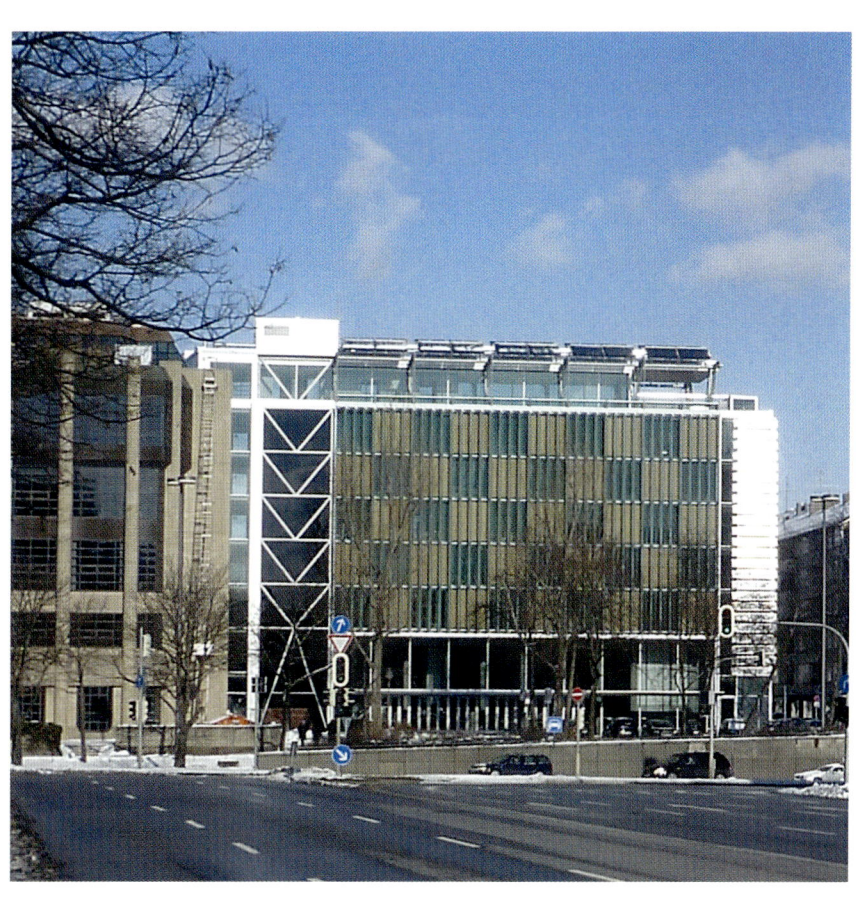

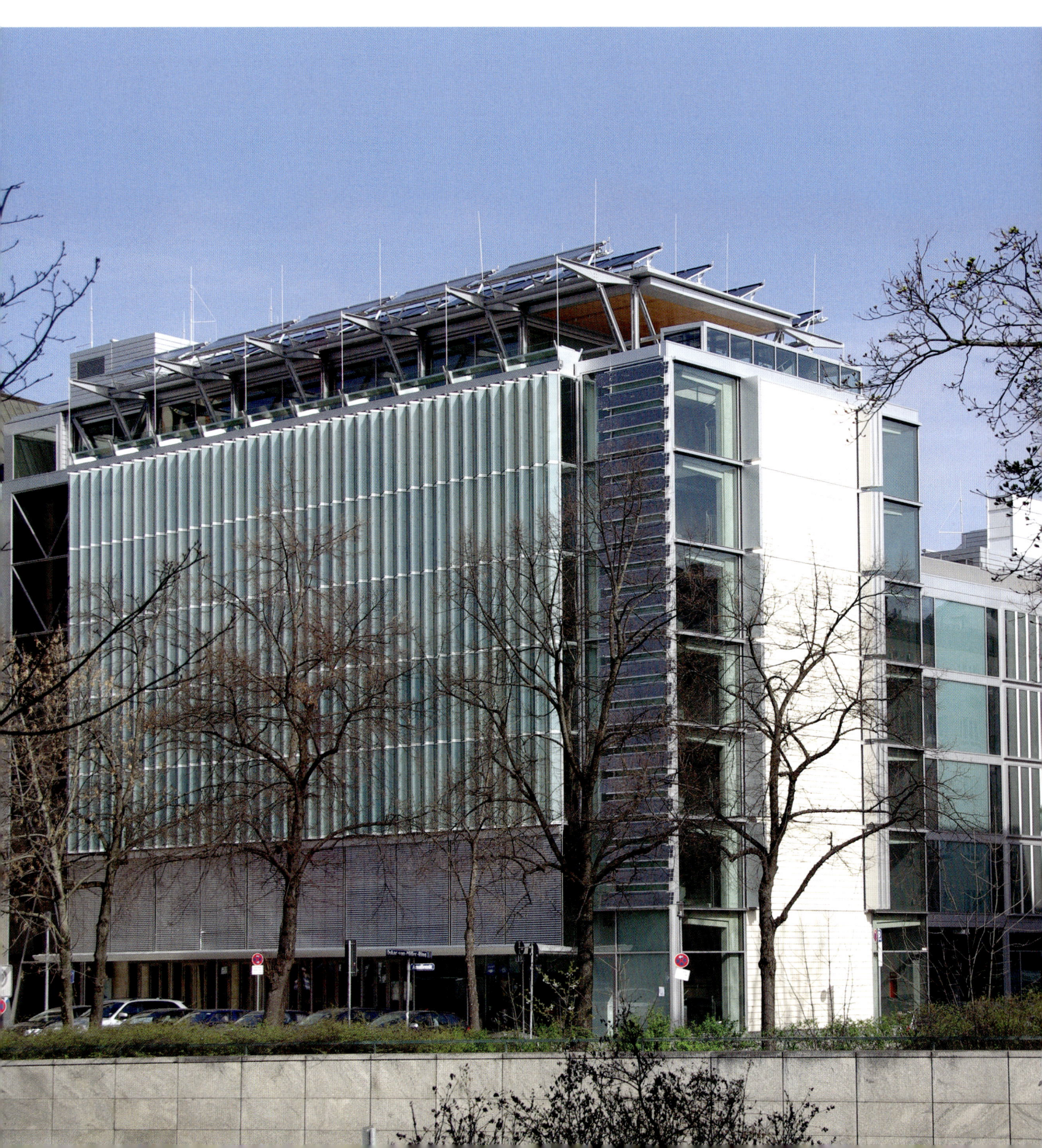

Oskar von Miller Forum
Thomas Herzog Ed.

Hirmer Verlag

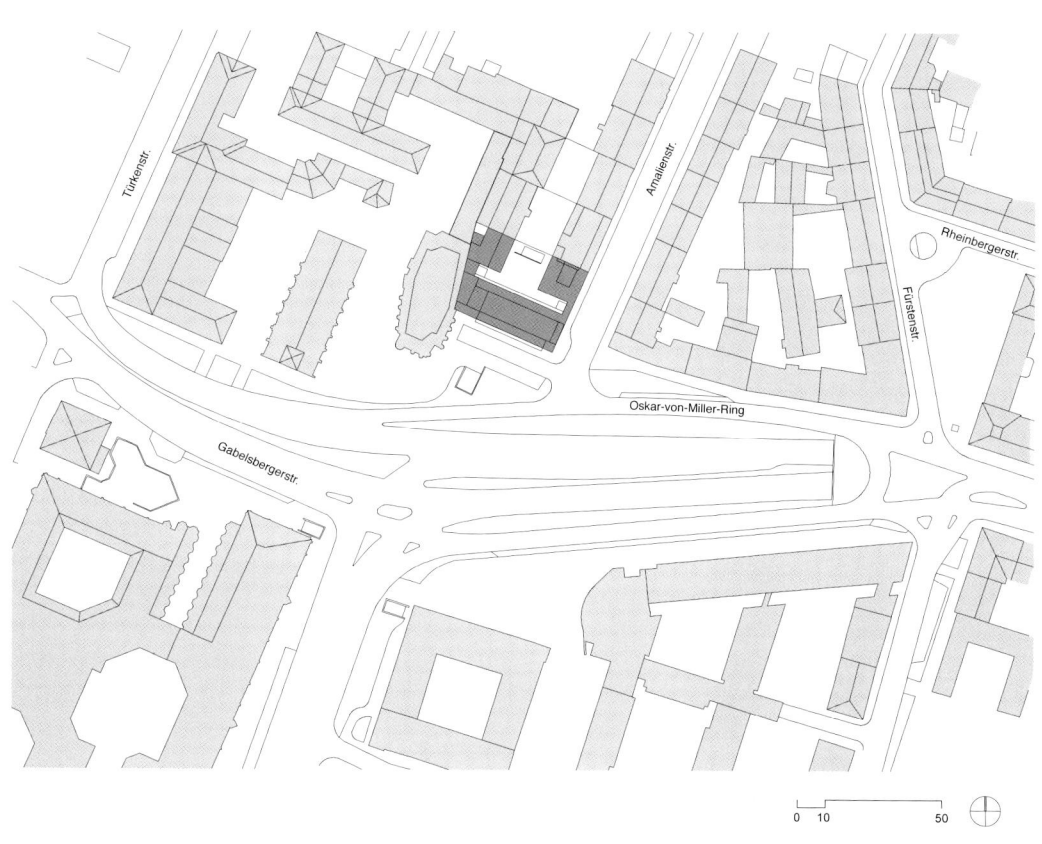

Inhalt		Contents
Stimmen zur Eröffnung	**9**	Comments made on the Occasion of the Opening
Projektbeschreibung	**10 18** Thomas Herzog	Description of the Project
Spezielle Konstruktionen und Produkte	**20 26** Thomas Herzog	Special Forms of Construction and Products
Energetische Bewertung	**33** Gerd Hauser	Assessment of Energy Performance
Freiraumplanung	**34** Christoph Valentien	Landscape Planning
Baugrunderkundung, Gründung und Baugrubenverbau	**36** Norbert Vogt	Soil Investigations, Foundations and Shoring of Excavations
Tragwerksplanung	**38 40** Kurt Stepan Thomas Winkler	Structural Planning
Natürliche Lüftung und Entrauchung der Obergeschosse im Südbau	**46 48** Thomas Herzog Roland Schneider	Natural Ventilation and Smoke Extract on the Upper Floors of the South Tract
Systeme der Gebäudetechnik	**50 56** Christian Dotzauer	Services Systems
Gebäudeautomation	**64** Werner Rösener	Automation in the Building
Elektro- und Informationstechnik	**66 68** Peter Hross	Electrical and Information Technology
Schallschutz und Raumakustik	**70** Gerhard Hilz	Sound Insulation and Spatial Acoustics
Entstehung und Zielsetzung des Projekts	**72 74** Thomas Herzog	The Origins of the Project and its Aims
„Die Wahl des Systems entscheidet" Hommage an Oskar von Miller	**76** Sabine Kammerl	"The Choice of System is Decisive" A Homage to Oskar von Miller
Gravuren	**79** Nikolaus Lang	Engravings
„L'artista e l'ingegnere" Leonardo Da Vinci, Künstler, Ingenieur und Architekt	**82** Rainer Wittenborn	"L'artista e l'ingegnere" Leonardo da Vinci, artist, engineer and architect
Projektdaten	**88**	Project data
Projektbeteiligte	**90**	Credits

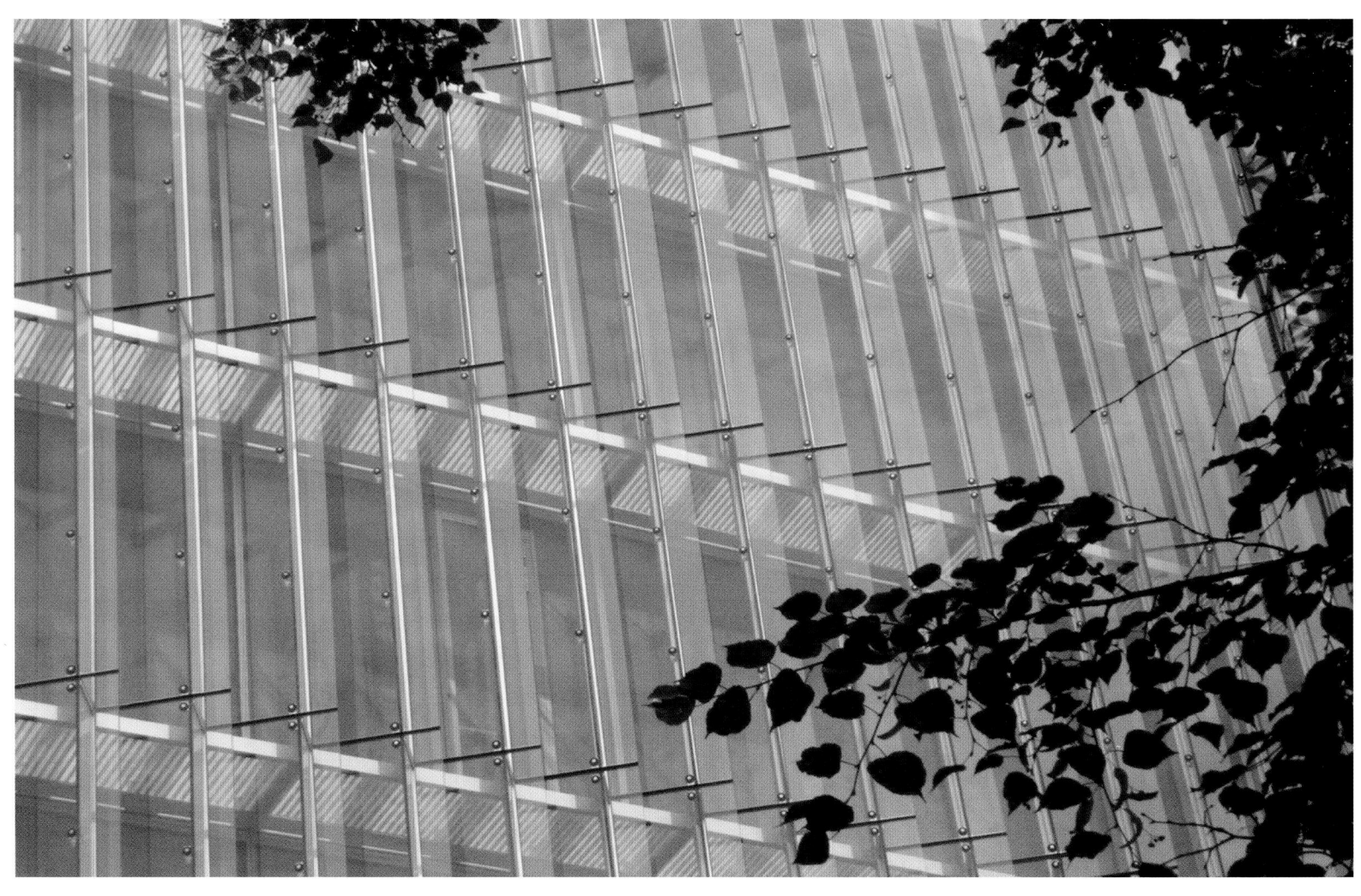

Beschlüsse der Stadtgestaltungskommission der Landeshauptstadt München vom 13.03.2007:
„Erstens, die Stadtgestaltungskommission begrüßt die vorgelegte Planung." (Einstimmig)
„Zweitens, die Stadtgestaltungskommission empfiehlt der Landeshauptstadt München, in planerische Überlegungen zur Aufwertung des Vorfeldes des Gebäudes einzutreten." (Einstimmig)

**Decisions taken by the Commission for Urban Design of the City of Munich,
capital of the Federal State of Bavaria on 13.03.2007:**
"First, the Commission for Urban Design welcomes the proposals that have been submitted." (unanimously)
"Second, the Commission for Urban Design recommends the state capital, Munich, to participate in formulating planning ideas to upgrade the approach area to the building." (unanimously)

Stimmen zur Eröffnung
Comments made on the Occasion of the Opening

Mit entschlossener Überzeugungskraft stritt Oskar von Miller, der gelernte Bauingenieur von der Technischen Universität München, für sein Lebenswerk – die Versorgung Bayerns mit elektrischer Energie – und wurde durch den Bau des Walchenseekraftwerks weltberühmt. Den meisten ist er als Gründer des Deutschen Museums in München bekannt. Mit dem Oskar von Miller Forum erhält das Bildungsland Bayern eine der modernsten und innovativsten Bildungs- und Austauschplattformen im Bereich des Bauwesens. Die künftigen Führungskräfte der Bauwirtschaft werden für ein internationales und interdisziplinäres Wirkungsfeld ausgebildet und sollen selbstbewusst und teamfähig gemacht werden für übergreifende Projektaufgaben. Sie sollen nicht nur gute Ingenieure und Architekten sein, sondern ihr Tun an übergeordneten, allgemeingültigen Werten orientieren. Die Auseinandersetzung mit ethischen Fragen gehört für mich zum unverzichtbaren Kern der Tätigkeit eines Akademikers.

Oskar von Miller, who studied building engineering at the Technische Universität München, fought with great conviction for his life achievement – providing Bavaria with electrical energy – and rose to world fame through the construction of the Walchensee power station. To most people, however, he is known as the founder of the Deutsches Museum in Munich. With the Oskar von Miller Forum, Bavaria – in its role as a land of scholarship and culture – has now acquired one of the most modern and innovative platforms for education and the exchange of ideas in the field of construction. Future leaders in the building sector will be trained here to engage in international and interdisciplinary fields of activity. Here, they should acquire self-confidence and the ability to work in a team on multi-disciplinary projects. They should not be just good engineers and architects; their actions should be based on higher values that have a universal validity. To my mind, a dialectic with ethical questions lies at the very heart of an academic's work.

Ministerpräsident des Freistaats Bayern Prime Minister of Bavaria **Horst Seehofer**

Dieses Bauwerk ist ein wunderschöner Beleg dafür, welch wichtige Funktion die Sozialpartner, die Tarifvertragsparteien der Bauwirtschaft in unserem Land haben und was wir, Arbeitgeber und Gewerkschaften, gemeinsam auf die Beine stellen können. Ohne die gemeinsame Sozialkasse, ohne starke Gewerkschaften und Arbeitgeberverbände wäre das, was hier geschaffen wurde, nicht möglich. Wenn Begabung und Leistung zusammenkommen, dann wird dieses Forum zu einem Raum für neue Ideen, die unser Land, Arbeitgeber und Arbeitnehmer gleichermaßen voranbringen.

This building is a superb demonstration of the important role played by the partners in society, the parties involved in collective bargaining in the building sector in our country, and what we, employers and trade unions, can achieve together. Without the joint social-security benefits office, without strong unions and employers' organizations, the things that have been achieved here would not have been possible. When talent and endeavour are united, this forum will become a stage for new ideas that will advance our state, employers and employees alike.

Bundesvorsitzender der Industriegewerkschaft Bauen-Agrar-Umwelt
Federal Chairman of the Industrial Union for Building, Agriculture and the Environment **Klaus Wiesehügel**

Aus vielen internationalen Studenten sollte eine Gruppe entstehen, die unterschiedliche Kulturen zusammenbringt. So werden über die Jahrzehnte viele Botschafter zurück in ihre Heimatländer gehen, die ein Stück Deutschland in ihren Herzen tragen und damit auch einen Beitrag zur Verständigung für gemeinsame Geschäfte leisten werden. Die Ingenieurausbildung erhält mit diesem Gebäude die Chance, eine neue internationale Dimension zu erschließen.

Through the many international students here, a group should develop that will bring different cultures together. In this way, numerous ambassadors will return to their own countries in future decades, bearing part of Germany in their hearts and thus contributing to an understanding for joint enterprises. With this building, the training of engineers acquires the opportunity to explore a new international dimension.

Präsident des Bayerischen Bauindustrieverbandes President of the Association for the Bavarian Building Industry **Thomas Bauer**

Wir setzen große Hoffnung auf die neue Nachbarschaft des Oskar von Miller Forums, das fördernd und fordernd die Aktivitäten der Universität in Richtung exzellenter Ausbildung junger Ingenieure im Bauwesen ergänzt. Im steinernen Relief über dem südlichen Einfahrtstor unserer Universität steht als Motto für die Identität der Hochschule „scientiis (et) artibus". In diesem Sinn engagieren sich die beiden Baufakultäten Architektur und Bauingenieurwesen im Spannungsfeld zwischen anspruchsvoller Wissenschaft und gestalterischem Können.

We place great hopes in our new neighbour, the Oskar von Miller Forum, which complements the activities of the university in supporting and promoting outstanding education for young engineers in the building sector. In the stone relief over the southern entrance gate to our university stands the motto that defines its identity as a place of higher education: "scientiis (et) artibus". To this end, the two building faculties – for architecture and civil engineering – are active in that exciting realm between higher science and design skills.

Präsident der Technischen Universität München President of the Technische Universität München **Wolfgang A. Herrmann**

Projektbeschreibung

Thomas Herzog

In städtebaulich prominenter Lage Münchens, an der Nahtstelle zwischen Altstadt und Universitäts- bzw. Museumsviertel, entstand ein internationales Begegnungszentrum. Es soll der Förderung der Ausbildung von exzellenten Ingenieuren im Bauwesen an der Technischen Universität München dienen. Träger ist die Stiftung Bayerisches Baugewerbe.

Innerhalb enger Vorgaben des Bebauungsplanes wurde ein Gebäude entwickelt, das aus drei Baukörpern besteht, welche U-förmig um einen zentralen Innenhof liegen. Es enthält Räume für ausgewählte Studiengäste (Master-Studenten, Meisterschüler, Doktoranden) und Appartements für Gastdozenten. Im Erdgeschoss stehen in einer über sechs Meter hohen, transparenten, flexibel nutzbaren Halle Membranfaltwände, die in verschiedenen Stellungen ganz unterschiedliche Formationen bilden können, wodurch der Raum auf vielfältige Weise für Ausstellungen, öffentliche Veranstaltungen, Vorträge, Empfänge oder Konferenzen nutzbar ist. Transparente, weit öffenbare Glasfassaden schaffen eine Verbindung zum grünen Hof, zu dem hin sich auch die beiden seitlichen Gebäude orientieren. Innen- und Außenraum sind zu einer differenzierten Gesamtheit verwoben.

Der öffentliche Freiraum im Vorfeld des Anwesens bedarf in naher Zukunft in Zusammenwirkung mit der Stadt München noch der Neugestaltung. Die Hauptfront des Gebäudes im Süden ist durch den Verkehrsfluss des Altstadtringes starken Immissionen ausgesetzt. Deshalb wurden die vom 2. bis zum 6. Obergeschoss gelegenen Schlafräume zur ruhigen Nordseite hin orientiert.

Auf der Südseite übernimmt eine speziell entwickelte, nach außen gefaltete, gläserne Doppelfassade Sonnen- und Schallschutzfunktionen. Über diesen Raum werden die vorgelagerten Gemeinschaftszonen der einzelnen Stockwerke, in denen sich Aufenthalts- bzw. Arbeitsbereiche, Essplatz und Küche befinden, natürlich belüftet.
Im 7. Obergeschoss liegen Räume für Begegnungen in kleinerem Rahmen, für Besprechungen, Seminarnutzung und Empfänge. Von einer überdeckten Loggia aus weitet sich der Ausblick nach Südosten auf die Silhouette der Stadt und reicht an klaren Tagen bis hin zur Kette der bayerischen Alpen.

Im Ostgebäude liegen Wohnungen für Gastdozenten und das Büro des Hausmeisters. Im Erdgeschoss steht den Gästen ein Bistro zur Verfügung.

Im Westgebäude orientiert sich zum begrünten Innenhof ein „Clubraum" mit einer kleinen Bibliothek, darüber Büros und Besprechungsräume der Direktion und ein kleines Appartement.

Im Rahmen der Vorplanungen wurden zunächst zusammen mit DS-Plan Stuttgart grundlegende Untersuchungen durchgeführt, um ein energetisch schlüssiges Gesamtkonzept zu finden. Die weitere Bearbeitung im eigentlichen Planungsteam führte letztlich zu anderen Lösungen, die dann realisiert wurden.

Die Heizung ist an die in der Amalienstraße verlaufende städtische Fernwärmeleitung angeschlossen. Sie wird durch thermische Solarkollektoren über der Dachebene ergänzt, die dort im Sommer auch als Verschatter dienen. Mittels der so gewonnenen Wärmeenergie erfolgt bei Bedarf dann auch eine solare Kühlung der Räume über Umwandlung mit einer Absorptionskältemaschine. Die Böden sind thermisch aktiviert und durchwegs mit heimischem Naturstein belegt.

Zusätzlich zur individuell regulierbaren, natürlichen Lüftung über die Fassaden können alle Nutzungsbereiche mechanisch belüftet werden. In den Zimmern der Studierenden garantiert eine klimaoptimierte Grundlüftung einen Minimal-Luftwechsel. Die Temperatur ist durch Einzelheizkörper raumweise regelbar. In diesem Bereich kühlt die Bauteilaktivierung. Geschlossene Fassadenteile sind stark wärmegedämmt. Sie haben eine Bekleidung aus großformatigen, hinterlüfteten, keramischen Platten.

Die meisten tragenden und aussteifenden Bauteile sind als Stahlbetonkonstruktion aus Fertigteilen entwickelt. Sie bleiben sichtbar als eine dem Kräfteverlauf entsprechend geformte Struktur und zeigen so das Potenzial dieser Bauweise in Präzision und Gestaltung.

Über dem Hauptgebäude steht eine selbstständige Stahlkonstruktion. Im Süden trägt sie die äußere Fassadenschicht. Im Norden sind daran Fluchtbalkone wie eine „Harfe" abgehängt. Lamellen mit silbergrau schimmernden Photovoltaik-Modulen schützen die großen Glasflächen des östlichen Treppenhauses im Sommerhalbjahr vor übermäßiger Wärmeentwicklung. Günstig zur Sonne hin exponiert, wird deren Ertrag ins öffentliche Netz eingespeist. Große, über Sensoren gesteuerte Faltläden regulieren den Strahlungseintrag der Sonne auf der Ostseite.

Die Geometrie der das Tragwerk des Südbaus in Längsrichtung aussteifenden Konstruktion bildet sich in Richtung Stadtzentrum in der Fassade als weithin sichtbares Zeichen ab. Die Architektur und das Design des Gebäudes integrieren den aktuellen Stand der Gebäudetechnologie in Bayern.

Großflächige künstlerische Eingriffe und Ergänzungen auf speziellen Wandflächen, die sich auf die Funktion und die kulturelle Dimension der Inhalte des Gebäudes beziehen, bestimmen maßgeblich Texturen, Raumwirkung und damit auch Teile der neuen Institution in ihrer physischen Gestalt.

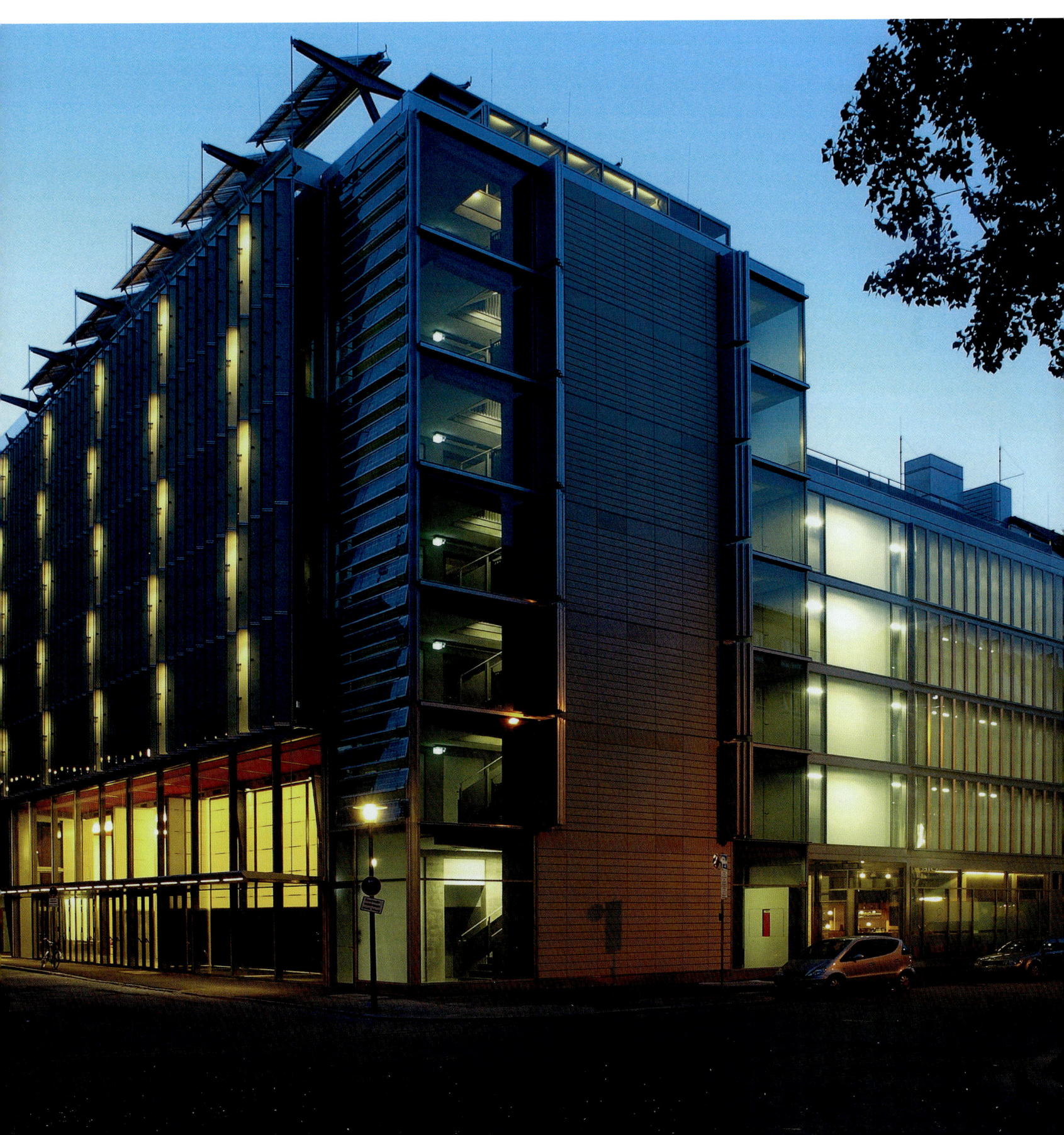

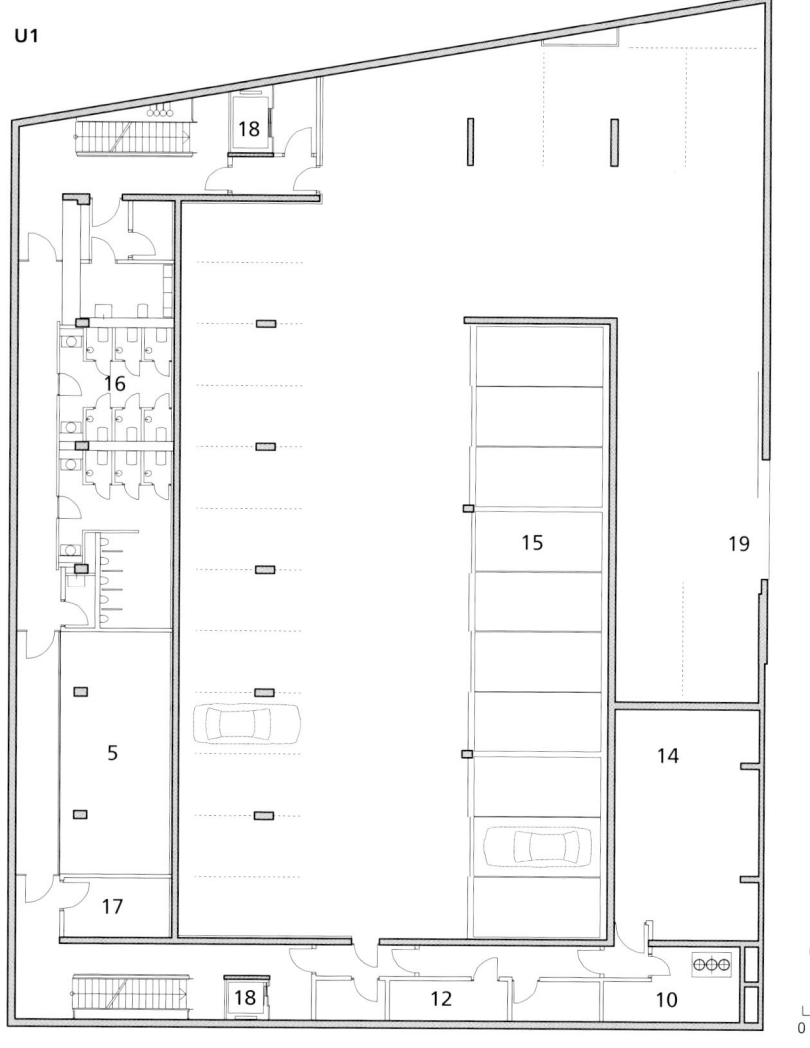
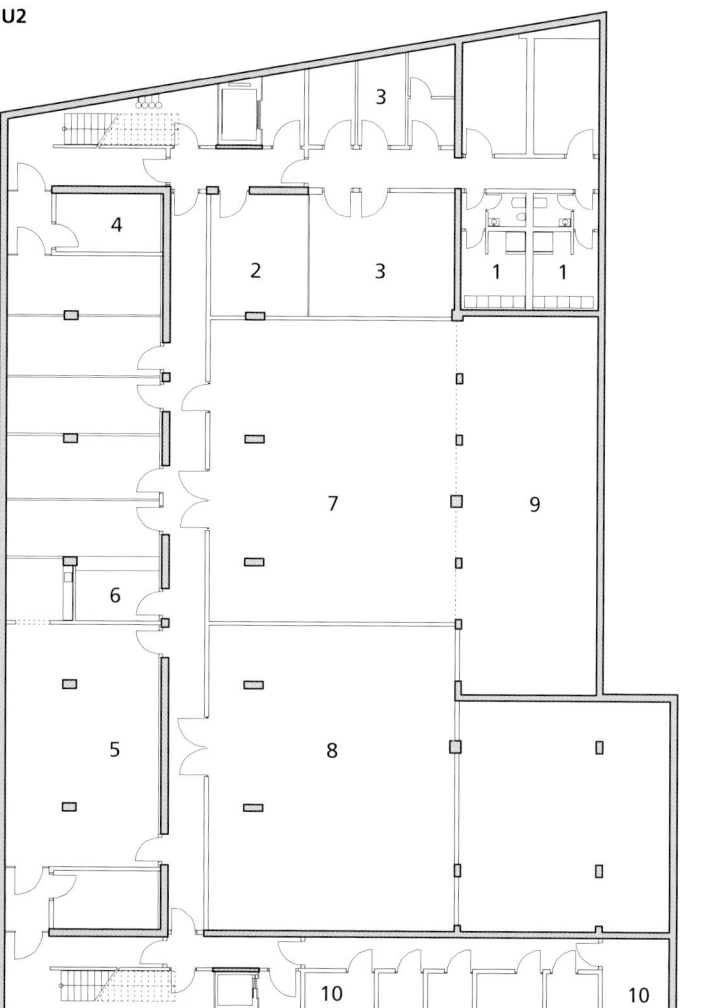

Untergeschosse
1. Personalumkleiden
2. Sprinklerzentrale
3. Lagerräume
4. Informationstechnologie
5. Partyraum
6. Waschmaschinen und Trockner
7. Kältezentrale
8. Lüftungszentrale
9. Batterieanlage/Notstromversorgung Sprinkler
10. Elektrotechnik
11. Diverse Technik
12. Hausanschluss Wasser, Abwasser
13. Trafo
14. Lüftung Tiefgarage/Entrauchung
15. Kombi-Parksystem
16. Sanitäranlage
17. Installationsraum
18. Aufzug
19. Zufahrt über vorhandene Großgarage

Basement floors
1. Staff changing room
2. Sprinkler plant
3. Storerooms
4. Information technology
5. Party room
6. Washing machines and dryers
7. Cooling plant
8. Ventilation plant
9. Battery room/Emergency power supply for sprinkler plant
10. Electrical installation
11. Various technical spaces
12. Main connections: water, waste water
13. Transformer
14. Basement garage ventilation/Smoke extract
15. Combined parking system
16. Sanitary plant
17. Services room
18. Lift
19. Access via existing basement garage

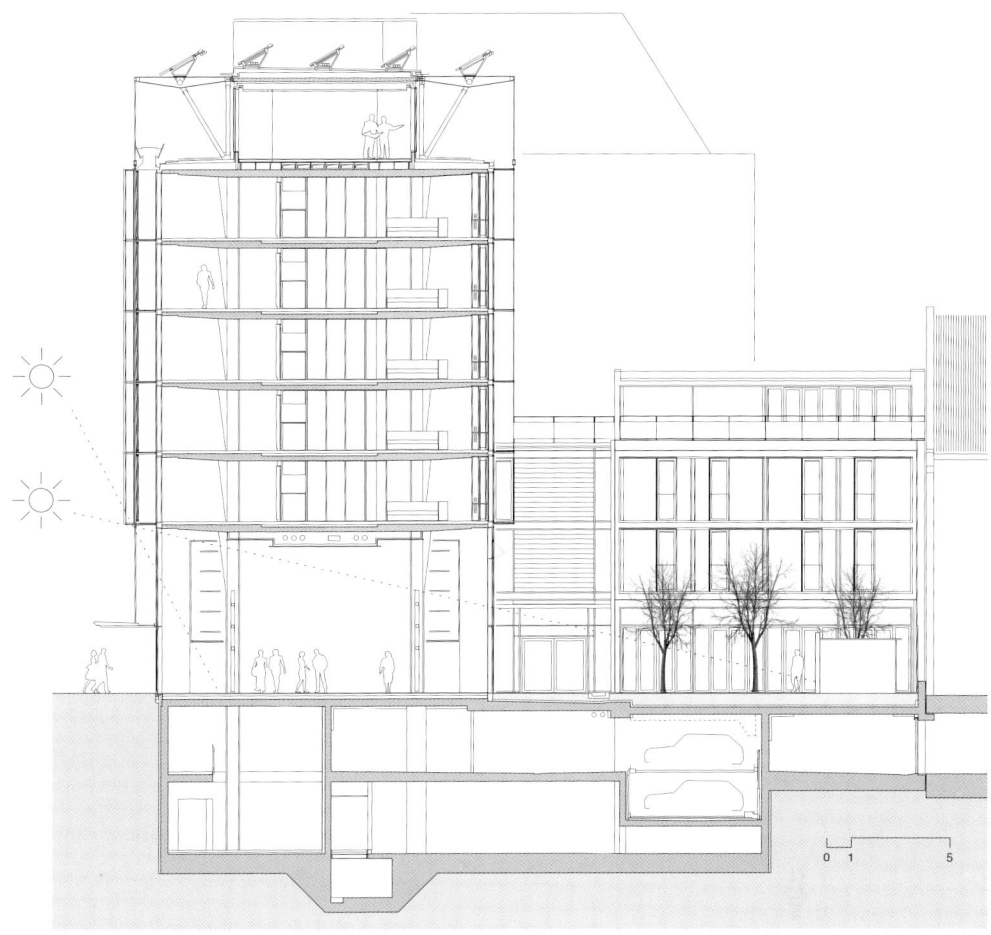

Querschnitt / Section

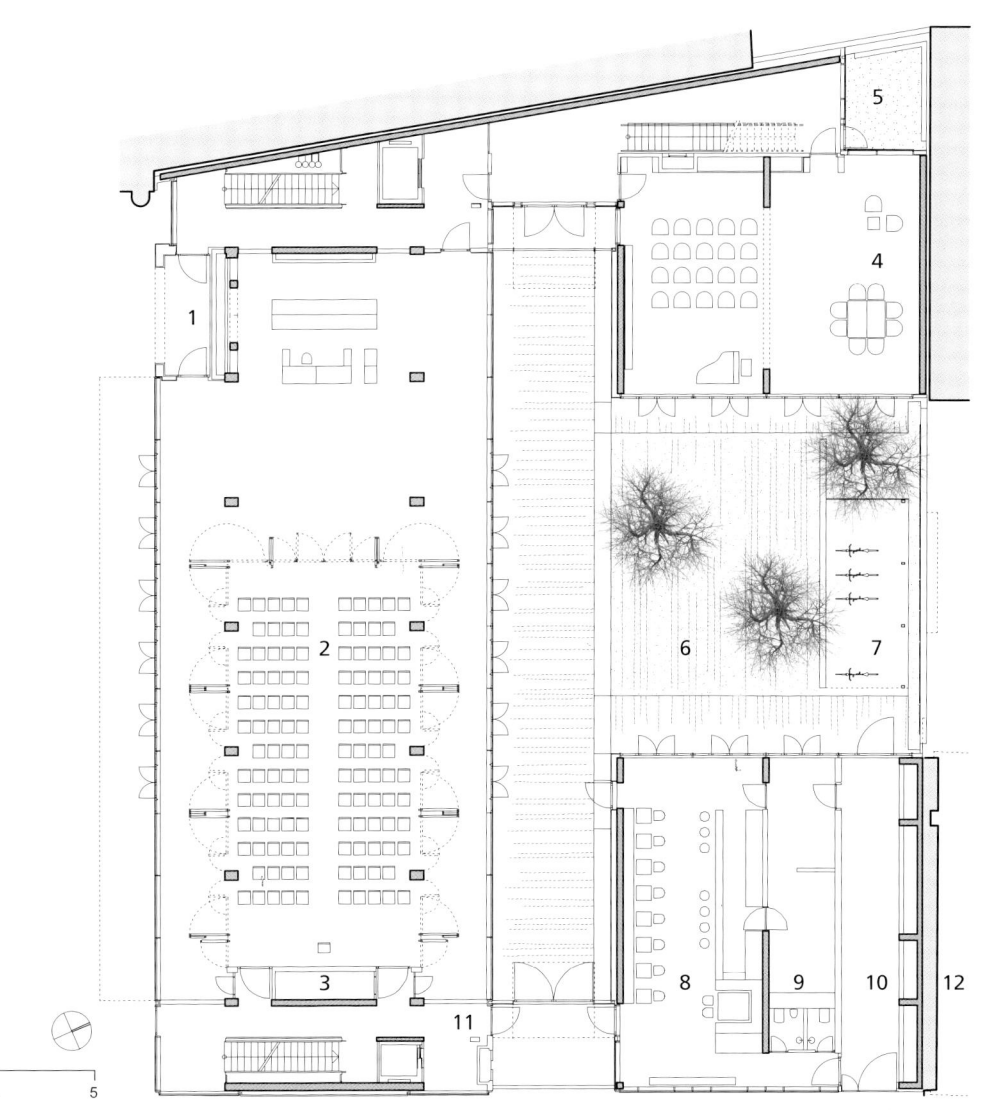

Erdgeschoss
1 Öffentlicher Haupteingang
2 Multifunktionale Halle
3 Medienraum
4 Bibliothek/Clubraum
5 Lichthof
6 Gartenhof
7 Fahrräder
8 Bistro
9 Küche
10 Müllraum
11 Haupteingang Wohnbereich
12 Installationsschacht

Ground floor
1 Main public entrance
2 Multi-purpose hall
3 Media space
4 Library/Clubroom
5 Patio
6 Garden courtyard
7 Bicycles
8 Bistro
9 Kitchen
10 Refuse room
11 Main access to living areas
12 Services duct

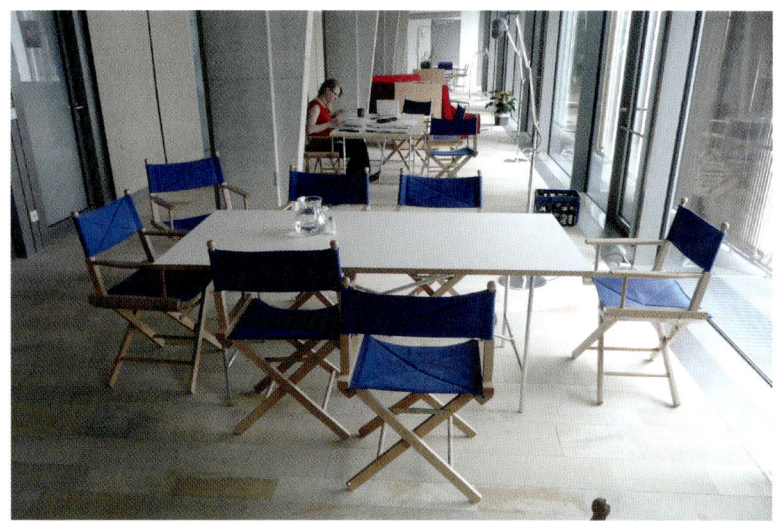

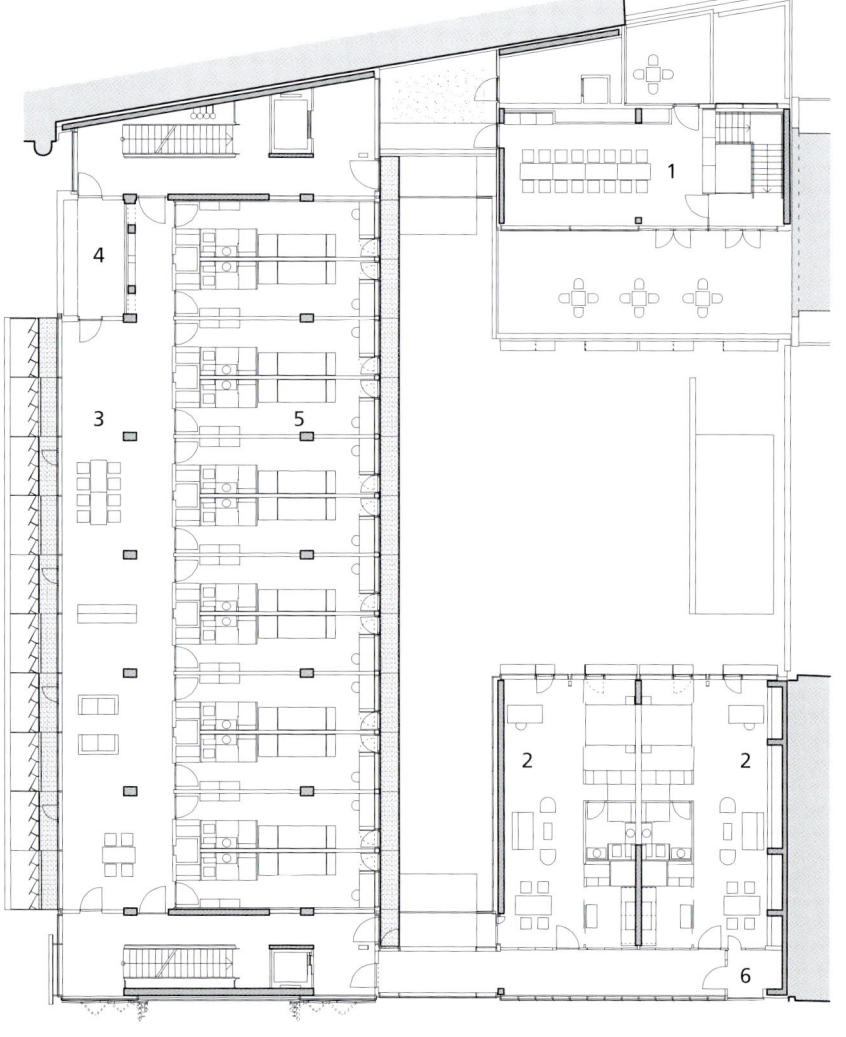

Regelgeschoss
1 Verwaltungsbereich
2 Appartement Dozenten
3 Gemeinsamer Wohnraum
4 Küche
5 Räume für Studiengäste
6 Loggia

Standard floors
1 Administration area
2 Lecturers' apartment
3 Communal living area
4 Kitchen
5 Rooms for study guests
6 Loggia

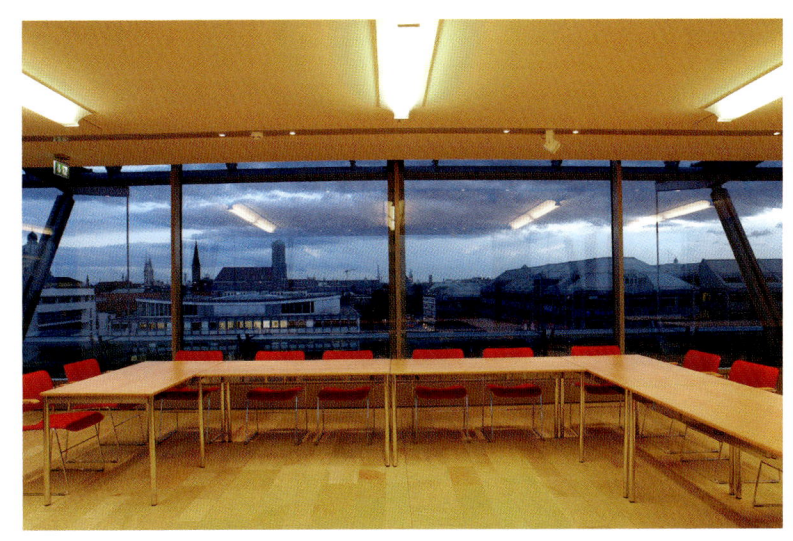

Dachgeschoss
1 Lüftungszentrale
2 Terrasse
3 Begrüntes Dach
4 Pantry
5 Sanitärräume
6 Seminar, Konferenz u.a.

Roof storey
1 Ventilation plant
2 Terrace
3 Planted roof
4 Pantry
5 Sanitary spaces
6 Seminars, conferences, etc.

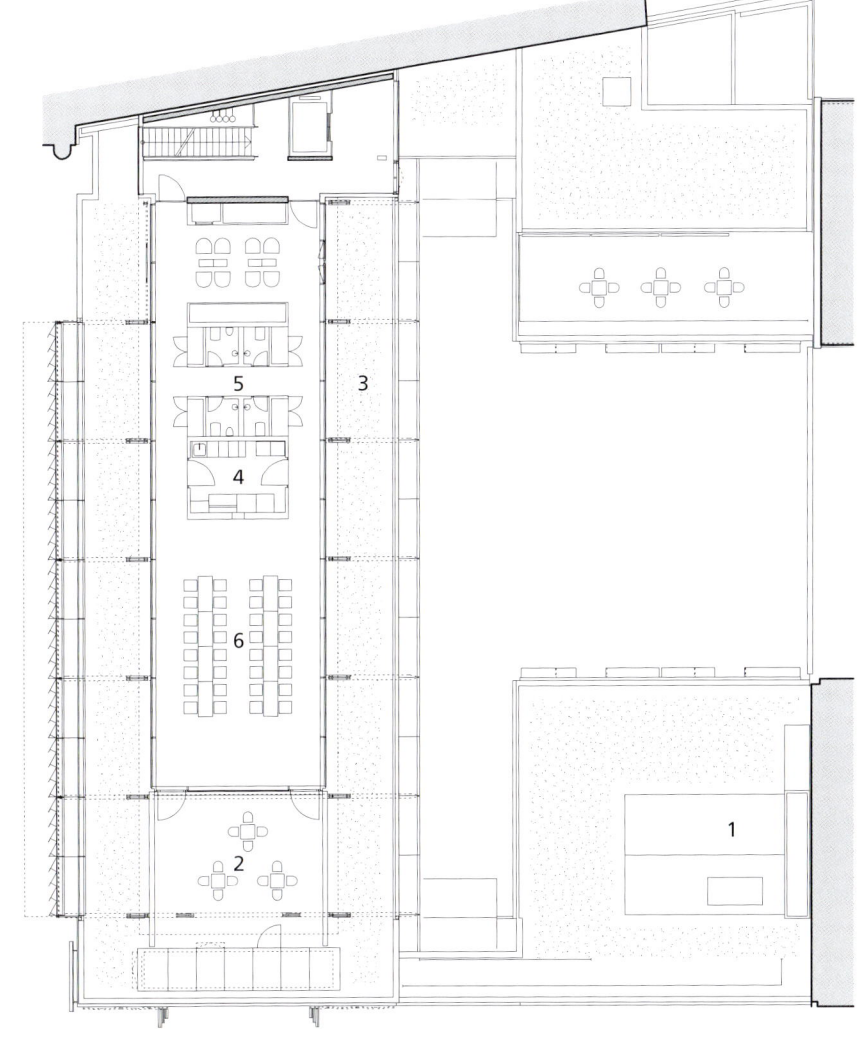

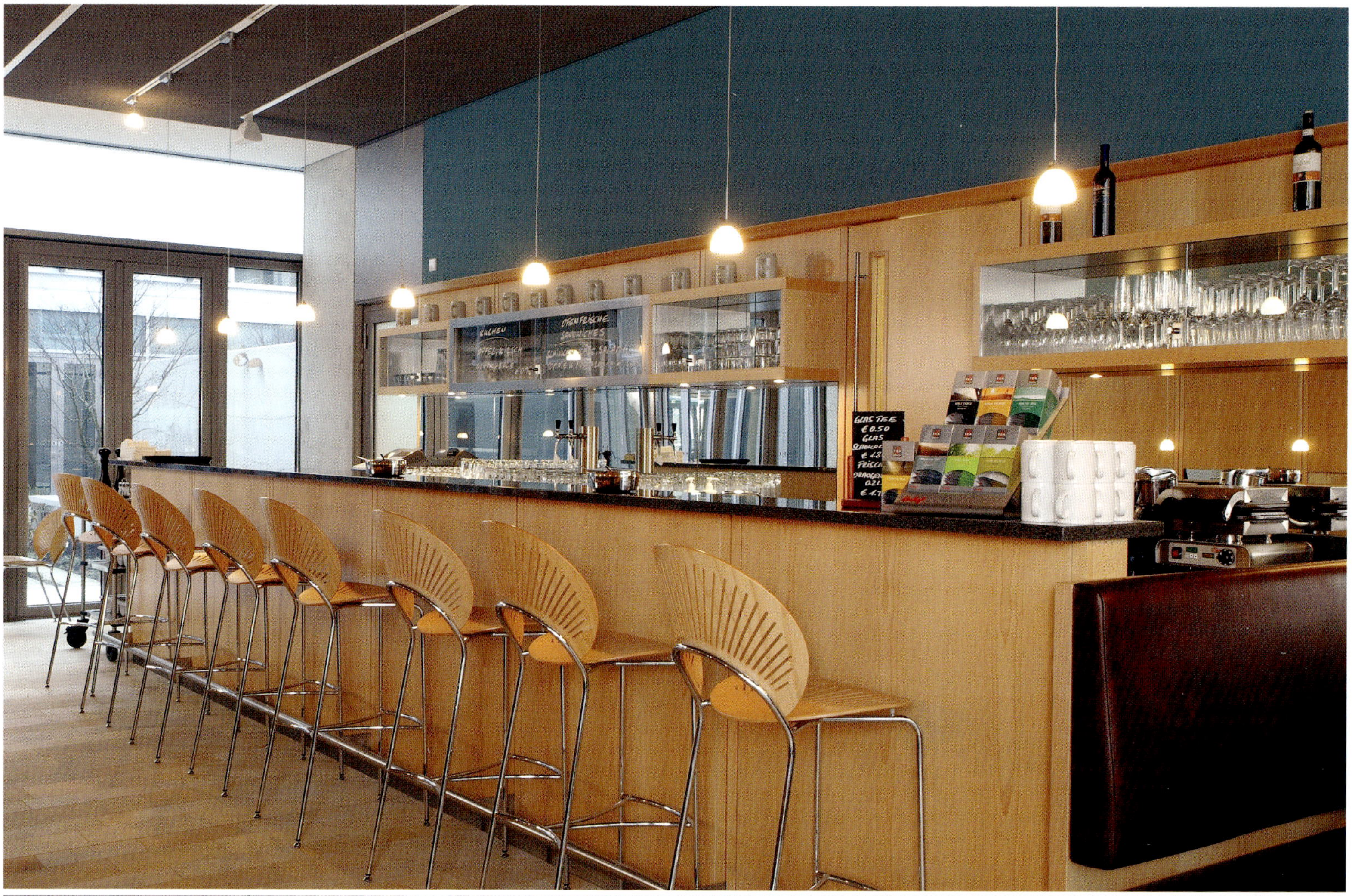

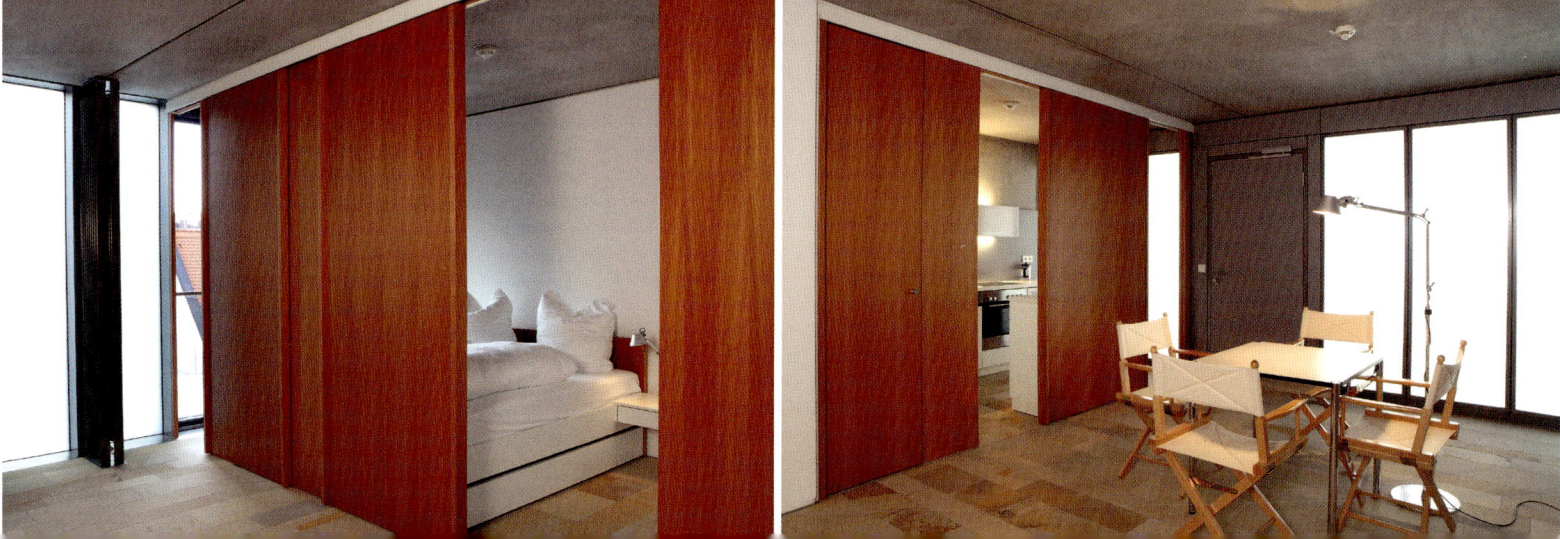

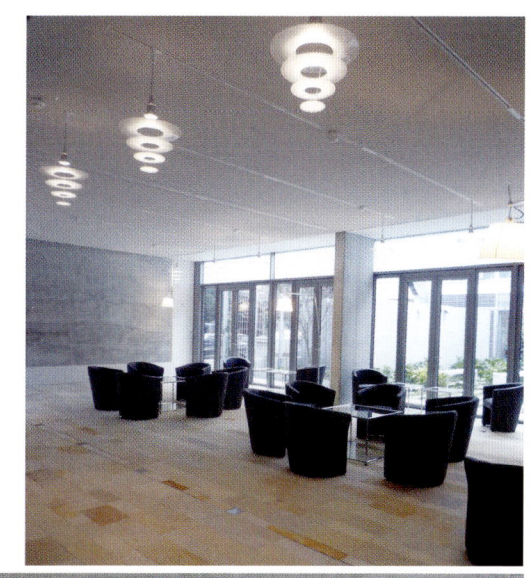

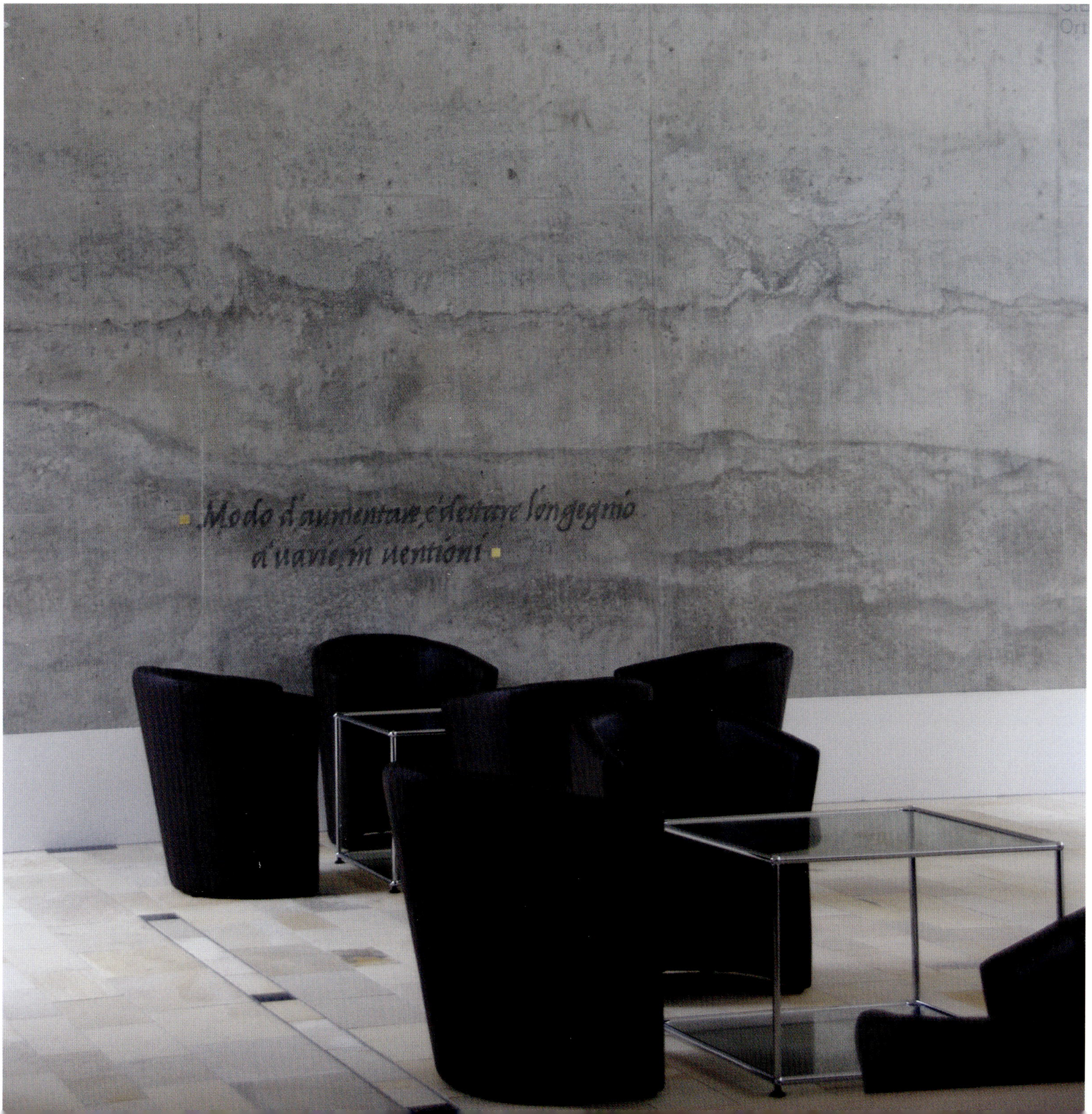

Description of the Project

Thomas Herzog

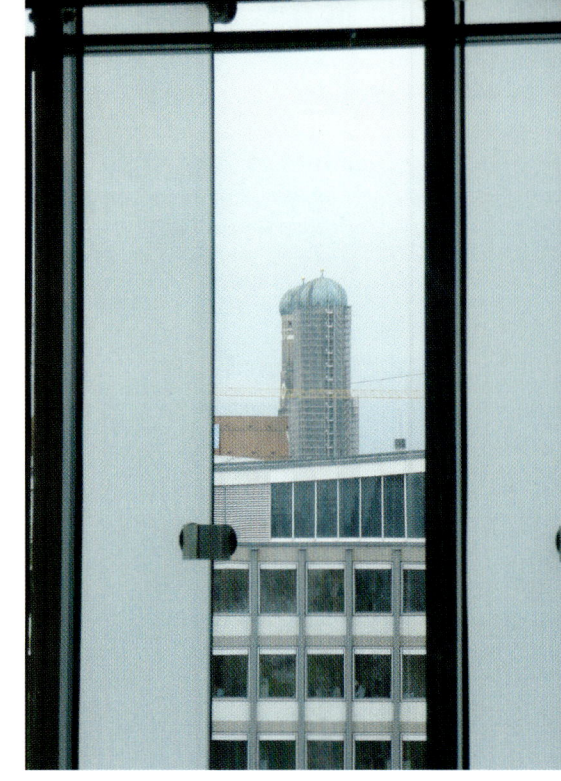

In a prominent urban location in Munich where the old part of the city meets the university and museum district, an international centre of communication has been created. Its purpose is to promote the education of outstanding engineers in the field of construction at the Technische Universität München (TUM) – the University of Technology. The sponsor is the Stiftung Bayerisches Baugewerbe (Bavarian Building Trades Foundation).

The building was designed to comply with the tight parameters of the development plan. It consists of three tracts laid out in a U-shaped form about a central courtyard. The complex contains rooms for selected guest students – those studying for a master's degree or doctorate, and people who are masters of a trade, for example – as well as apartments for visiting lecturers. In the more than six-metre-high flexible, transparent hall on the ground floor are folding membrane partitions that can be moved into various positions to create quite different layouts. As a result, this space can accommodate a wide range of functions, including exhibitions and public events, lectures, receptions and conferences. Transparent glazed facades that can be extensively opened create a link with the planted courtyard outside, which is flanked by the two wings of the building. Indoor and outdoor space are thus interwoven to create a subtly varied whole. The public open space in front of the development is urgently in need of redesign in collaboration with the Munich municipal authorities. The main front of the new building, which faces south, is subject to heavy pollution from traffic on the inner-city ring road. For that reason, the bedrooms – on the second to sixth floors – were located on the quiet north face.

On the south side, a specially developed double-skin glazed facade, folded on the outside, provides solar and acoustic screening. Above the facade space, the outer communal zones on the various floors, housing lounge and working areas, the dining room and kitchen, are naturally ventilated.

On the seventh floor are spaces for smaller group meetings, discussions, seminars and receptions. From a covered loggia, there is a view to the south-east over the skyline of the city, and on clear days, one can see the Bavarian Alps in the distance.

In the east wing are dwellings for guest lecturers as well as the caretaker's office. A bistro for guests has been installed on the ground floor. In the west wing, oriented to the planted courtyard, is a "clubroom" with a small library, and above this offices and discussion spaces for the administration, as well as a small apartment.

The pre-planning was carried out with DS-Plan Stuttgart. Basic investigations were done to find a logical overall energy concept. Further work of the actual planning team finally led to a different solution which was then realised.

The heating system is connected to the nearby municipal district-heating supply in Amalienstrasse and is complemented by solar thermal collectors above roof level that also serve as a means of sunshading in summer. The thermal energy generated in this way can also be converted by an absorption chiller to operate a solar cooling system for the rooms when required. The floors are thermally activated and finished throughout with stone from the region.

In addition to individually regulable natural ventilation via the facades, all user areas can be mechanically ventilated. In the students' rooms, a climatically optimized basic ventilation system guarantees a minimum air change. Temperatures can be controlled on a room-by-room basis by means of individual radiators. In these areas, cooling is achieved by thermal activation of the floors.

The closed sections of the facade have a high degree of thermal insulation and are clad with a rear-ventilated skin of large-scale ceramic tiles.

Most of the load-bearing and bracing construction consists of precast reinforced concrete elements. These were left visible to reveal a structure laid out in accordance with the flow of forces. In this way, they demonstrate the potential of this form of construction in terms of precision and design.

On top of the main building is an independent steel structure, over the south side of which the outer facade layer extends. Suspended from this structure on the north side is a construction known as the "harp", consisting of escape balconies and a series of vertical rods.

Louvres with shimmering silver-grey photovoltaic units screen the large glazed areas of the eastern staircase from overheating in the summer months. Exposed to the sun on this side, they generate power that is fed into the public network. Large folding shutters controlled by sensors regulate the gains from insolation on the east face.

The geometry of the construction bracing the load-bearing structure of the southern tract in the longitudinal direction (i.e. facing the city centre) creates a bold image in the facade that is visible from afar. State-of-the-art Bavarian constructional technology is integrated into the architectural design of this building.

Large-scale art projects and additions to certain wall surfaces reflect the function and cultural dimension of the building. They have a strong influence on the texture and spatial part of this new institution and thus on its character and physical presence.

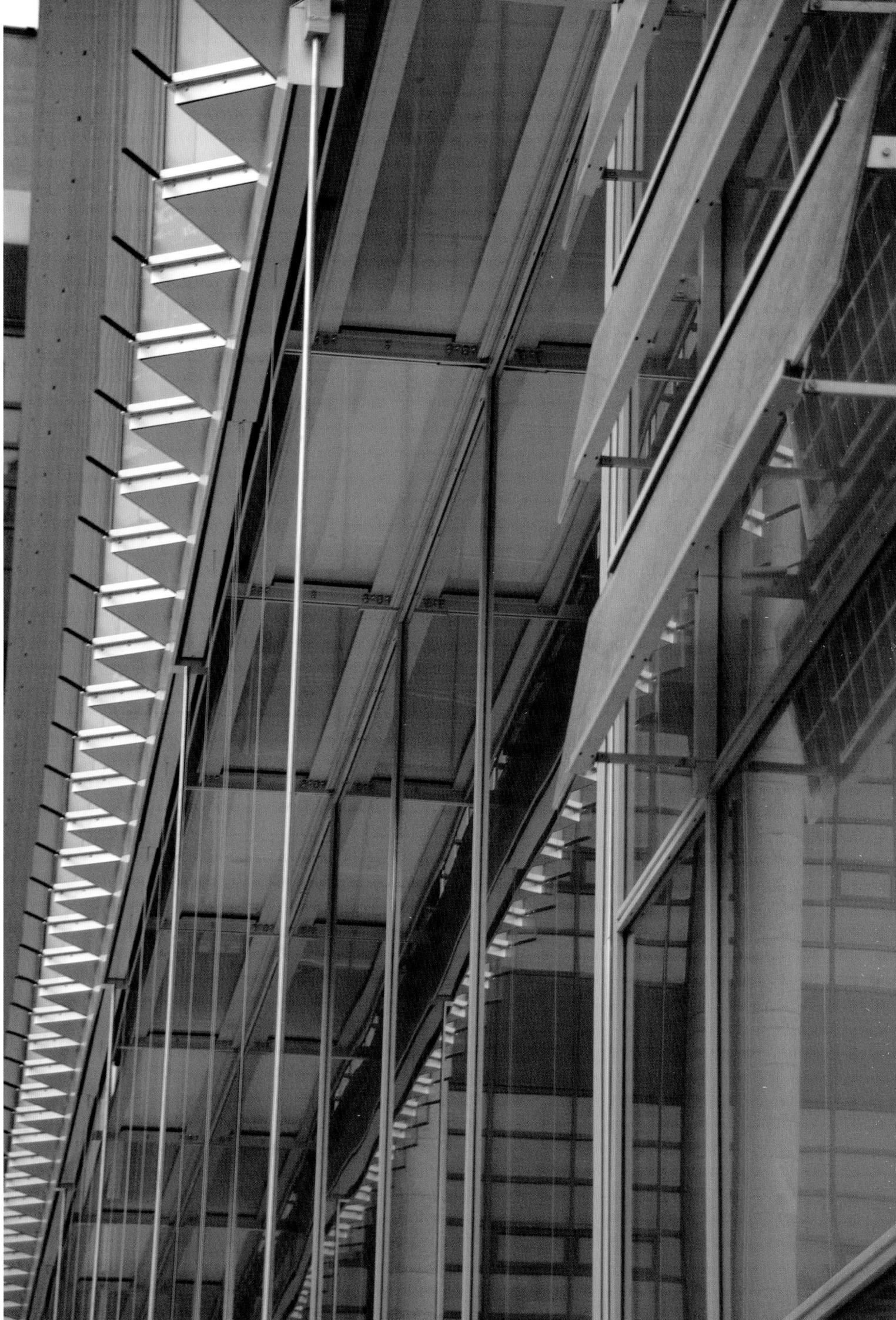

Spezielle Konstruktionen und Produkte

Thomas Herzog

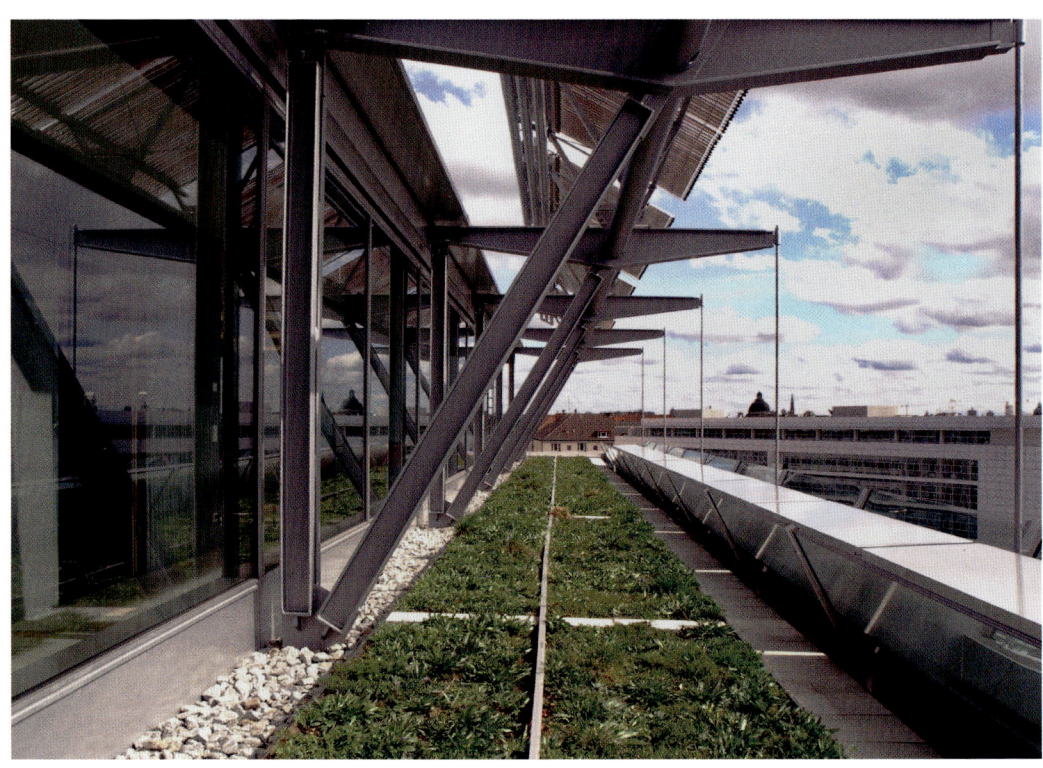

Teil der Architekten- und Ingenieuraufgabe war es, an dafür geeigneter Stelle Technologien, Bauweisen, Komponenten, Materialien oder Produkte einzusetzen, die nach heutigem Stand der Technik hinsichtlich Gebrauchstauglichkeit und Gestaltung hohen Ansprüchen genügen. Beispiele hierfür:

Ausleger

Die äußeren Fassadenebenen des Südbaus hängen an großen Trägern, die über die Dachebene des 7. Obergeschosses zu beiden Seiten auskragen. Die Stahlkonstruktionen auf Höhe des Terrassengeschosses zeigen skulpturale Elemente heutigen Ingenieurbaus. Die gesamte Dachfläche ist in voller Breite mit Hochleistungsröhrenkollektoren überdeckt, deren Hightech-Eleganz sich dem Betrachter auch vom Raum des Dachgeschosses aus mitteilt. Der gesamte Erdgeschossbereich wird in Höhe der Halle beidseits von jeder außenstehenden, senkrechten Tragkonstruktion freigehalten, wodurch maximale Durchlässigkeit erreicht wird.

Die Gebäudehülle

Die **Doppelfassade** im Süden besteht in ihrer inneren Lage aus raumhohen, gut wärmedämmenden Isolierglasscheiben mit einigen Lüftungsöffnungen zum Fassadenzwischenraum hin. Die äußere Hülle ist aus abwechselnd transparenten und transluzenten Glasscheiben mit Punkthalterungen aneinandergekoppelt. Die transparente Scheibe ragt dabei randlos nach außen vor. Die Faltung der Fläche erhöht die Stabilität gegen Horizontalkräfte. Es besteht die Möglichkeit der Umrüstung mit öffenbaren Fensterflügeln falls der Verkehr des Altstadtringes wesentlich abnehmen sollte.

Zwischen den beiden gläsernen Ebenen erfolgt eine vertikal durchgehende Schachtlüftung. Neben den positiven Auswirkungen für den Schallschutz prägt das spezielle

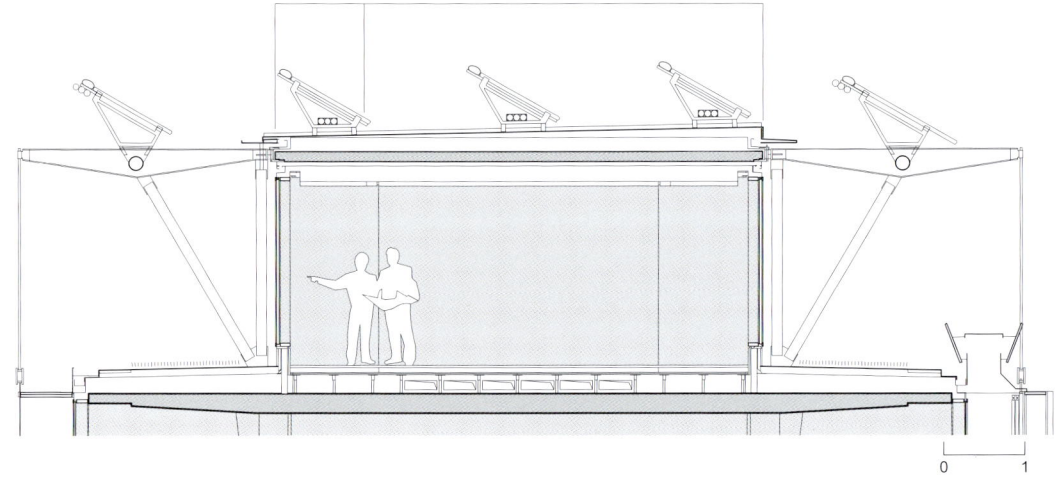

Erscheinungsbild die Identität des Gebäudes in Richtung Innenstadt.

Große **Schiebeläden** mit Holzlamellen sind im Hohlraum der Doppelfassade wirksame Verschatter gegen die im Sommer unerwünschte Aufheizung des Aufenthaltsbereiches. Sie werden je nach Bedarf geschossweise auf die ganze Länge der Südfront ausgefahren oder auf die Hälfte der verglasten Südfassade übereinandergeschoben. In jedem Fall bestimmt die Wirkung der großen Holzflächen ganz wesentlich die Atmosphäre der Gemeinschaftsräume in den Etagen für die Studierenden. Mehrfach reflektiertes eindringendes Licht bestimmt zudem den Farbwert der großen Flächen.

Die auf der gegenüberliegenden Nordseite abgehängte „Harfe" hält die Bodenroste der Fluchtbalkone. Die engstehenden, in Querrichtung auf Brüstungshöhe verbundenen Rundstäbe aus nichtrostendem Stahl bilden zudem eine Absturzsicherung.

Leichte Lüftungspaneele mit Vakuumdämmung bestimmen wesentlich den Charakter der Fassaden von dem Ost- und dem Westgebäude zum Hof hin. Die tiefen Räume der Baukörper sind wegen der Aussicht und zum Zweck maximaler Nutzung des Tageslichtes weitgehend verglast. Die dafür erforderliche Wärmedämmwirkung war nur mit einer hochwertigen Dreischeiben-Konstruktion realisierbar. Es wurden leichte Holzpaneele konstruiert, mit Decklagen aus Bootssperrholz und einer neuartigen Vakuumdämmung im Innern, die den Messwerten zufolge eine etwa um den Faktor 6 geringere Wärmeleitwirkung gegenüber konventionellen Schaum- oder Mineralwolledämmschichten haben. Entsprechend schlank konnten die Lüftungsflügel ausgebildet werden. Nur auf solche Weise – d.h. durch vollständige Verlegung des mit großer Sorgfalt und Vorsicht vorzunehmenden Einbaus der Dämmelemente im Werk – erscheint

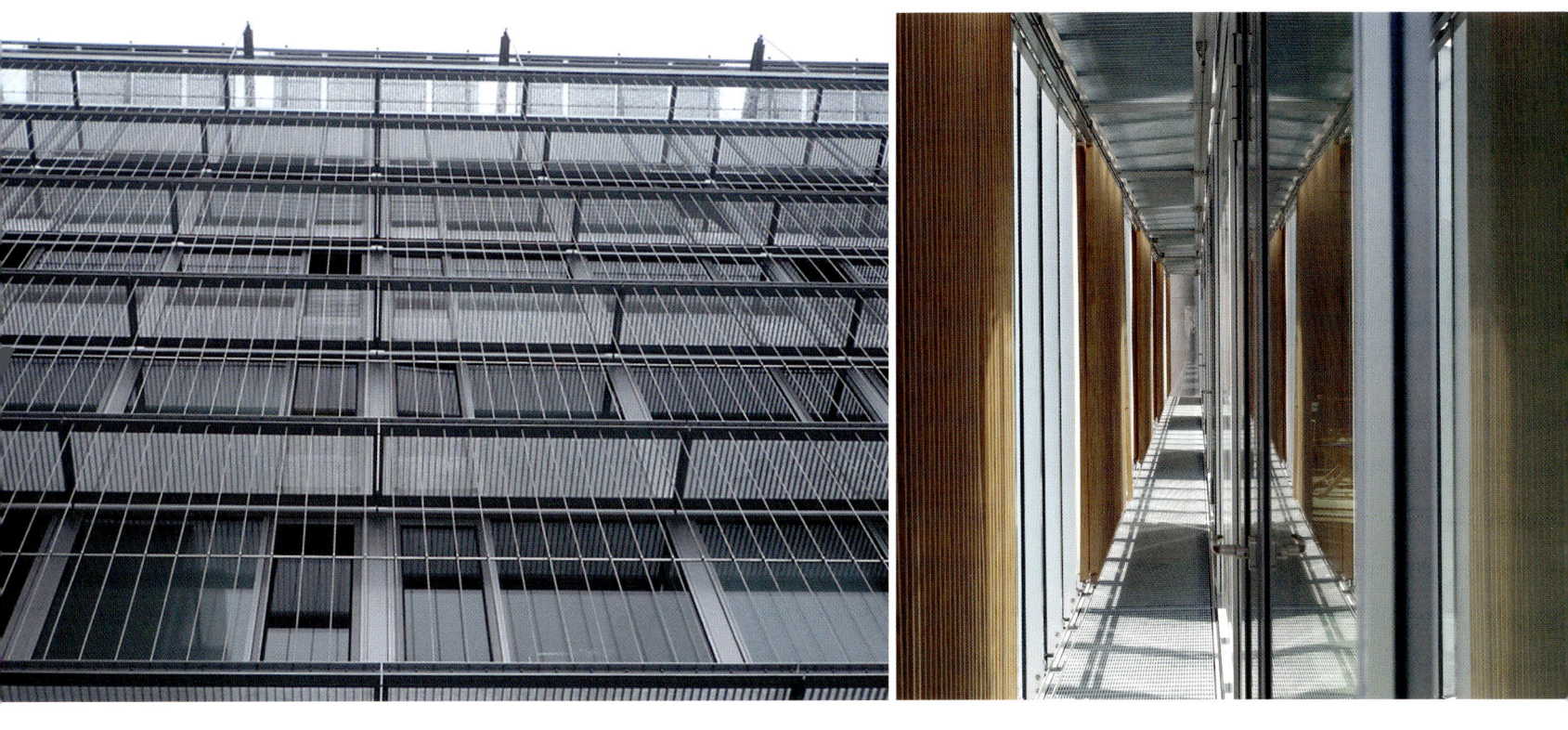

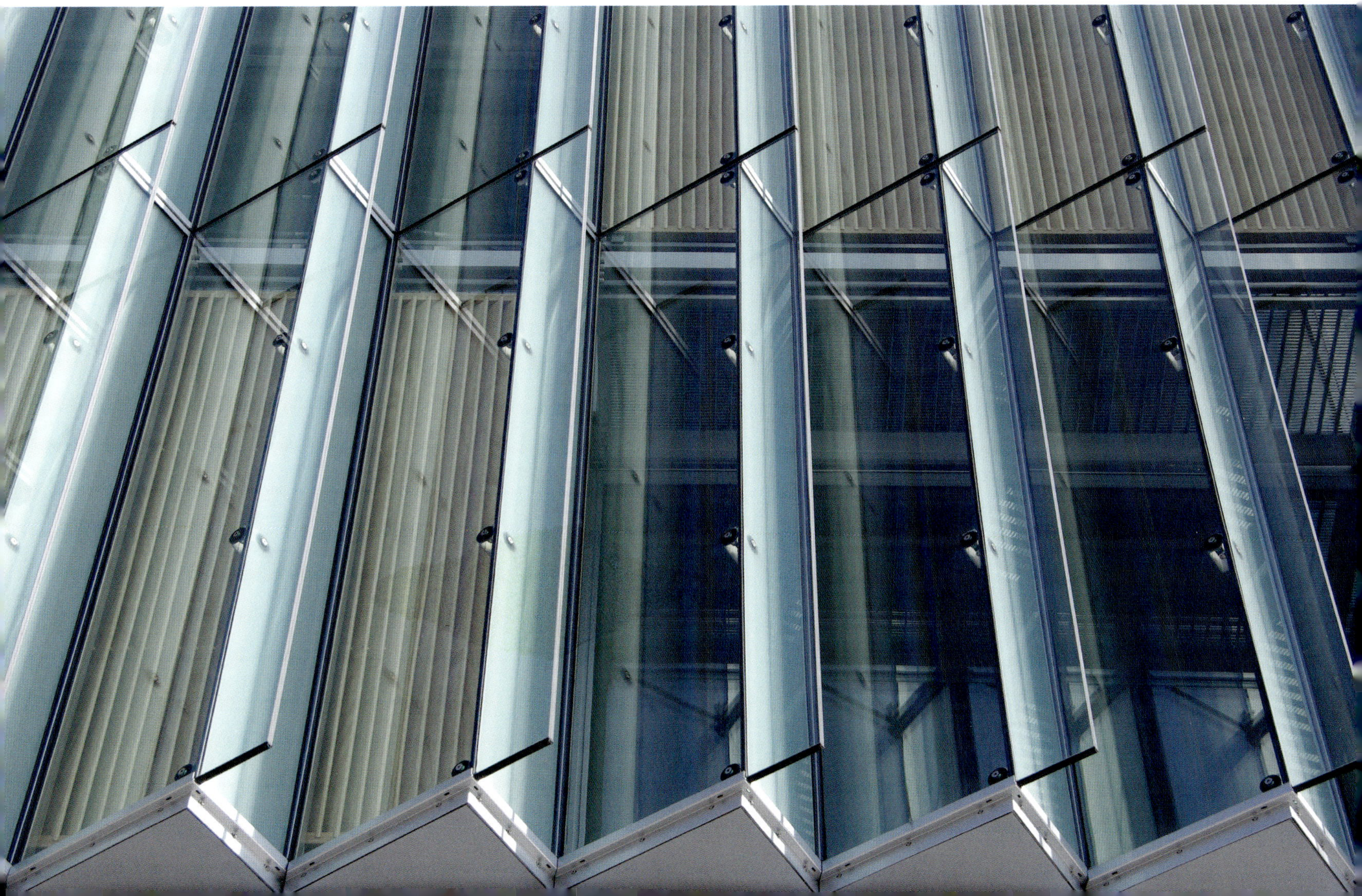

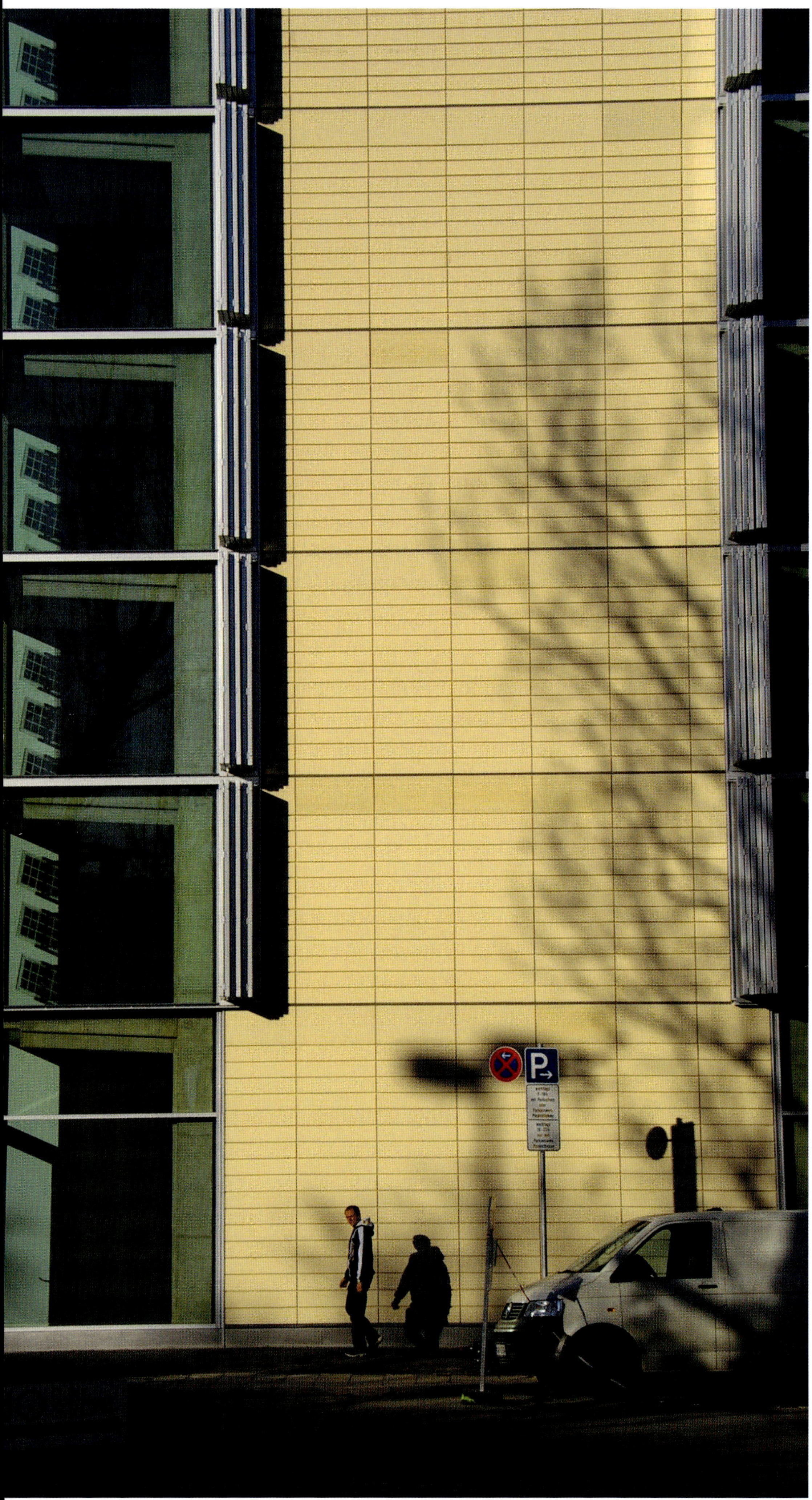

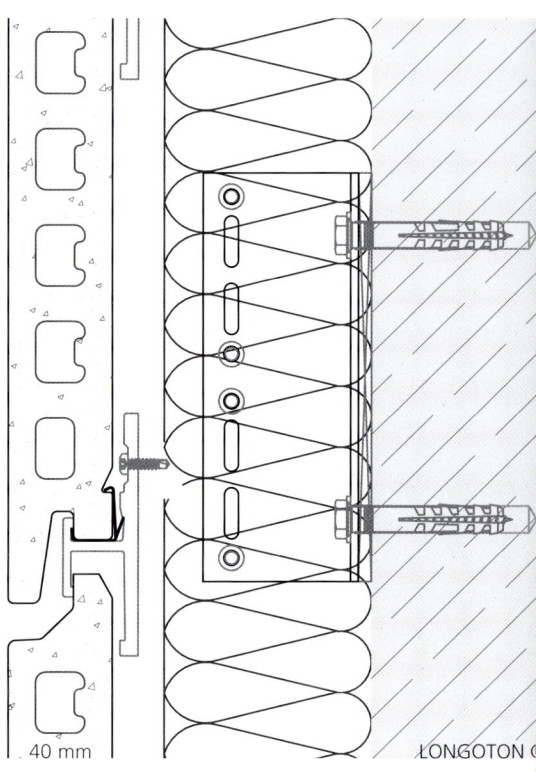

40 mm   LONGOTON

die Anwendung dieses hochleistungsfähigen neuen Baumaterials aussichtsreich, weil Beschädigungen, wie sie auf Baustellen leicht vorkommen, und Fertigungsungenauigkeiten unbedingt vermieden werden müssen.

Die östliche gläserne Front zur Amalienstraße belichtet in den Obergeschossen die inneren, transluzenten Wände der Dozentenappartements. In der gläsernen Außenhaut liegen feine Metallreflektoren als horizontale Profile. Ein schmaler Streifen verbleibt in jedem Fassadenbauteil vollständig transparent, um die Sichtverbindung nach außen zu erhalten. Diese Stellen, die von der vormittäglichen Sonne durchdrungen und damit im Sommer auch zu unerwünschter Aufheizung führen würden, sind, um dies zu verhindern, durch nach außen stehende senkrechte Bleche teilweise verschattet.

Hinterlüftete, wärmegedämmte Keramikfassaden bekleiden die geschlossenen Wandfronten sowohl zur Außenseite nach Osten wie auch im Hofbereich. Die von uns seinerzeit in Zusammenarbeit mit einem niederbayerischen Ziegelwerk entwickelte Konstruktion wurde vom heutigen Hersteller in fertigungstechnisch hoher Kompetenz und durch jahrzehntelange Perfektionierung zu großformatigen Bauteilen weiterentwickelt, deren Formate und Farbgebung hier in bewusstem Bezug zum städtischen Kontext der nahen Ludwigstraße stehen.

Die Bauteilaktivierung der Stahlbetondecken als ein Prinzip der großflächigen Raumtemperierung mit sehr geringer Differenz zur Raumlufttemperatur, wie wir sie erstmals vor über 10 Jahren bei größeren Bauvorhaben eingesetzt haben, wurde inzwischen ein vielfach praktizierter erfolg-

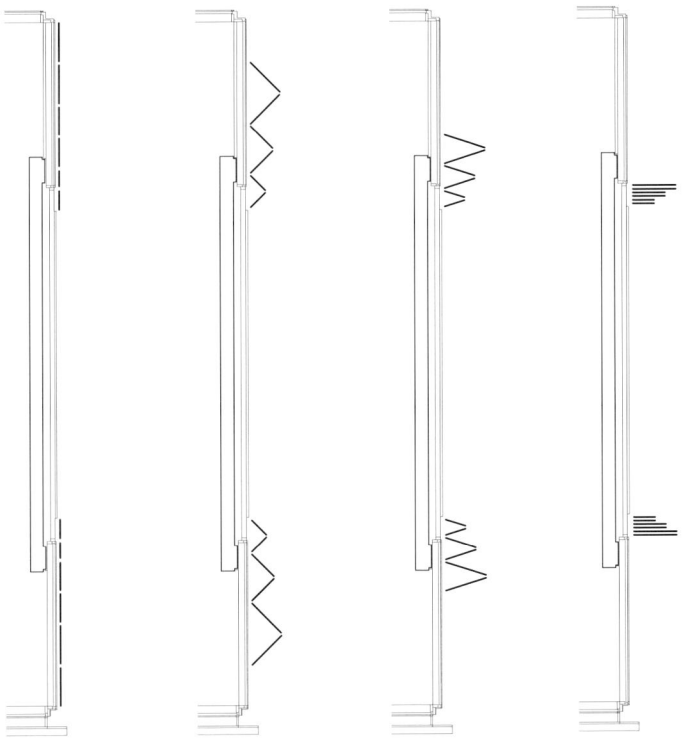
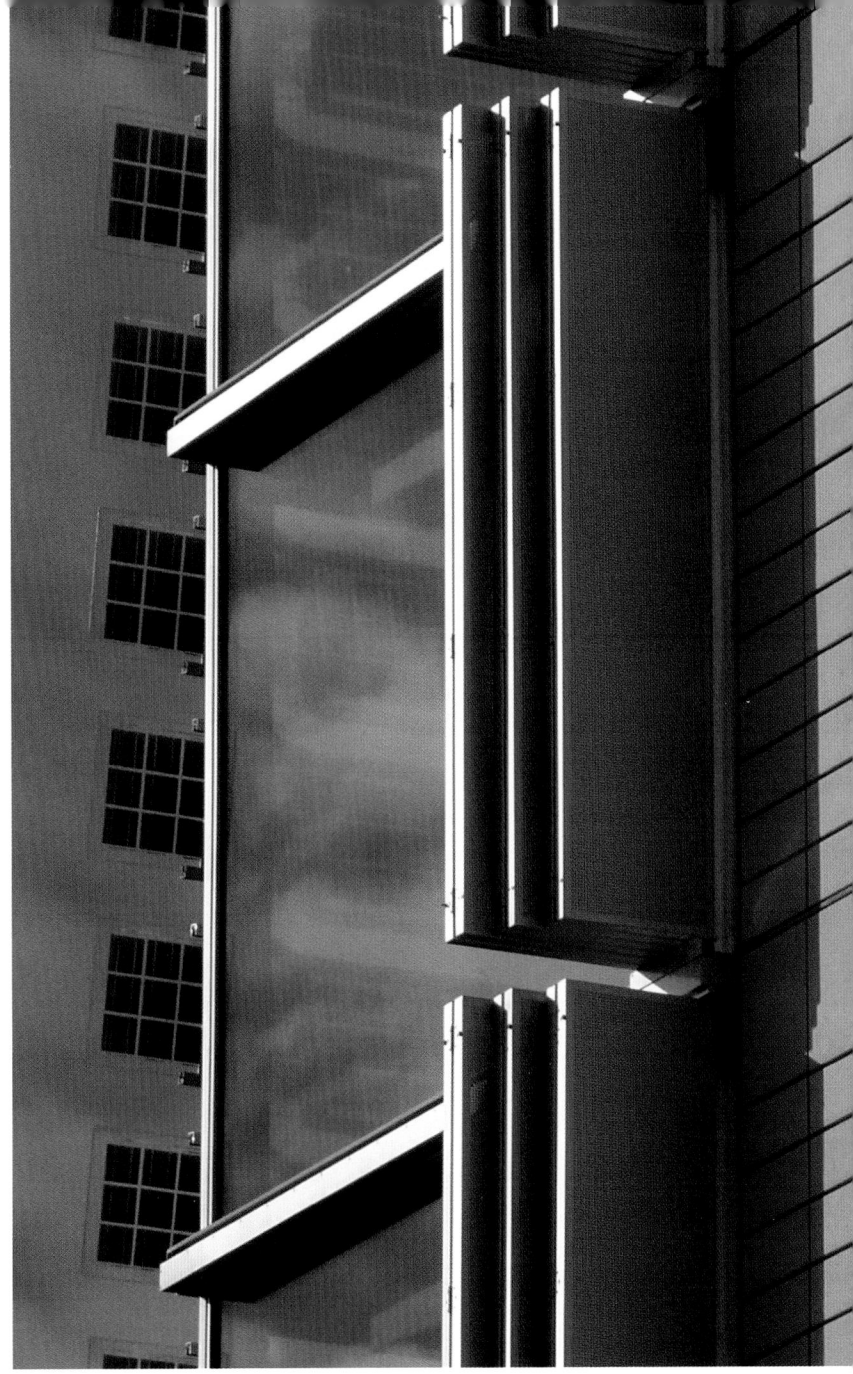

reicher Standard. Wärmeabgabe oder Kühlung über die großen, raumbildenden Flächen von Boden und Decke sind physiologisch komfortabel, ebenso wie die Wirkung von Strahlung bei weitgehender Vermeidung von Konvektion der Raumluft. Die Dimensionierung von Stahlbetondecken hat damit nicht nur Bezug zu den statischen Notwendigkeiten, sondern ihre thermische Speicherfähigkeit ermöglicht auch die Nutzung von Umweltenergie selbst bei nur geringem Temperaturniveau.

Fußböden

Alle Bodenoberflächen des Gebäudekomplexes bestehen aus Naturstein. Verkehrsflächen und Flächen mit starker Nutzung durch Publikum sind mit dunklem, weitgehend unempfindlichem „Anröchter Dolomit" belegt, alle Einzelräume und Gemeinschaftsräume mit dem für Bayern so charakteristischen Sollnhofener Jura, der bruchrau verwendet wurde, um sowohl die große Farbvielfalt als auch die zahlreichen, ablesbaren Einschlüsse in diesem heimischen Sedimentgestein zur Wirkung zu bringen.

Die Bäder

Um in den relativ schmalen Studentenzimmern durchwegs eigene Duschbäder realisieren zu können und gleichzeitig den dafür erforderlichen Flächenbedarf zu minimieren, wurde ein in der Größe veränderbarer Nassraum entwickelt. Wird das Bad nicht benutzt oder dient es nur als Toilette, so bedarf es dazu nur eines Raumes von minimaler Breite. Soll jedoch das Bad ganzflächig verfügbar sein, so lassen sich die beiden eine Doppeltür bildenden Glasflächen um 90 Grad nach außen schwenken, wodurch ein Teil des Vorraums temporär dazugewonnen wird. Das Bad hat also nur bei Benutzung die wünschenswerte Größe, ist ansonsten aber auf die Tiefe eines größeren Schrankes reduziert.

Der technischen Logik des Trockenbaus folgend, wie er für den Innenausbau weitgehend eingesetzt wurde, sind auch die Bäder, soweit ihre Wände nicht aus Glastafeln bestehen, aus großflächigem, leicht zu reinigendem, an den Übergangsstellen der Flächen weich gerundetem Corean. Einzelne großflächige Wandteile mit bereits integrierten Objekten kamen vom Hersteller und wurden vor Ort nur noch zusammengesetzt.

Möbel

Gäste des Hauses sollen sehen, dass in Bayern schon immer die Tradition eines modernen Designverständnisses gepflegt wurde. Sie begegnen hier Originalen bedeutender Designklassiker, um so ein Stück eigene Erfahrung machen zu können, was im Idealfall auch der persönlichen ästhetischen Bildung dient.

Von besonderer Bedeutung sind dabei Objekte des täglichen Bedarfs und der häufigen Handhabung. Eine Designlinie für die beweglichen Einrichtungsgegenstände und Leuchten ist im gesamten Gebäude durchgehalten. Beispiele:

Kubische USM-Möbel von Fritz Haller
Arbeits- und Esstische von Egon Eiermann
Stehleuchten, Arbeitsleuchten, Wandleuchten von Michele de Lucchi
Garderobenständer von Fritz Frenkler
Stapelstühle für die Halle und das Dachgeschoss von David Rowland
Stühle und Barhocker im Bistro von Nanna Ditzel
Stehtische und Bürostühle von Wilkhahn
Piktogramme von Otl Aicher

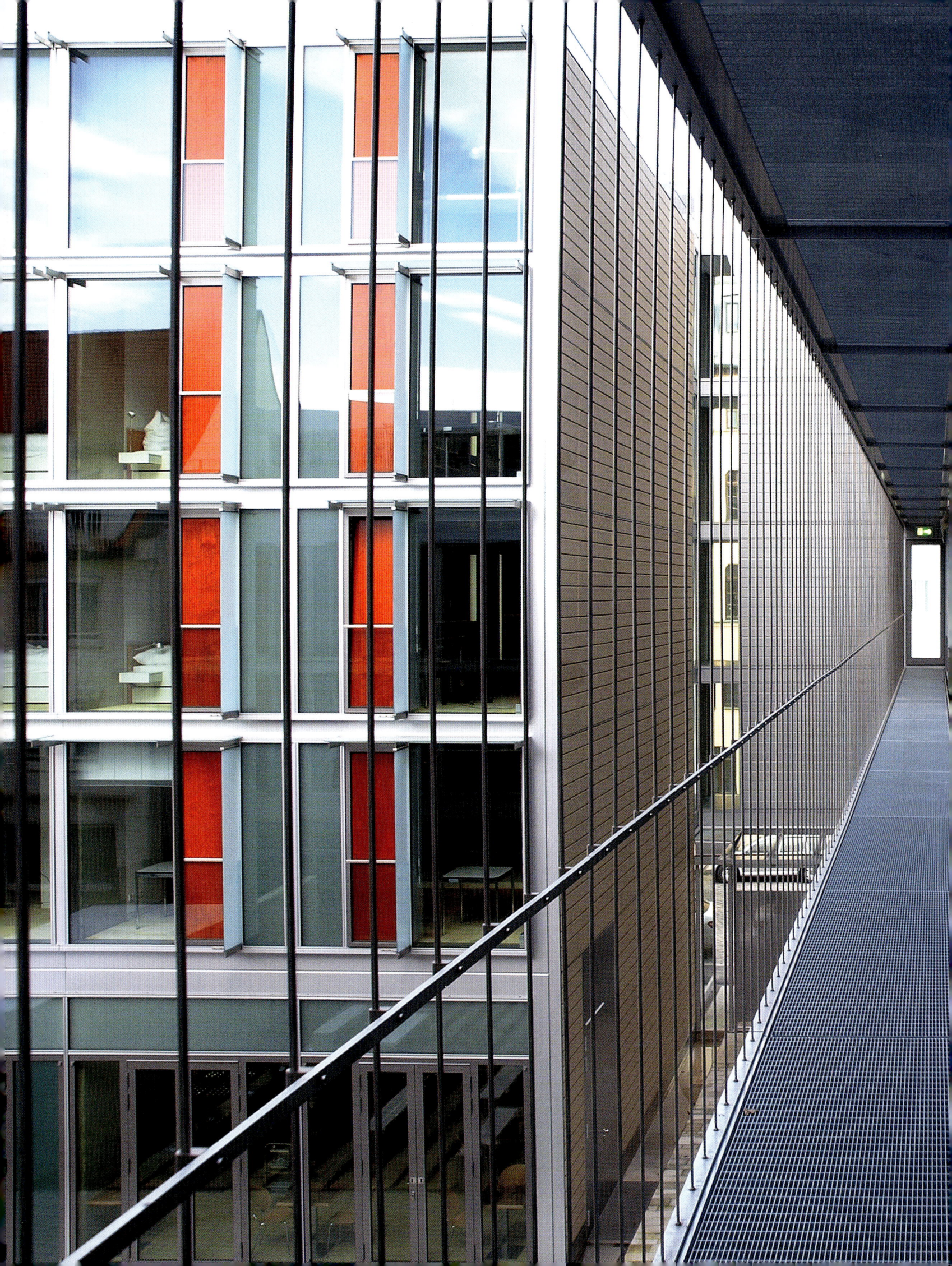

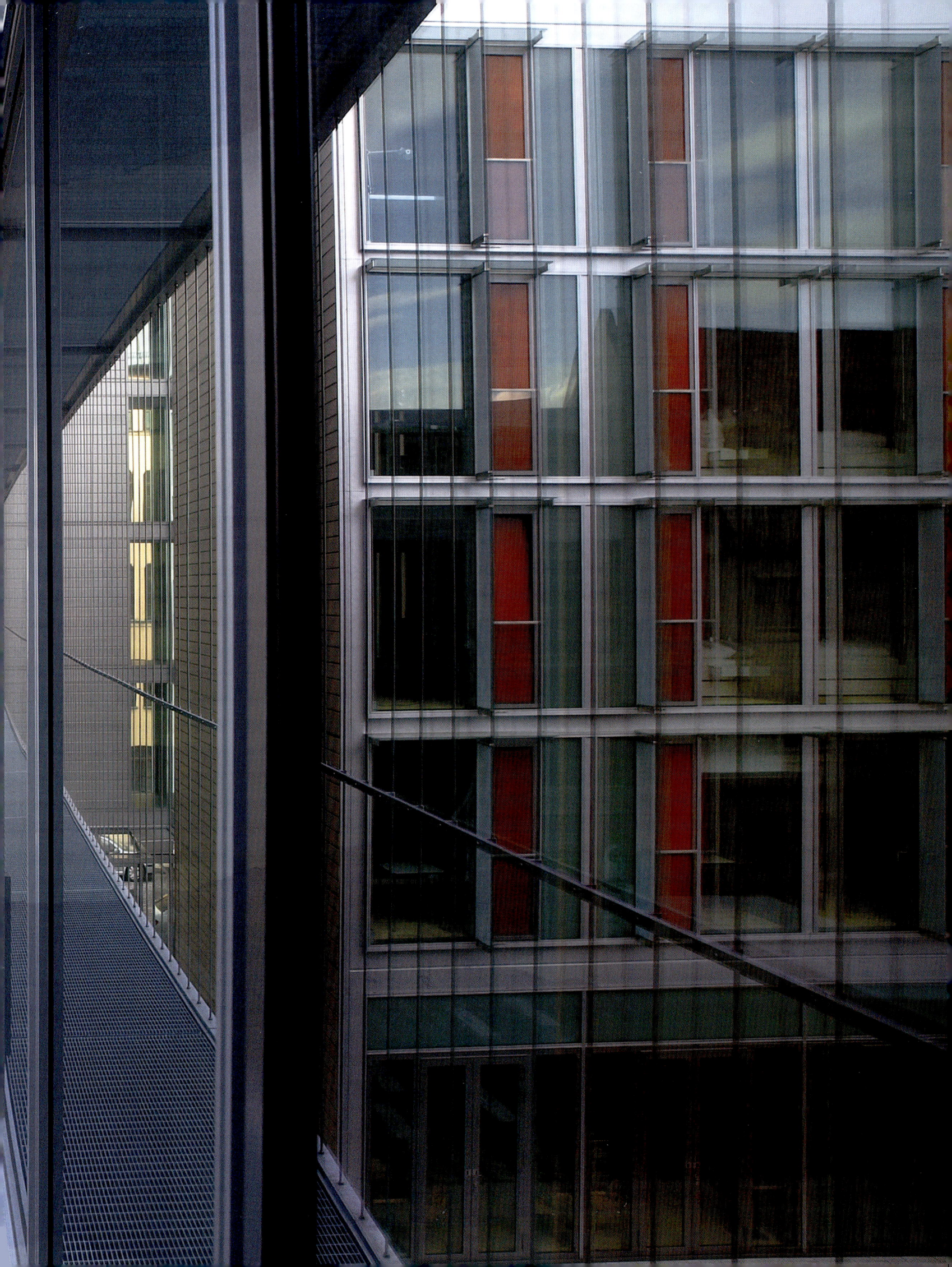

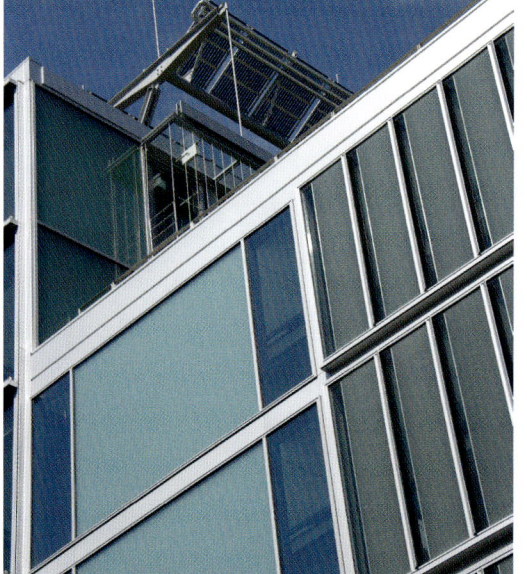

Special Forms of Construction and Products

Thomas Herzog

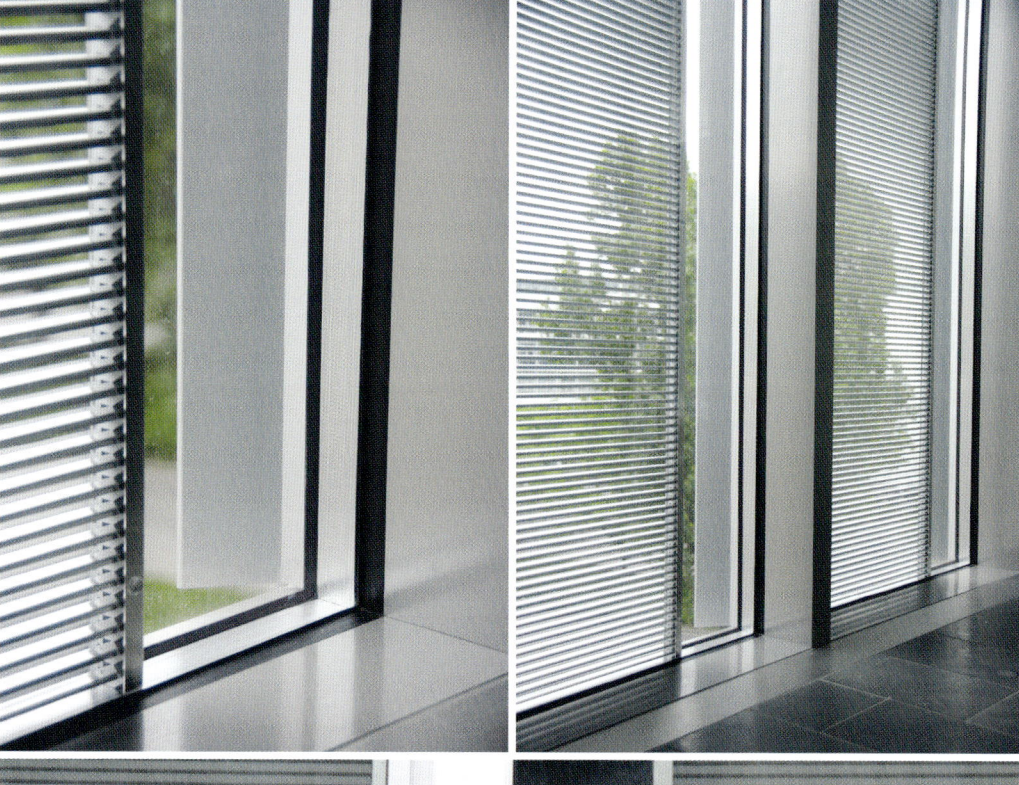

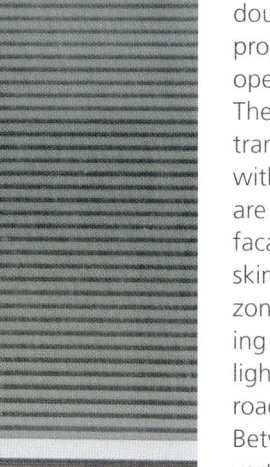

OKASOLAR RETRO O

One aspect of the architectural and engineering task was to apply state-of-the-art technology and forms of construction in the appropriate places, as well as materials, components and products that would comply with high modern technical standards in terms of function and design.
Examples of this are outlined below.

Steel arms

The outer facade planes of the south tract are suspended from large girders that cantilever out on both sides of the building above the seventh-floor roof level. The steel structures at the level of the terrace storey are sculpture-like modern engineering elements. The entire roof area is covered with high-performance tubular collectors, the state-of-the-art elegance of which is also visible from the space in the roof storey. A maximum of transparency was ensured by keeping both sides of the ground floor free of external vertical load-bearing elements for the full height of the hall.

The building envelope

The inner layer of the **double-skin facade** on the south side consists of room-height double glazing with good thermal-insulation properties and with a number of ventilation openings to the facade intermediate space. The outer skin is formed with alternately transparent and translucent panes of glass with point fixings. The transparent panes are frameless and project slightly beyond the facade plane. The folded construction of the skin increases stability and resistance to horizontal forces. Scope is allowed for converting the present system to one with opening lights, should traffic on the inner-city ring road be significantly reduced in the future. Between the two glazed skins, a continuous vertical intermediate space was created as a means of ventilation. In addition to the positive effect this has in terms of sound insulation, the special appearance of this form of construction defines the identity of the building on the side facing the city centre. Large **sliding shutters** with wooden louvres in the intermediate space between the two skins of the outer wall form an effective means of shading, reducing unwanted heat gains in summer in the lounge areas. According to needs, the shutters can be extended floor by floor over the entire length of the south face; alternatively, they can be pushed back over each other to cover half the area of this glazed front. At all events, the effect of the large areas of wood has a great influence on the atmosphere in the communal spaces on the floors where students live. After repeated reflection, the light that enters also determines the colour values of these large areas.

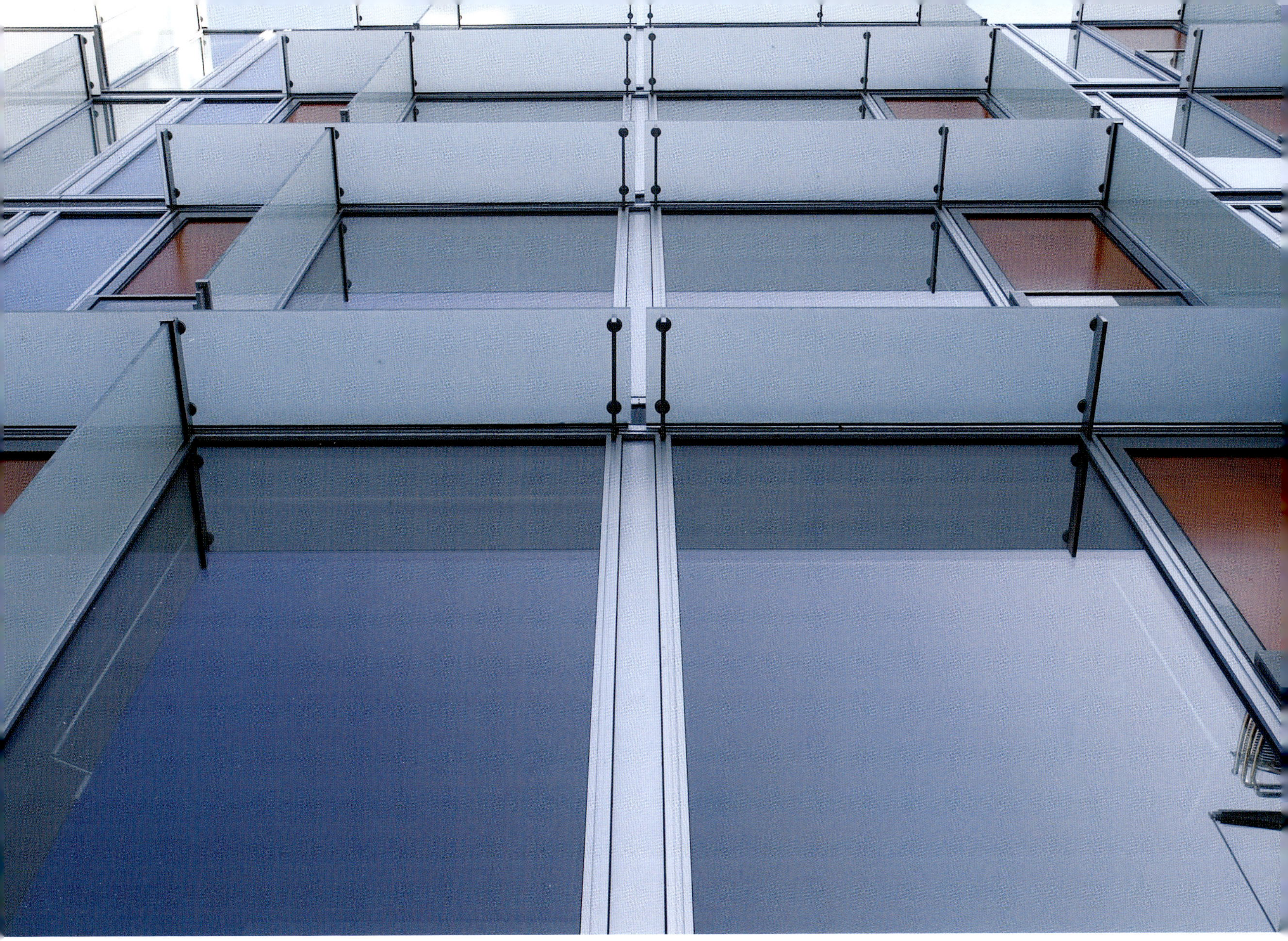

The "**harp**" suspended on the north face supports the escape-balcony gratings. Furthermore, the closely spaced, inox rods, which are connected horizontally at balustrade height, form a barrier to prevent people falling from the balconies.

The facades to the east and west tracts overlooking the courtyard are distinguished to a large extent by **lightweight ventilation panels with vacuum insulation**. The deep spaces in these tracts are extensively glazed in order to provide good views out and to maximize the exploitation of daylight. The requisite thermal-insulation effect could, therefore, be achieved only with high-quality triple glazing. Lightweight wood panels were constructed with a marine plywood lining and with a newly developed form of vacuum insulation internally. This has a thermal transmission that measurements show to be lower than that of conventional foam or mineral-wool insulation by a factor of 6. As a result, it was possible to design the panels with correspondingly slender dimensions. But only if the elements are fabricated completely at works, together with the insulation, and the panels are hung in position on site with the greatest of care does the use of this top-grade new building material appear to hold any promise for the future, since lack of precision in the manufacturing process and the damage that can so easily be caused on site have to be avoided at all costs.

The daylight that enters through the **glazed eastern front** overlooking Amalienstrasse falls on the translucent internal walls of the lecturers' apartments on the upper floors. In the glazed outer skin, there are slender hori-

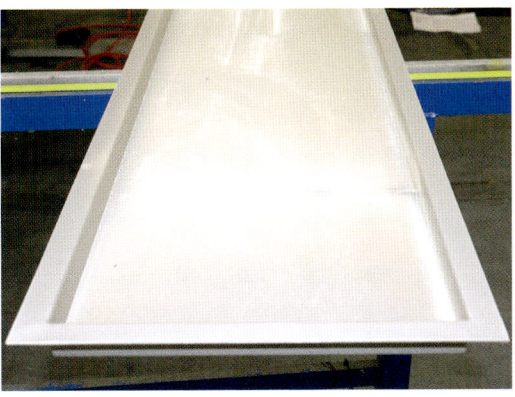
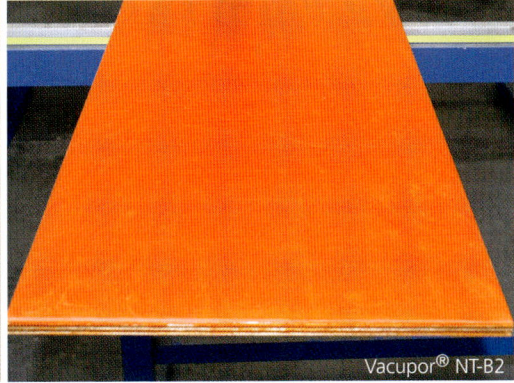
Vacupor® NT-B2

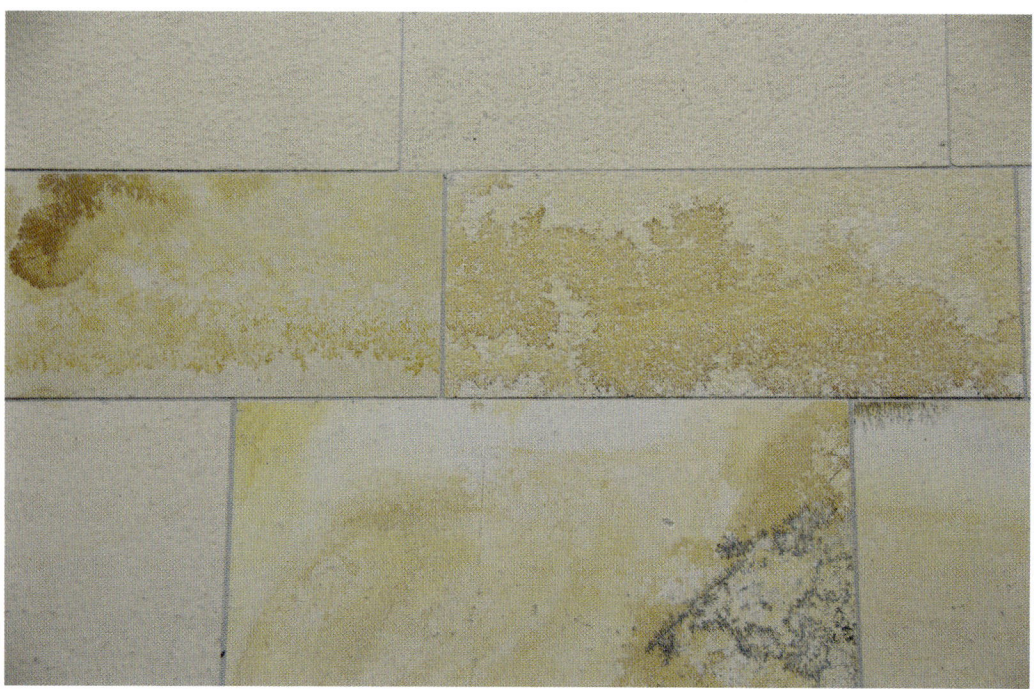

zontal metal sections that act as reflectors. A narrow transparent strip in each facade element maintains a visual link with the outside. In order to prevent unwanted heat gains in summer caused by the morning sun penetrating these strips, vertical sheet-metal sections were fitted externally to provide partial shading.

The closed areas of the east-facing outer walls as well as those overlooking the courtyard are clad with **rear-ventilated, thermally insulated ceramic facade panels**. This form of construction, which we created at an earlier date in collaboration with a brickworks in Lower Bavaria, was developed further by the present manufacturer with a high-quality finish to produce – after decades of perfectioning – a large-scale building element. The size, shape and coloration of these panels consciously reflect the urban surroundings of Ludwigstraße.

Activation of building components
The activation of building components in the form of the reinforced concrete floors is an underlying principle of the large-area spatial heating concept. This system, which is based on a very small difference between the temperature of the component and that of the air in the rooms, is one we applied for the first time more than ten years ago in a larger building scheme. In the meantime, it has found widespread application and has become a successful standard. The emission of heating or cooling energy via the large areas of floors and ceilings ensures a physiologically comfortable sensation akin to the effect of radiant heat in internal spaces where air convection is avoided. The dimensions of the reinforced concrete floors, therefore, were determined not only by structural needs, but also by the requisite thermal storage capacity. In this way, the exploitation of environmental energy becomes possible even at low temperature levels.

Floor finishes
All floors in this development were paved with stone. Circulation areas and other surfaces that are subject to heavy wear are covered with dark Anröchte "dolomite", a stone with great resilience. Individual rooms and communal spaces are paved with Sollnhofen Jura, a characteristic Bavarian product that is used in its rough quarried state. In this form, the great diversity of colour and the many particles enclosed within this native sedimentary stone are effectively brought out.

Bathrooms
To install individual shower facilities in the relatively narrow student apartments, while at the same time minimizing the area required, a wet room was developed that could be varied in size. If the sanitary space is not used as a bathroom or serves merely as a WC, a space of only minimum width is necessary. If the bathroom is to be available over its full area, the glazed double doors can be turned outwards by 90°, allowing part of the lobby to be incorporated temporarily for this purpose. The bathroom then has the requisite size; otherwise it can be reduced to the depth of a largish cupboard.

The technical logic of dry forms of construction was extensively applied in the internal finishings. Accordingly, where the bathroom walls do not consist of glass, large-area easy-to-clean Corean panels were used to enclose these spaces. The panels are gently curved at the junctions with other elements. Individual large-area wall units with integrated fittings were supplied by the manufacturer and simply had to be assembled on site.

Furnishings
Guests of the house should appreciate that a modern understanding of design has a long tradition in Bavaria. This was to be made apparent through visual perception and the use of important, original design classics. In this way, guests can expand their own experience, a process that should ideally further their aesthetic education. Of special importance in this respect is regular contact with everyday objects – objects that often have a physical proximity and form an important counterpart to one's own person. A specific design line for movable furnishings, fittings, lamps, etc. has been observed throughout the building.

Examples of these include:
Cubic USM furnishings by Fritz Haller
Working and dining tables by Egon Eiermann
Standard lamps, working lamps and wall lamps by Michele de Lucchi
Clothes stands by Fritz Frenkler
Stackable chairs for the hall and roof storey by David Rowland
Chairs and bar stools in the bistro by Nanna Ditzel
Stand-up tables and office chairs by Wilkhahn
Pictographs by Otl Aicher

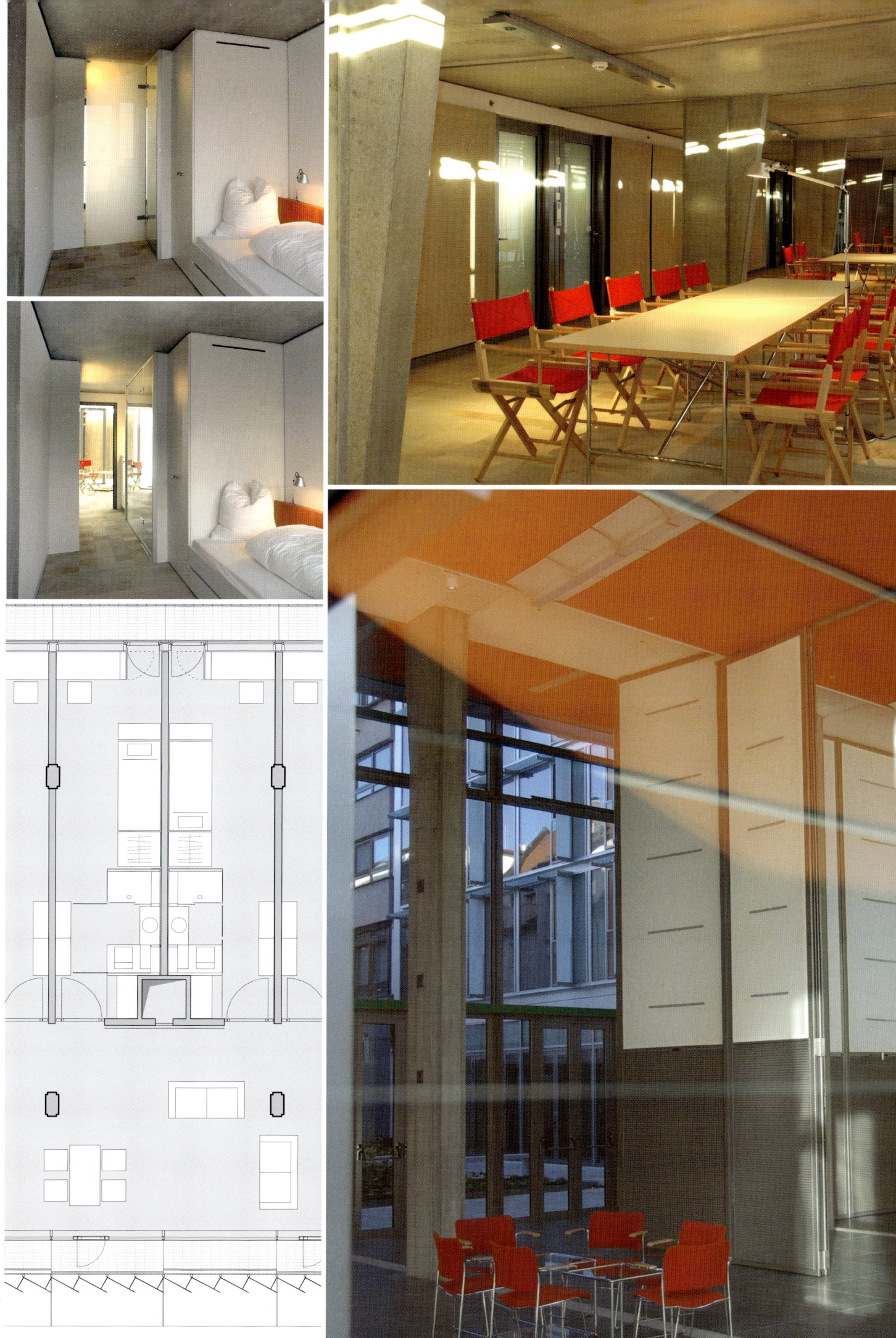

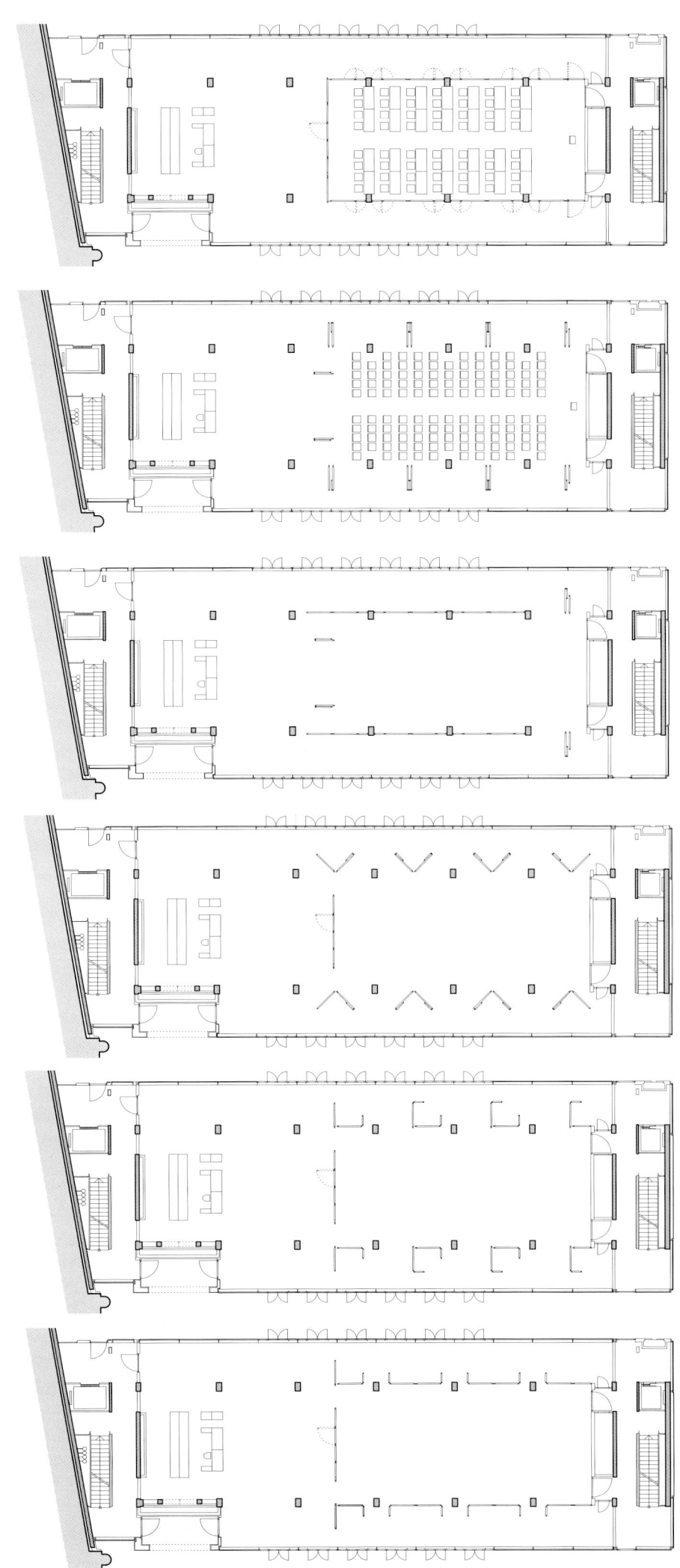

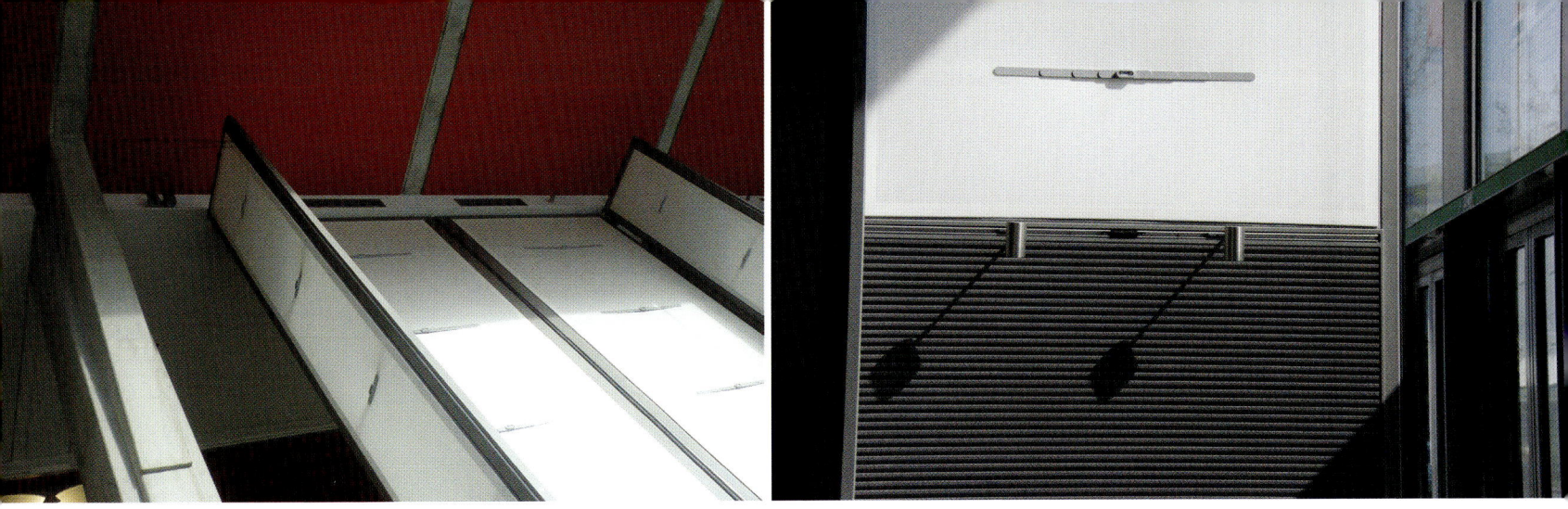

Das verstellbare Wandsystem

Für die Möglichkeit der räumlichen Abtrennung zum Veranstaltungssaal innerhalb der großen Halle wurde ein Wandsystem entwickelt, das über Türhöhe aus einer mehrlagigen transluzenten Membrankonstruktion besteht, die sowohl Tageslicht von außen als auch nach Sonnenuntergang Kunstlicht von Innen wirkungsvoll durchdringt. Monumentalität wird dadurch vermieden und die hell schimmernden Membranflächen verhindern einen optisch hermetischen räumlichen Abschluss des inneren Saales.

Movable wall system

To allow a realm to be created for special events within the large hall space, a wall system was developed, comprising a multilayer, translucent membrane structure that extends above door height. This construction is effectively penetrated by both daylight and, after dusk, by the internal artificial lighting. As a result, any sense of monumentality is avoided, and the brightly gleaming surfaces of the membrane help to overcome the impression of a visually hermetic spatial enclosure within the hall.

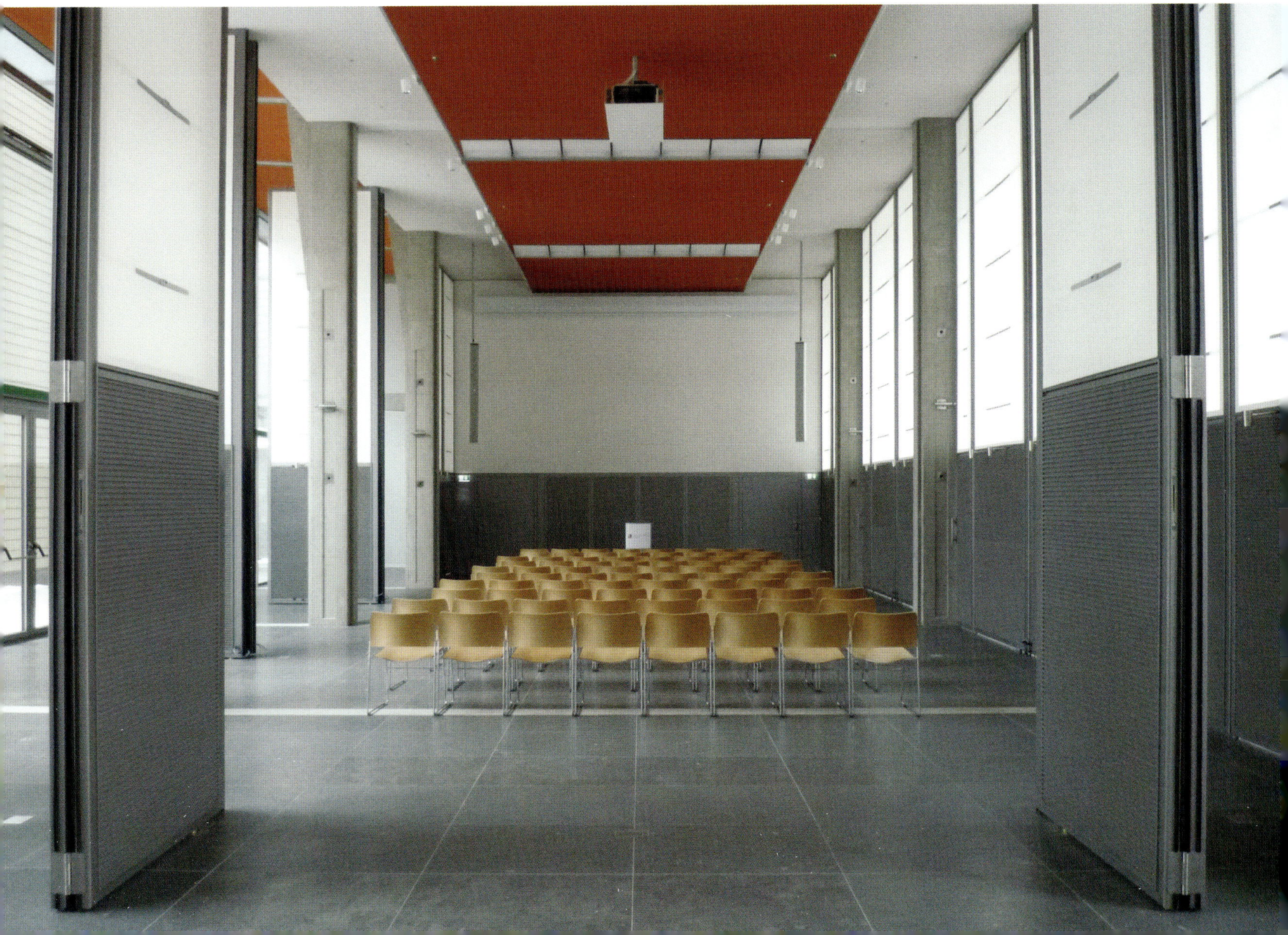

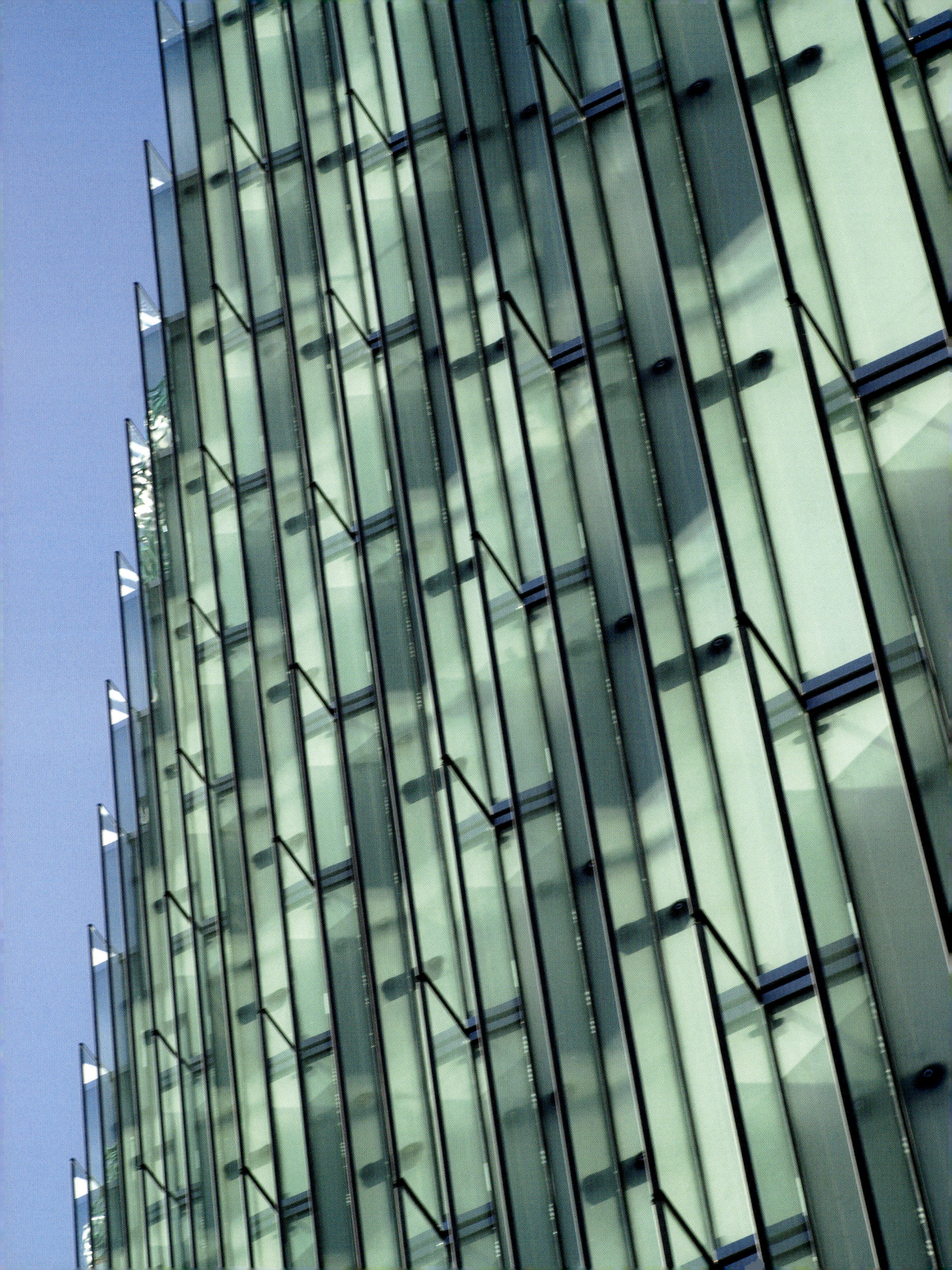

Energetische Bewertung
Assessment of Energy Performance

Gerd Hauser

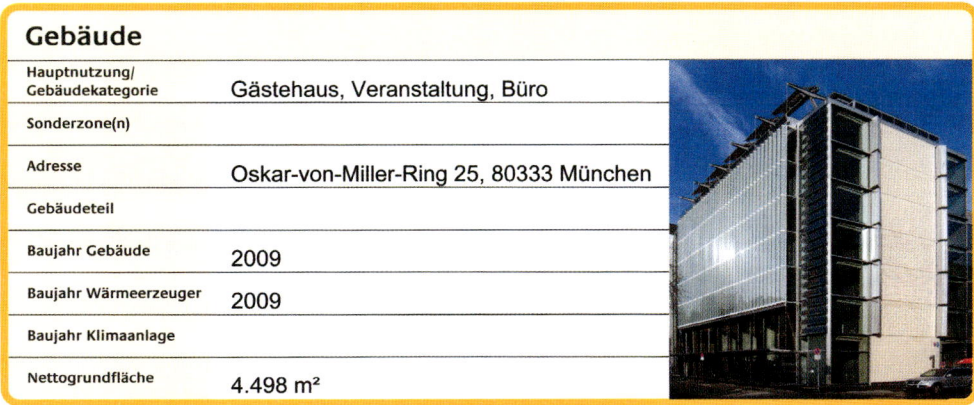

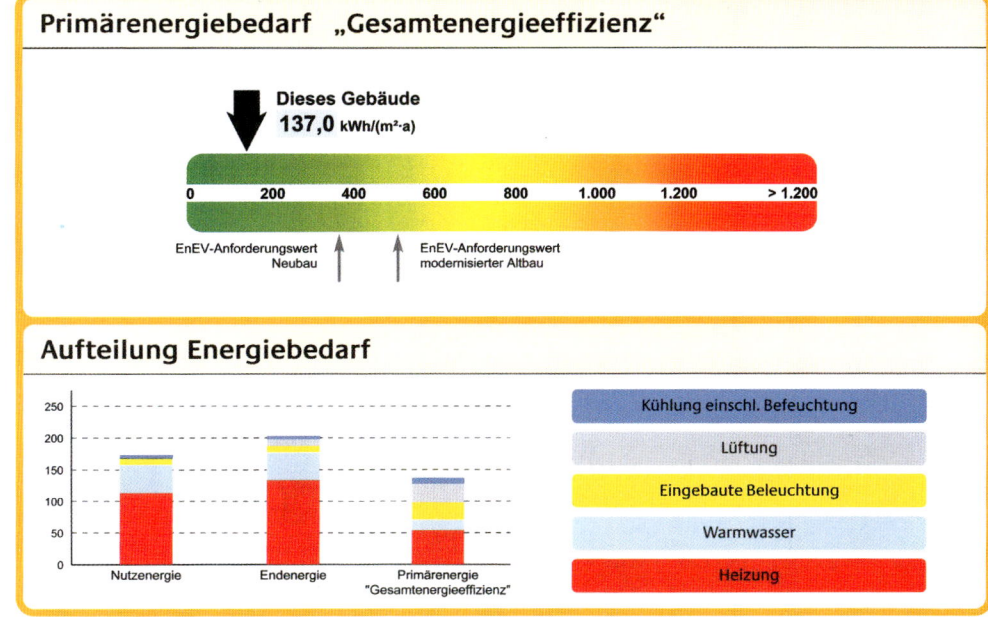

Schulen und Universitäten als Hort der Ausbildung und Erziehung von Kindern und Jugendlichen sind das geeignete Objekt, um Nachhaltigkeit zu vermitteln und umzusetzen. Zu keiner Zeit unseres Lebens sind wir so aufnahmefähig wie in diesem Alter und können von einer hohen Qualität der Raumakustik, des Schallschutzes, der Tageslicht- und Kunstlichtversorgung, der Luft sowie einer hohen thermisch-hygrischen Behaglichkeit infolge eines guten baulichen Wärmeschutzes profitieren, die ökologischen und ökonomischen Auswirkungen durch Demonstration erfahren und die Vorzüge erkennen, damit wir dann auch an anderen Orten ähnliche Qualitäten anstreben. Gerade in Deutschland sind wir gehalten, in Ausbildungsstätten und dazugehörigen Einrichtungen die bestmöglichen Bedingungen sicherzustellen, entsteht dort doch unsere wesentliche, nachwachsende Ressource.

Das Oskar von Miller Forum, ein von der bayrischen Bauwirtschaft zur Erweiterung der Bildungsmöglichkeiten des Nachwuchses an den Baufakultäten der Technischen Universität München realisiertes Gästehaus für exzellente Lehrende, Lernende und junge Meister leistet als Begegnungs- und Kommunikationszentrum in diesem Zusammenhang einen wesentlichen Beitrag. Dabei wird im Gegensatz zu üblichen Schul- und Universitätsgebäuden durch die zusätzlichen Nutzungen das Erfahrungsspektrum erheblich erweitert.

Zur Bewusstseinsstärkung der Nutzer und zahlreichen Besucher des Oskar von Miller Forums für Fragestellungen der Erzeugung, Verteilung, Speicherung und des Verbrauchs von Energie und deren Einordnung in den Gesamtzusammenhang der Nachhaltigkeit wurde für das Oskar von Miller Forum ein Energiepass erstellt und die Qualität hinsichtlich Nachhaltigkeit nachgewiesen. Die Primär-Energiekennzahl von 137 kWh/(m²a) belegt die hohe Qualität des Oskar von Miller Forums auch in Hinblick auf die Nachhaltigkeit des Gebäudes.

As centres for the education and training of children and young people, schools and universities are the ideal objects through which to communicate and implement the goals of sustainability. At no other time in our lives are we so receptive; and we can profit and learn from high-quality spatial acoustics, sound insulation, natural and artificial lighting, the purity of the air, as well as a high level of hygro-thermal comfort as the outcome of good thermal insulation in a building. Via a process of demonstration, we can come to appreciate the environmental and economic effects that play a role in all these things and to recognize their advantages, so that we may aspire to similar qualities in other locations. In Germany in particular, we are obliged to ensure the best possible conditions in places of education and related institutions, for it is there that our most important regenerable resource has its origins.

The Oskar von Miller Forum, a residence realized by the Bavarian building sector to extend educational facilities for the younger generation in the building faculties of the Technische Universität München (TUM), accommodates outstanding teaching staff, students and young masters of the building trades. In this respect, the institution makes a major contribution as a meeting place and centre for communication. In contrast to the usual school and university buildings, the forum also provides functions that considerably broaden one's range of experience. As a means of heightening the awareness of users and the many visitors to the Oskar von Miller Forum in terms of the production, distribution, storage and consumption of energy and their role and significance in the overall context of sustainability, an energy certificate was issued for the Oskar von Miller Forum, attesting its quality in this respect. A primary-energy index of 137 kWh/(m²a) confirms the high standards of the Oskar von Miller Forum and its environmental quality.

Freiraumplanung

Landscape Planning

Christoph Valentien

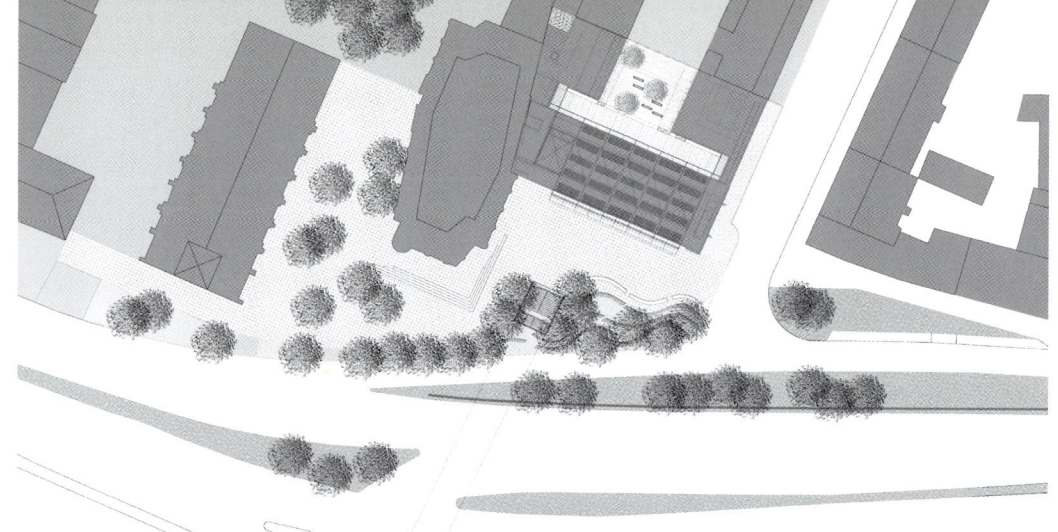

Eine hohe, offene Glashalle bildet das Herzstück der dichten Gebäudegruppe des Oskar von Miller Forums. Der Raum lebt von dem Bezug zwischen zwei Freiräumen, von eng und weit, privat und öffentlich; die große Halle lädt ein, wird Teil des öffentlichen Raumes.

Der kleine intime Innenhof ist luftig gestaltet, dunkles Grün steht im Kontrast zu hellen Plattenbändern und weißen Blüten, Lichtpunkte im Schatten des Hofes.

Der öffentliche Vorplatz ist eine wichtige Verbindungszone zwischen dem Haus der Kunst und den Pinakotheken, aber auch von der Amalienstraße zur Innenstadt. Stark belastet durch den Verkehr des Oskar-von-Miller-Rings, wirkt der Platz heute wenig einladend und wird schnell durchquert. Dies entspricht nicht seiner Bedeutung im Stadtraum, zumal er auch gemeinsamer Vorplatz der St. Markus Kirche und des Oskar von Miller Forums ist. Er sollte am Tage wie bei abendlichen Veranstaltungen nicht nur Passage, sondern auch ein angenehmer und freundlicher öffentlicher Raum sein.

Es wird vorgeschlagen, die verschiedenen Bereiche bis hin zur Kirche durch einheitliche und großzügig gestaltete Beläge zu verbinden und zugeordnete, differenzierte Aufenthaltsräume zu schaffen. Vor dem Oskar von Miller Forum entstünde eine attraktive Vorzone, die bei Veranstaltungen auch für Außengastronomie genutzt werden könnte. Der Ring wird abgeschirmt durch hohe Bäume. Eine Kulisse geschwungener Eibenhecken, vor denen eine breite lange Bank liegt, lässt eine eigene Atmosphäre entstehen, eine kleine Oase in der lauten Stadt, ein Gewinn auch für das Quartier.

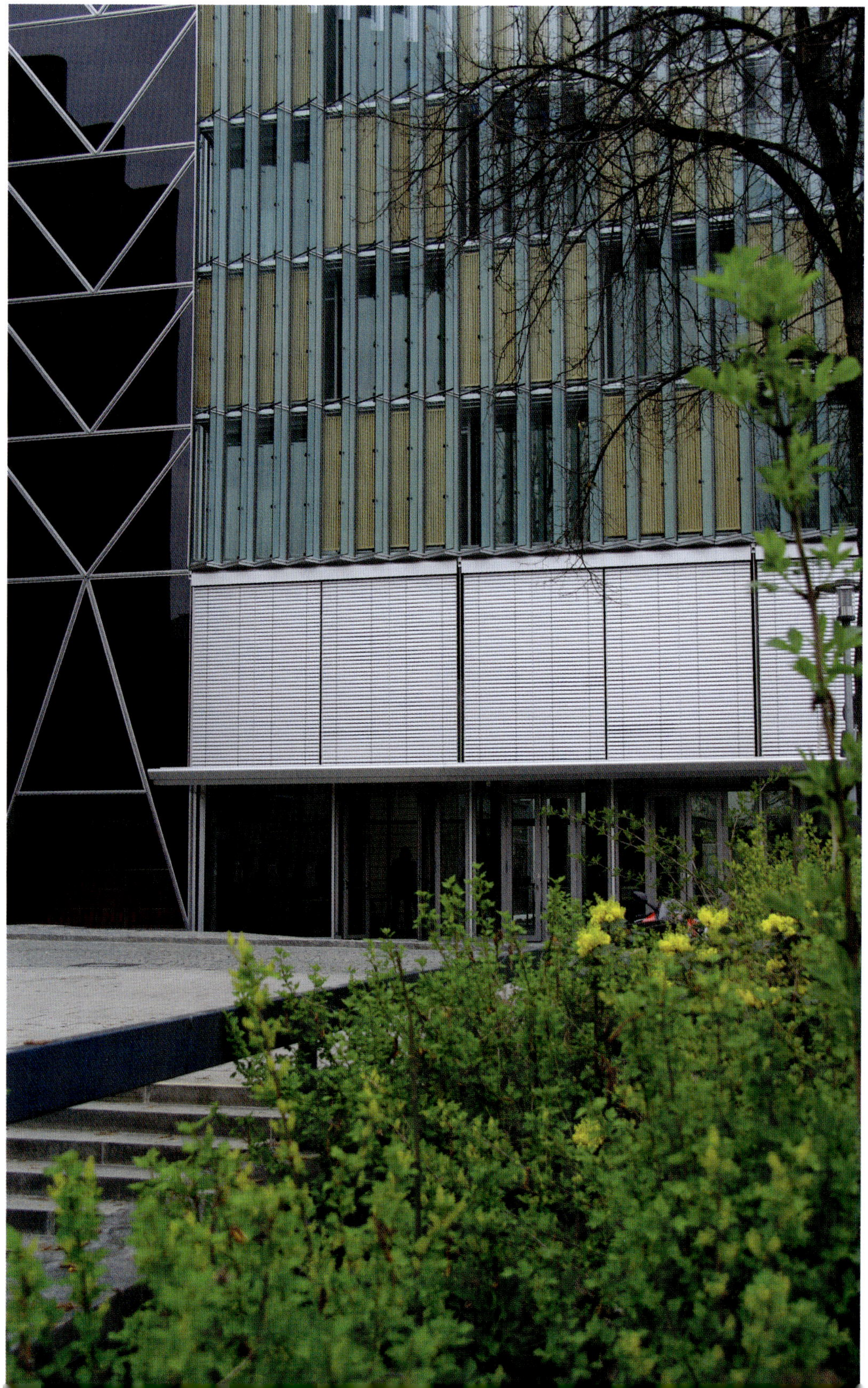

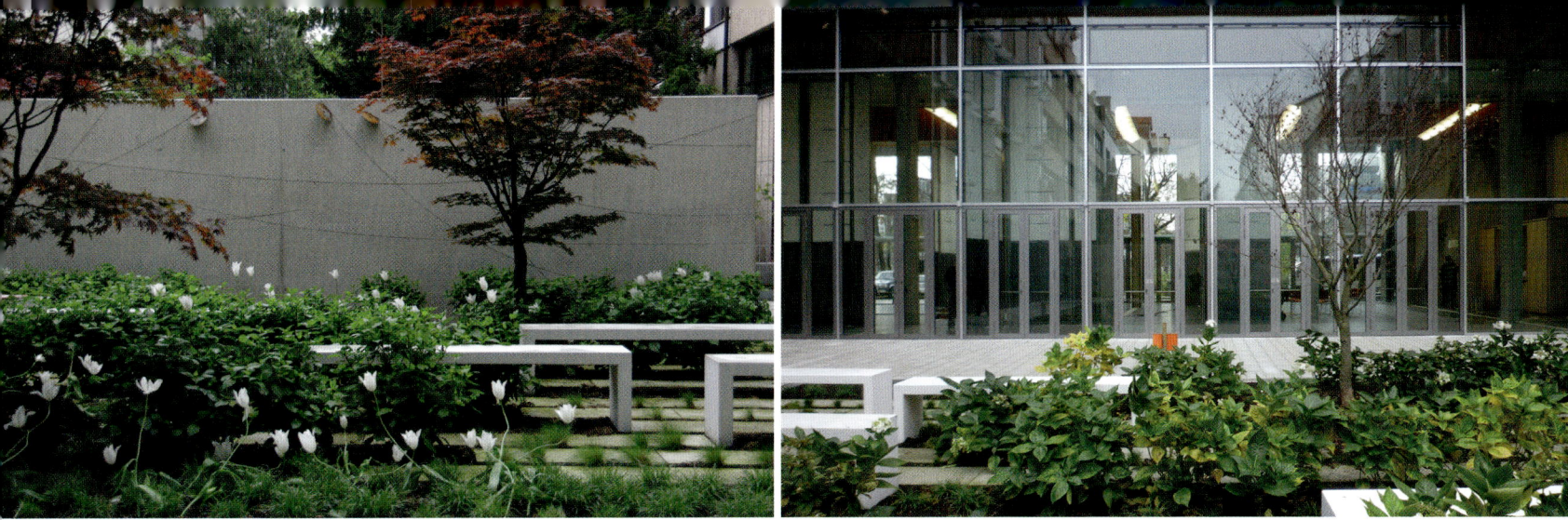

At the heart of the compact group of buildings comprising the Oskar von Miller Forum is an open glazed hall, the vitality of which is based on the relationship between two open areas and on the contrast between constriction and breadth, private and communal activities. This large hall is an inviting space and also forms part of the public realm. The small, intimate courtyard has an airy design: dark green is contrasted with light-coloured strips of concrete paving and white blossoms that form spots of light in the shade of the open space. The public forecourt is an important connecting zone between the well-known art gallery Haus der Kunst and the various Pinakothek galleries. It also forms a link between Amalienstrasse and the inner city. At present, this space suffers from the heavy traffic on the Oskar-von-Miller-Ring road and is not particularly inviting. People tend to cross it quickly without heeding the surroundings, which does not reflect its significance as part of the urban space, especially as it forms a common access area for St Mark's Church and the Oskar von Miller Forum. By day and also when evening events take place here, it should function not just as a through route: it should be a friendly, attractive public space.

Suggestions have been made to link the various areas as far as the church by means of unified pavings with a generous layout and to create a series of related yet distinct recreational spaces. According to these plans, an attractive approach zone would be formed in front of the Oskar von Miller Forum that could also be used for special events with outdoor catering. The ring road would be screened off by tall trees, and a background of curving yew hedges with a long, broad bench in front would help to create a special atmosphere: a little oasis in the noisy city, a gain for the entire neighbourhood.

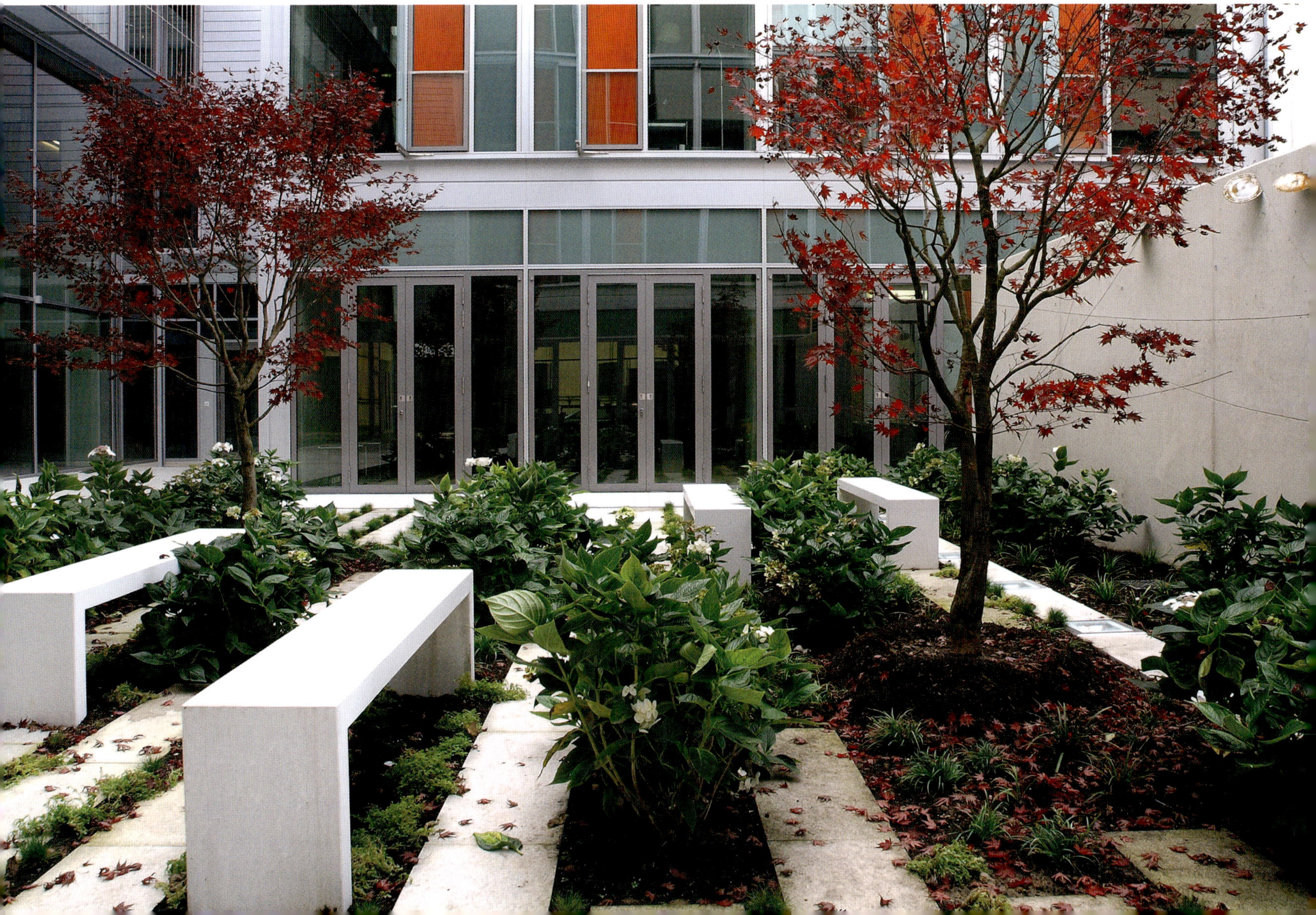

Baugrunderkundung, Gründung und Baugrubenverbau

Soil Investigations, Foundations and Shoring of Excavations

Norbert Vogt

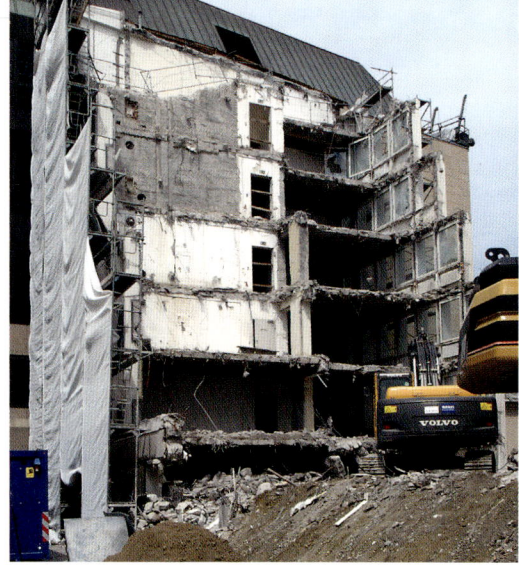
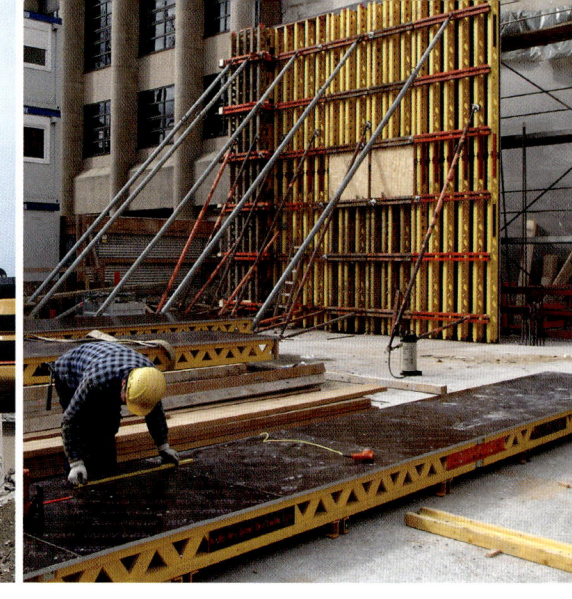

Im Bauwerksbereich befanden sich zuoberst nur locker gelagerte Auffüllungen, darunter gewachsene quartäre Kiese der Münchner Schotterebene bis zu Tiefen zwischen etwa 8 m und 12 m unter Geländeoberfläche in mitteldichter bis dichter Lagerung. Zur Tiefe folgen mit sehr großer Mächtigkeit tertiäre Bodenschichten in einer Wechsellagerung aus Feinsanden, Tonen und Schluffen. Vom im Westen direkt an das Baufeld angrenzenden Bank- und Verwaltungsgebäude standen aus dem Jahre 1973 Ergebnisse von 5 Aufschlussbohrungen zur Verfügung. Zwei dieser Aufschlussbohrungen liegen direkt an der Grundstücksgrenze. Auf der Ostseite des Baufeldes, an der Amalienstraße, und an der Südseite am Oskar-von-Miller-Ring wurden weitere Bohrungen als Rammkernbohrungen mit einem Bohrdurchmesser von 178 mm und Tiefen von ca. 14 m niedergebracht. Die Gründungssohle der zwei Untergeschosse liegt auf sehr gut tragfähigen Schichten nahe der Grenze zwischen Quartär und Tertiär. Das Bauwerk konnte daher mit einer einfachen tragenden Bodenplatte flach gegründet werden. Das Grundwasser steht hier ca. 7 m unter Gelände an. Deshalb wurden die Bauwerkssohle und -wände wasserundurchlässig als weiße Wanne ausgebildet. Auch die Baugrubenumschließung musste wegen des ca. 1 m über der Baugrubensohle anstehenden Grundwassers im untersten Bereich als dichte Wand ausgeführt werden. Sie bindet unten in dichte Tone ein, so dass beim Abpumpen des Grundwassers innerhalb der Baugrube von außen kein Wasser nachströmt. Hier konnte im Westen die vorhandene Schlitzwand aus der Errichtung des erwähnten Bank- und Verwaltungsgebäudes genutzt werden. Entlang der Nordseite wurde eine überschnittene Bohrpfahlwand eingebracht. Die südliche und östliche Begrenzung der Baugrube wurde mit der Sonderform eines Trägerverbaues gesichert. Dabei stehen vertikale Stahlträger im Abstand von etwa 2,30 m voneinander vor der Grundstücksgrenze im Innern des Grundstücks und die Ausfachung zwischen diesen Trägern zur Bildung der Wand direkt an der Grundstücksgrenze oder etwas außerhalb. Die wasserundurchlässige Ausfachung im Baugrubentiefsten wurde mit Hilfe von Düsenstrahllamellen geschaffen. Dabei wird unter sehr hohem Druck und mit großer Fließgeschwindigkeit Zementsuspension in den Boden eingebracht, die das Bodengefüge auflöst und den Boden mit ihr durchsetzt, wodurch ein fester und dichter Boden-Beton entsteht. Die Erd- und Wasserdruckkräfte auf die Baugrubenumschließung wurden durch eine einfache Rückverankerung aller Stahlträger, die deutlich unter die Baugrubensohle hinab reichen, aufgenommen. Bei der Ausführung der Verbauarbeiten gab es unerwartete Schwierigkeiten im Bereich der sehr locker gelagerten Auffüllung, die dort durch eine Verkittungsinjektion gemeistert werden konnten.

The uppermost layers of soil in the construction area consisted of loose filling. Beneath this was undisturbed Quarternary gravel belonging to the Munich gravel plain, which extends down to depths between 8 and 12 metres beneath the surface in medium-dense to dense strata. These are followed by Tertiary layers of considerable thickness in alternating strata of fine sand, clays and silts. Findings were available from five exploratory borings made in 1973 for the bank and administration building directly adjoining the forum site to the west. Two of these borings were located directly on the site boundary. On the eastern side of the site along Amalienstrasse and on the south side adjoining Oskar-von-Miller Ring, further dynamic probes were driven with a diameter of 178 mm and to depths of approximately 14 metres. The floor slab beneath the two basement storeys was laid on strata with a high bearing capacity close to the boundary between Quarternary and Tertiary layers. This allowed the structure to be supported on a simple, load-bearing slab at the base of the excavation. The groundwater level was roughly seven metres below ground level, as a result of which the base slab and the basement walls were constructed in a waterproof concrete box.

The lower sections of the excavation retaining walls also had to be watertight, since the groundwater level was roughly one metre above the bottom of the excavation. At the base, the retaining walls were anchored in dense clays, to prevent the inflow of groundwater through the base of the excavation. On the western side, it was possible to use the existing diaphragm wall constructed when the above-mentioned bank and administration building was erected. Along the northern edge of the site, an overlapping bored-pile wall was built. The southern and eastern sides of the excavation were secured with a modified form of king-post shoring. Vertical steel sections were placed within the site boundary at roughly 2.30-metre centres. The infill between the steel sections was placed directly on the line of the site boundary or somewhat outside it.

The waterproof infill sections of the wall in the deepest part of the excavation were formed by jet grouting. With this system, a cement suspension was injected into the ground under very high pressure and high flow rate. The composition of the ground was broken up and turned into a hard, dense soil-concrete mixture. The lateral earth and water pressures on the retaining structures were resisted by a single row of ground anchors, one per steel section. The anchors were sufficiently long to extend below the bottom of the excavation. During the installation of the retaining structures unexpected difficulties arose due to layers of loose infill. These were overcome by injecting cement suspension into the ground.

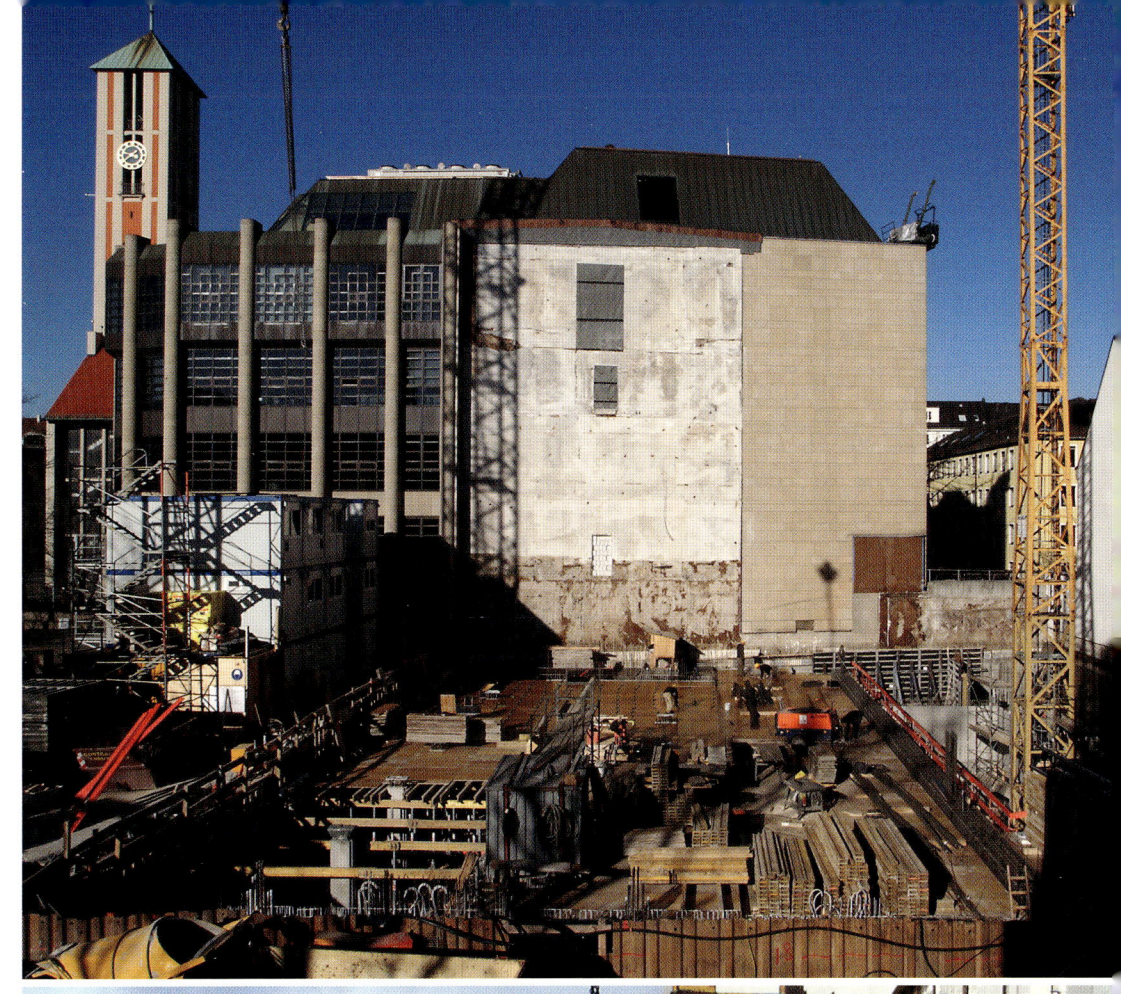

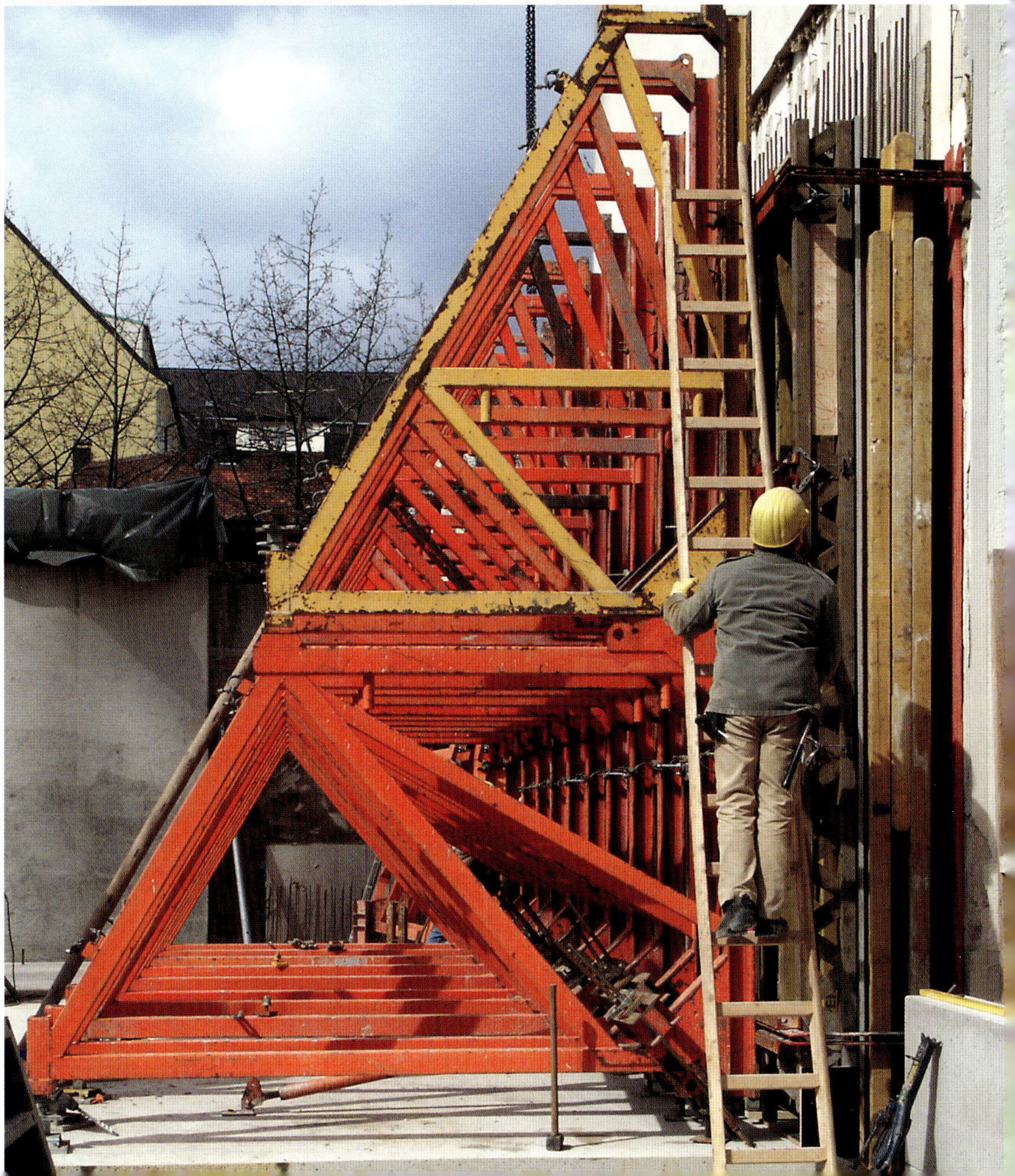

Tragwerksplanung

Structural Planning

Kurt Stepan, Thomas Winkler

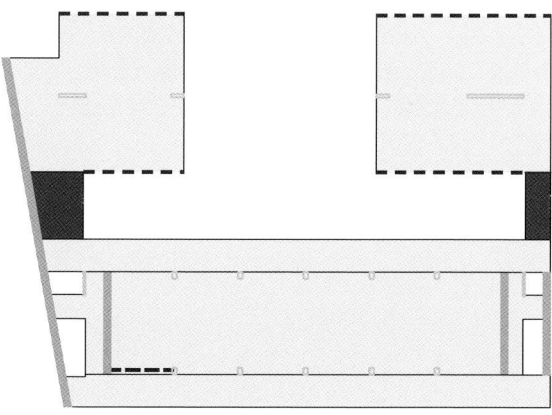

Über das gesamte Baugrundstück von ca. 40x32 m erstrecken sich 2 Untergeschosse und 3 darauf aufbauende Gebäudeteile. Der Südbau am Oskar-von-Miller-Ring hat eine Grundfläche von ca. 38x14 m und erreicht mit 7 Obergeschossen sowie einem Dachgeschoss eine Höhe von ca. 25 m. Der Ostbau an der Amalienstraße besteht aus 5 Obergeschossen auf einer Fläche von ca. 14x12 m und ist ca. 17 m hoch. Der Westbau mit 4 Obergeschossen und einer Grundfläche von ca. 9x12 m hat eine Höhe von ca. 13 m. Die beiden Nebengebäude sind über flurbreite Stege mit dem Hauptgebäude verbunden.

Der gesamte Gebäudekomplex wurde in Stahlbetonbauweise sowohl mit unterzugslosen Flachdecken als auch konventionellen ein- und zweiachsigen Deckenplatten realisiert. Die Aussteifung der Gebäude erfolgt über die sich aus dem Gesamtkonzept ohnehin ergebenden Deckenscheiben und je zwei in Ost-/Westrichtung wirkende Wandscheiben im Seiten- und Rückgebäude sowie vier in Nord-/Südrichtung orientierte im Hauptgebäude. Da die in Ost-/Westrichtung und in Nord-/Südrichtung wirkenden Wände in verschiedenen Gebäudeteilen liegen, kommt den Verbindungsstegen eine zentrale Bedeutung zu. Erst durch die kraftschlüssige Verbindung des Seiten- und Rückgebäudes mit dem Hauptgebäude über die Stege wird die Gesamtstabilität des Tragsystems erreicht. Hierdurch konnte auf zusätzliche Querwände verzichtet werden. Für die Aussteifung der oberen Geschosse des Hauptgebäudes, das die beiden anderen überragt, wurden geschossweise zwischen zwei Stützen und den Decken V-förmige Verbände eingefügt, so dass sich ein durchgängiges vertikales Fachwerksystem ergibt.

Aussteifungssystem
Bracing system

- - - Wandscheiben Ost-/Westrichtung
Wall diaphragms in east-west direction

▓ Wandscheiben Nord-/Südrichtung
Wall diaphragms in north-south direction

■ Verbindungsstege
Linking bridges

Querschnitte Baugrubenverbau
1 Grundstücksgrenze
2 Freiraum für vorhandene Sparten
3 Abbruch bis +- 0,00
4 Schalungen + Kiesschüttung + Abbruch Bodenplatte + Fundamente auf 1,0 x 1,0 m im Bereich der späteren Träger
5 Abbruch der Decke und Auffüllung des Kellers mit Bauschutt
6 Einbau der Verbauträger
7 Abbruch der Lichtschachtelemente
8 Einbau des Spartenverbaues
9 Einbau der Gurtung und Holzsteifen
10–12 Abschnittsweiser Aushub und Abbruch der Kellerwand mit Einbau weiterer Gurtungen und Holzsteifen
13 Einbau der Ruckverankerung
14 Abschnittsweiser Aushub und Abbruch der Kellerwand mit Einbau der Spritzbetonschale mit Abstandshaltern
15 Aushub in Tiefenschnitten und Einbau der Spritzbetonschale mit Abstandshaltern
16 Einbau der Injektionsdichtschürze
17 Endgültiger Aushub und Einbau der Spritzbetonschale mit Abstandshaltern

Cross-sections through basement shoring
1 Site boundary
2 Space for existing services
3 Demolition down to level ± 0.00
4 Shoring + gravel filling + demolition of base slab + 1.0 x 1.0 m foundations in the area of subsequent girder beams
5 Demolition of floor slab and filling of basement with rubble
6 Insertion of shoring girders
7 Demolition of light-shaft elements
8 Insertion of shoring for services space
9 Insertion of booms and timber stays
10–12 Excavation in stages and demolition of basement wall, with insertion of further booms and timber stays
13 Execution of rear anchoring
14 Excavation in stages and demolition of basement wall; execution of injected-concrete shell with distance pieces
15 Excavation in stages by depth and execution of injected-concrete shell with distance pieces
16 Execution of sealing apron with injected concrete
17 Final excavation and construction of injected-concrete base of tank with distance pieces

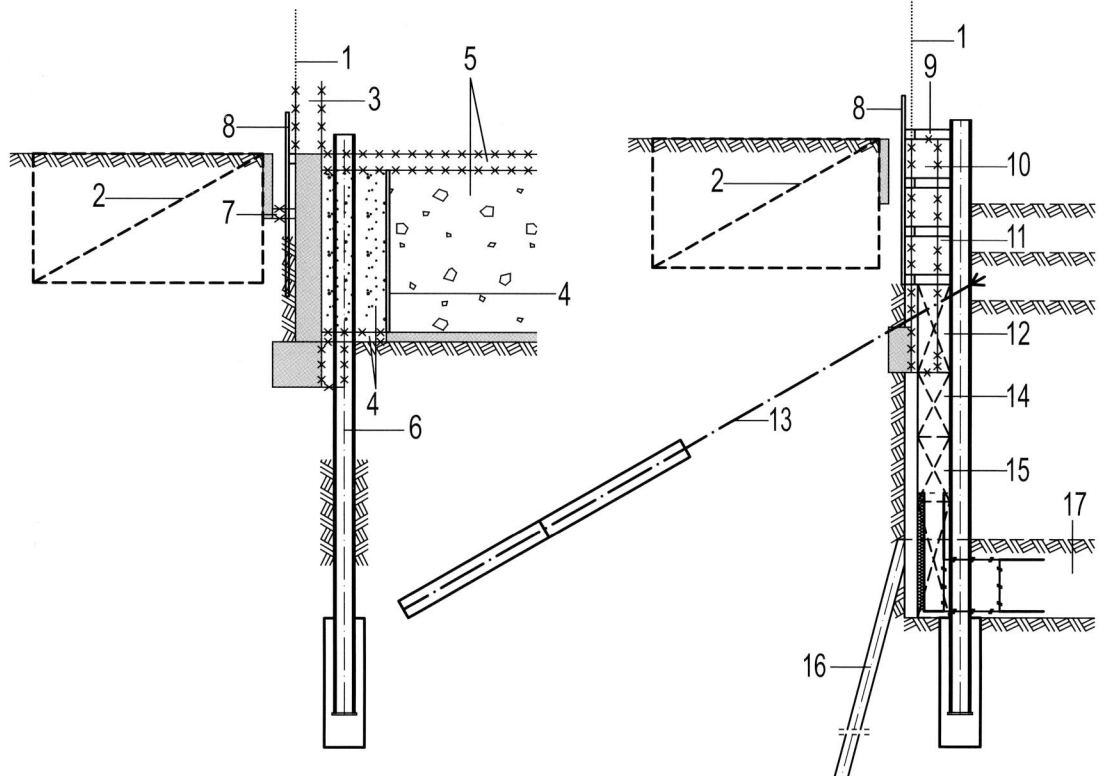

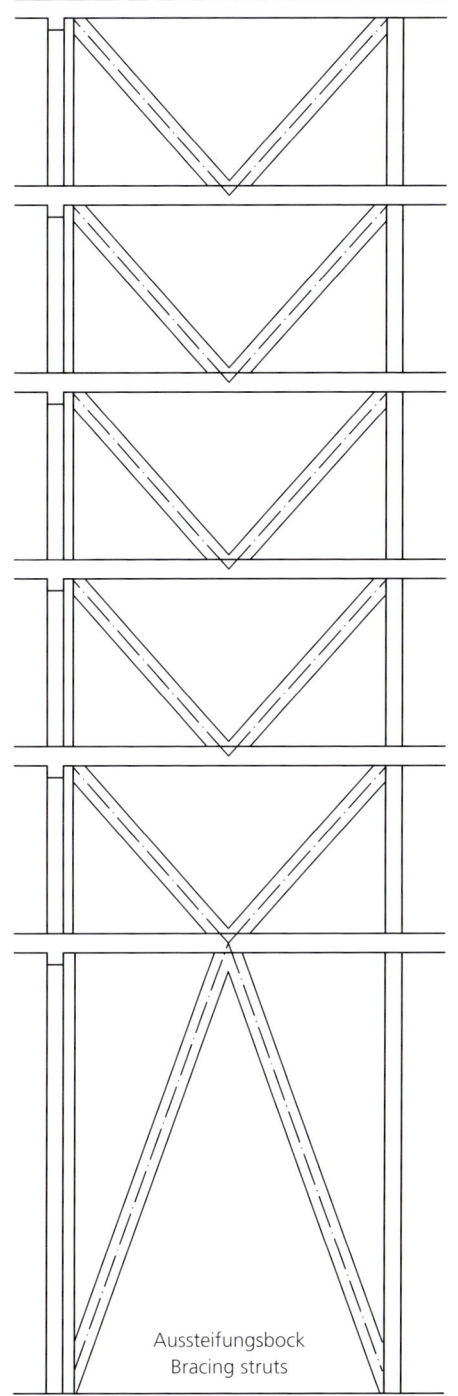

Aussteifungsbock
Bracing struts

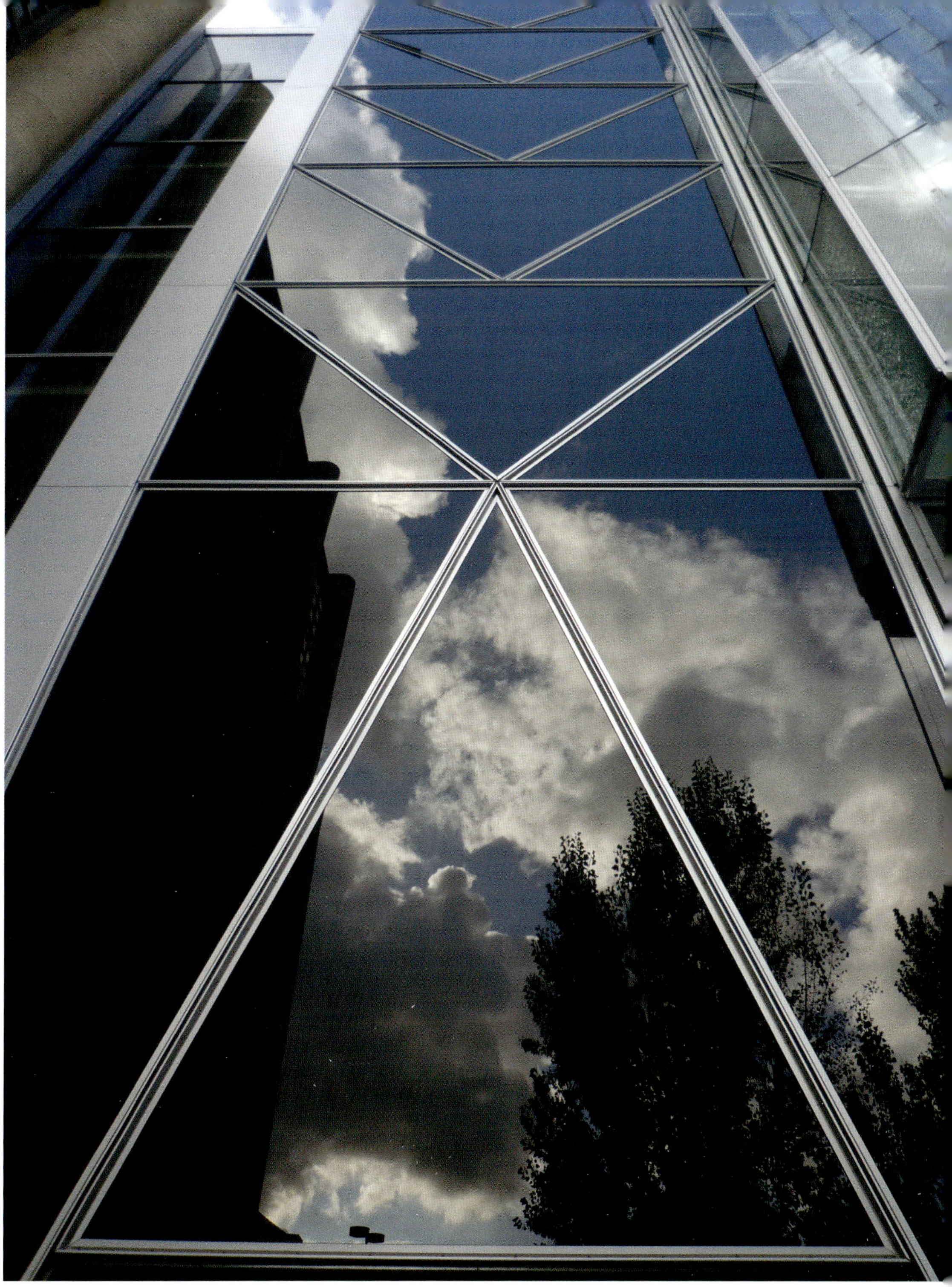

Durch die Optimierung des Aussteifungssystems wurde ein Höchstmaß an Transparenz erreicht, die bei einem Blick durch das Gebäude in den Innenhof sichtbar wird. In vielfältigen Variantenuntersuchungen wurde ein Deckensystem entwickelt, das einerseits den statischen Erfordernissen gerecht wird und andererseits eine offene und flexible räumliche Struktur ermöglicht.

Die punktgestützten Flachdecken ruhen in Gebäudequerrichtung auf nur zwei Stützen. Das Deckenfeld wird beidseitig zu den Fassaden hin durch zwei weit auskragende Platten ergänzt. Die weite Auskragung wurde durch eine konsequente Einspannung der Decken in die Stützen erreicht.

Die Deckenspannweiten und Querschnittabmessungen wurden so abgeglichen, dass sich in jede Richtung eine optimale Querschnittausnutzung und ein ausgewogenes Verformungsbild ergeben. Der Beanspruchung folgend verringert sich die Deckenstärke der Kragplatten zu den Fassaden hin. In den Räumen aller Geschosse teilt sich dies als architektonisch gewollter Effekt mit. Im inneren Deckenfeld wurde der Querschnitt oberseitig ausgenommen, so dass hier Trassen der technischen Gebäudeausrüstung geführt werden können.

Zur Erzielung einer hohen Sichtbetonqualität wurden die Stützen als Fertigteile und die Decken aus Filigranplatten in einer Breite von 2,40 m und Längen von bis zu 13,30 m hergestellt.

Die Untergeschosse, als weiße Wanne mit einer tragender Bodenplatte ausgebildet, nehmen im Grundriss nahezu die gesamte Grundstücksfläche ein und grenzen unmittelbar an die nachbarliche Bebauung bzw. den öffentlichen Grund an. Es war daher eine ca. 7,50 m tiefe Baugrube mit senkrechten Verbauwänden erforderlich. Entlang der Nachbarbebauungen konnten die Baugrubenwände mit konventionellen Bauweisen, wasserdichter überschnittener Bohrpfahlwand und Teilunterfangungen, erstellt werden. Aufgrund der dichten Spartenbelegung entlang der Grundstücksgrenze zum öffentlichen Grund hin war es jedoch nicht möglich, eine Baugrubenwand außerhalb des bestehenden bzw. neu zu errichtenden Gebäudes anzuordnen. Hier kam eine Sonderform eines Trägerverbaues mit im Gebäude liegenden Verbauträgern zum Einsatz.

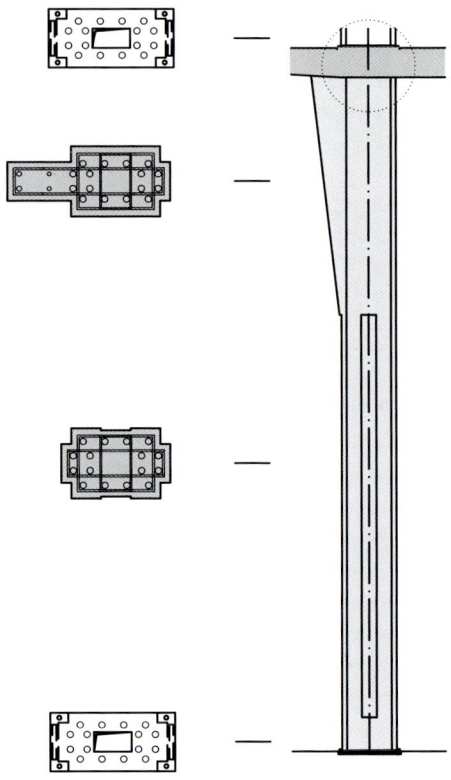

Vorgefertigte Stahlbetonstütze
Precast concrete column

The two basement storeys of the building extend over the entire area of the site, which is roughly 40 x 32 metres in extent. The three tracts of the forum were erected on top of the basement structure. The southern tract facing Oskar-von-Miller-Ring has a footprint of approximately 38 x 14 metres and reaches a height of about 25 metres, with seven above-ground floors plus a roof storey. The east tract along Amalienstrasse, with a footprint ca. 14 x 12 metres in size, consists of five above-ground storeys and is roughly 17 metres high. The four-storey-high west tract, with a footprint of approximately 9 x 12 metres, rises to a height of roughly 13 metres. The two side tracts are linked to the main building by bridges of the same width as the internal corridors into which they continue. The entire complex was constructed in reinforced concrete with both flat-slab floors (without downstand beams) and conventional uni- and biaxial floor slabs. The building is braced using the floor slabs as diaphragms connecting to two shear walls in the east-west direction in the two side tracts as well as to four shear walls that run in the north-south direction in the main building. Since these east-west and north-south bracing walls are situated in different sections of the development, the linking bridges are of crucial significance. Only with a rigid, load-bearing connection of the side tracts to the main section of the building by means of these walkways was it possible to ensure the overall stability of the load-bearing system. As a result, further cross-walls were not necessary. To brace the upper floors of the main building, which rise above the side tracts, diagonal elements were inserted on each floor in a V-shaped form between two columns and the floors, creating a continuous, vertical framing system. By optimizing the bracing walls in this way, a maximum of transparency was achieved, which is evident when one looks through the building to the internal

Zunächst wurde das bestehende Gebäude bis zur Oberkante des Untergeschosses abgetragen, der Keller verfüllt und dann die Untergeschossdecke abgebrochen. Anschließend wurden die Verbauträger durch den verfüllten Kellerbereich und die noch bestehende Bodenplatte eingebracht. Im Folgenden wurden die Außenwände schrittweise abgetragen und die außen liegenden Leitungs- und Versorgungstrassen mit einem Spartenverbau, der sich gegen die Verbauträger abstützt, gesichert. Nach Erreichen von spartenfreien Zonen konnten die Verbauträger mit Erdankern rückverankert werden und das Bestandsgebäude weiter abgebrochen werden. Im Weiteren wurde die Baugrubenwand mittels Spritzbeton ausgefacht. Die Sohlabdichtung erfolgte mit einer Injektionsdichtschürze. Die neuen Außenwände wurden zunächst nur abschnittsweise zwischen den Verbauträgern ausgeführt. Nach Einbau der Decke über dem 1. Untergeschoss übernahmen sie die Erddrucklasten aus der Verbauwand, so dass dann die Verbauträger ausgebaut werden konnten. Im Anschluss wurden die offen gebliebenen Wandabschnitte geschlossen.

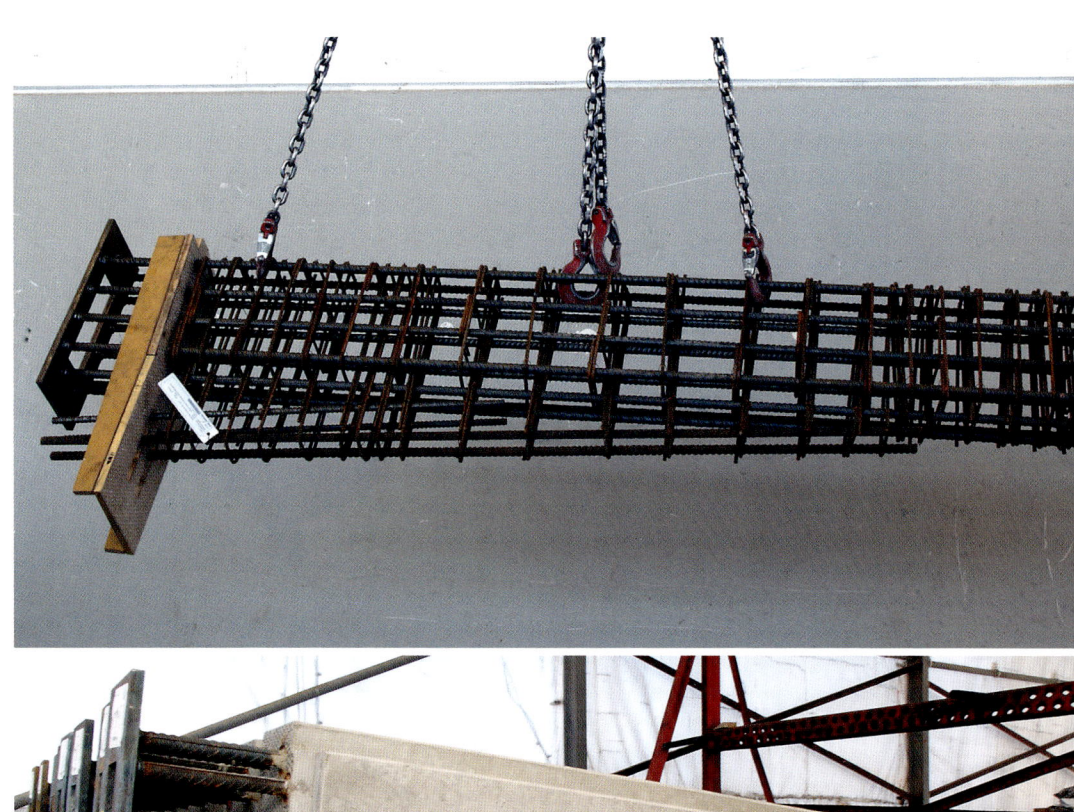

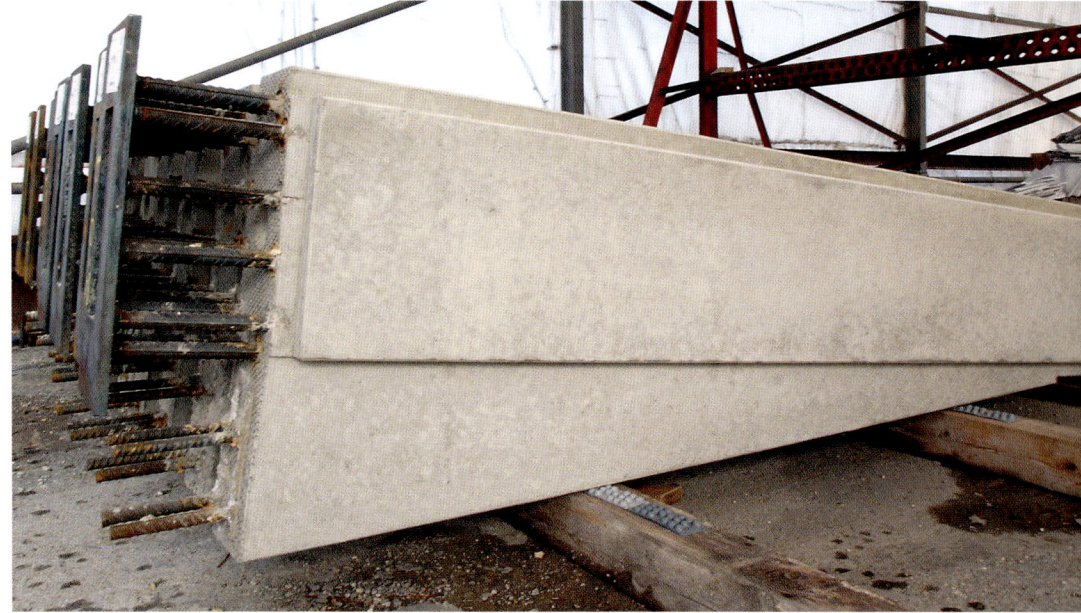

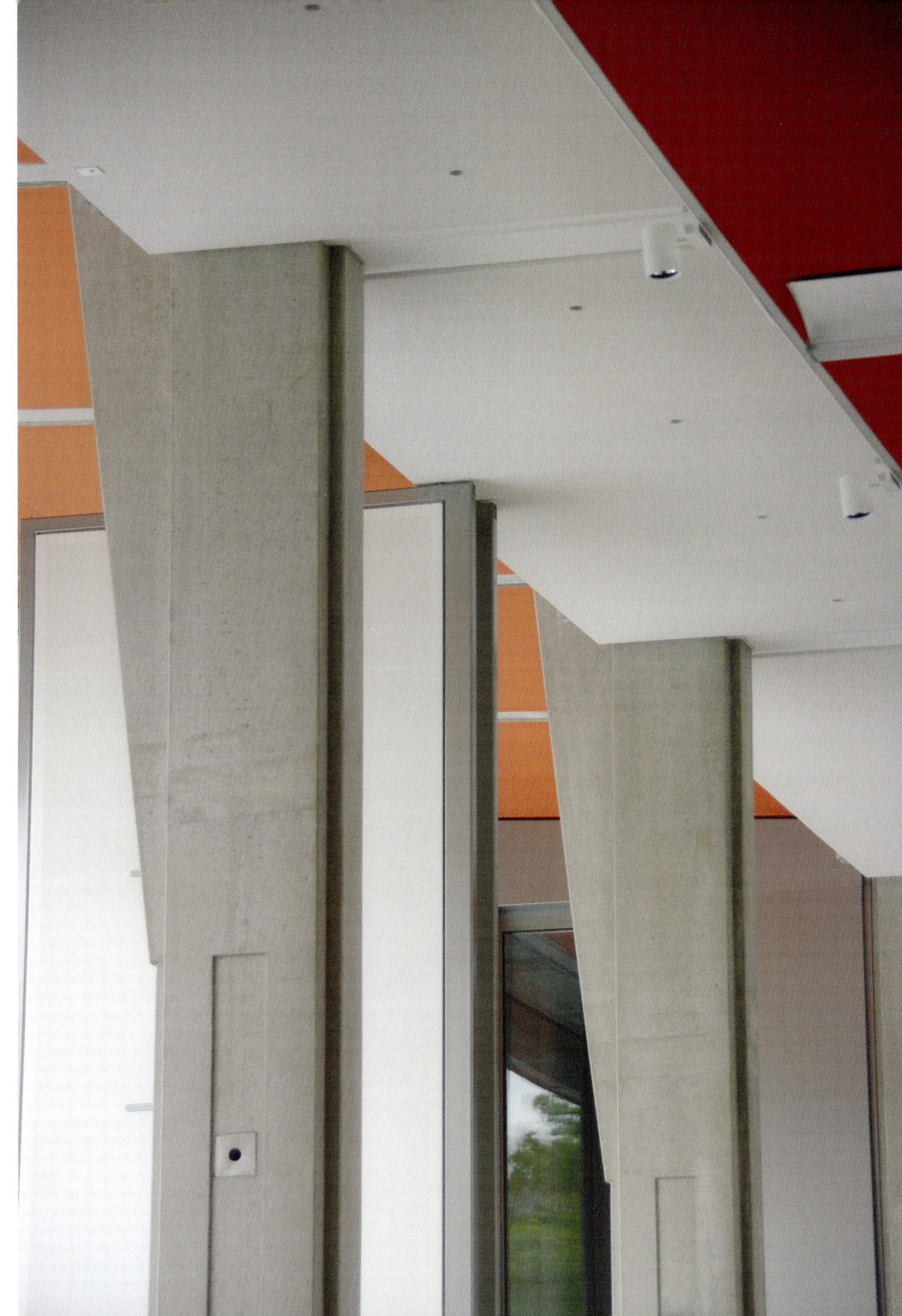

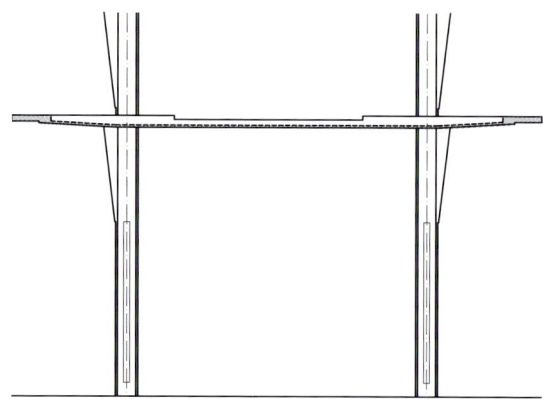

Deckenquerschnitt
Vorgefertigte Elementplatte mit Ortbetonergänzung

Section through floor slab
Precast concrete slabs with in-situ concrete filling

courtyard. Through the investigation of many different alternatives, a floor system was developed that not only met the structural requirements, but also allowed the creation of an open, flexible spatial structure. Flat slabs are supported in the lateral direction of the building by only two rows of columns. The central floor bays are assisted by the cantilevers towards the facades. The generous cantilevers were achieved by systematically anchoring the slabs in the columns. The floor spans and cross-sections were chosen in such a way to optimise the forces and balance out the deflections in both directions. Reflecting the degree of loading, the thickness of the cantilevered slabs decreases towards the facades. This is visible in the various floors as a deliberate architectural feature. The top surface of the central bays was recessed to accommodate service runs and technical installation. In order to obtain high-quality exposed-concrete surfaces, the columns were precast, and the floors were constructed in the form of semi-precast slabs 2.40 metres wide and up to 13.30 metres long. The basement storeys, constructed as a waterproof concrete tank with a loadbearing base slab, occupy almost the entire area of the site and directly adjoin the neighbouring buildings or public land. With an excavation roughly 7.50 metres deep, this necessitated the construction of vertical retaining walls as shoring. Adjoining the neighbouring buildings, it was possible to execute the excavation in a conventional form with watertight overlapping bored-pile walls and underpinning in part. In view of the dense layout of the various services along the site boundary to the public area, however, it was not possible to insert shoring around the excavation outside the existing building and also outside the proposed new building. In this case, therefore, a modified form of king-post shoring was used with the posts inside the building. The existing structure was first demolished down to the top of the basement. The basement was then filled and the floor above broken out. After this, the king posts were inserted through the basement filling and the existing base slab. The outer walls were then removed in stages, and the external service and installation ducts were secured with shoring supported against the inner steel sections. On reaching the zones where there were no service runs, it was possible to anchor the shoring beams in the earth and to demolish the rest of the existing building. The remaining sections of the retaining walls were then formed with sprayed concrete, and the edge of the basement floor was sealed with a raking injected apron extending below the actual slab. First of all, the sections of the external wall between the king posts were constructed. After concreting the floor slab over the first basement level, the earth pressures were then transferred to the slab, so that the king posts could be removed. Finally the remaining sections of the external walls were concreted.

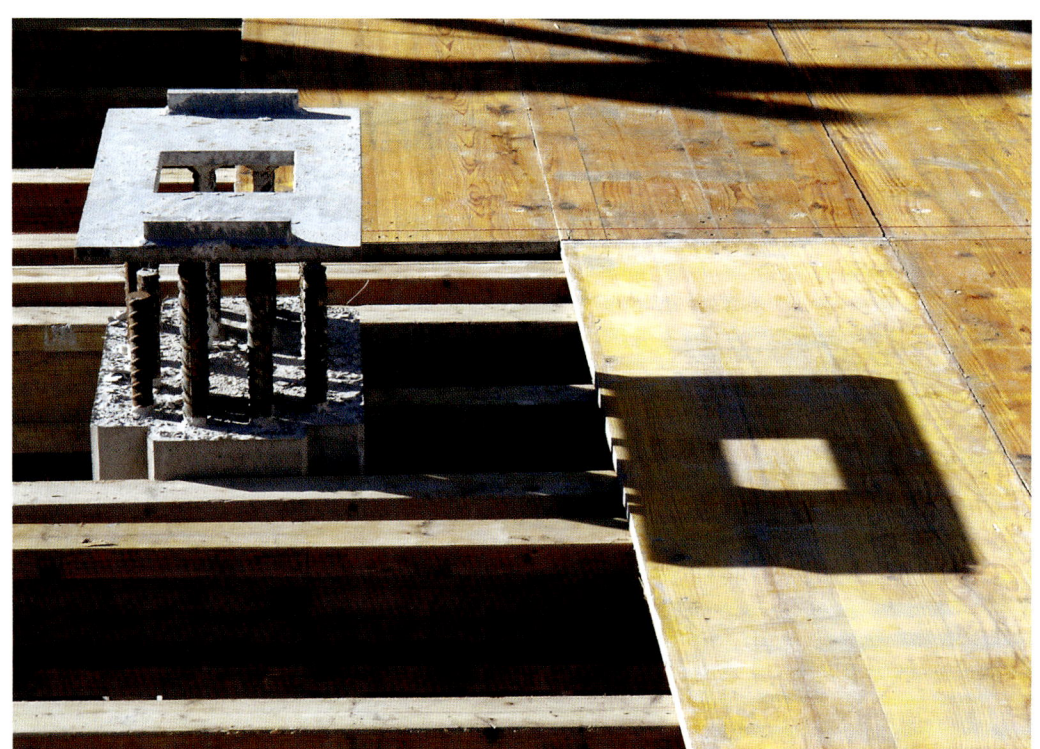

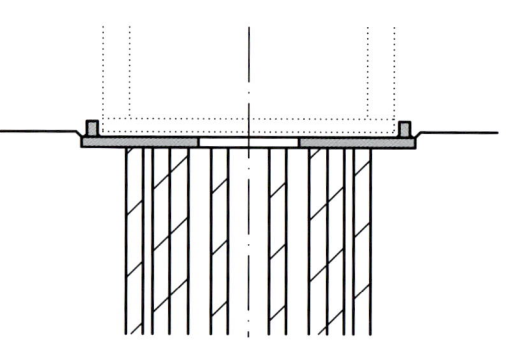

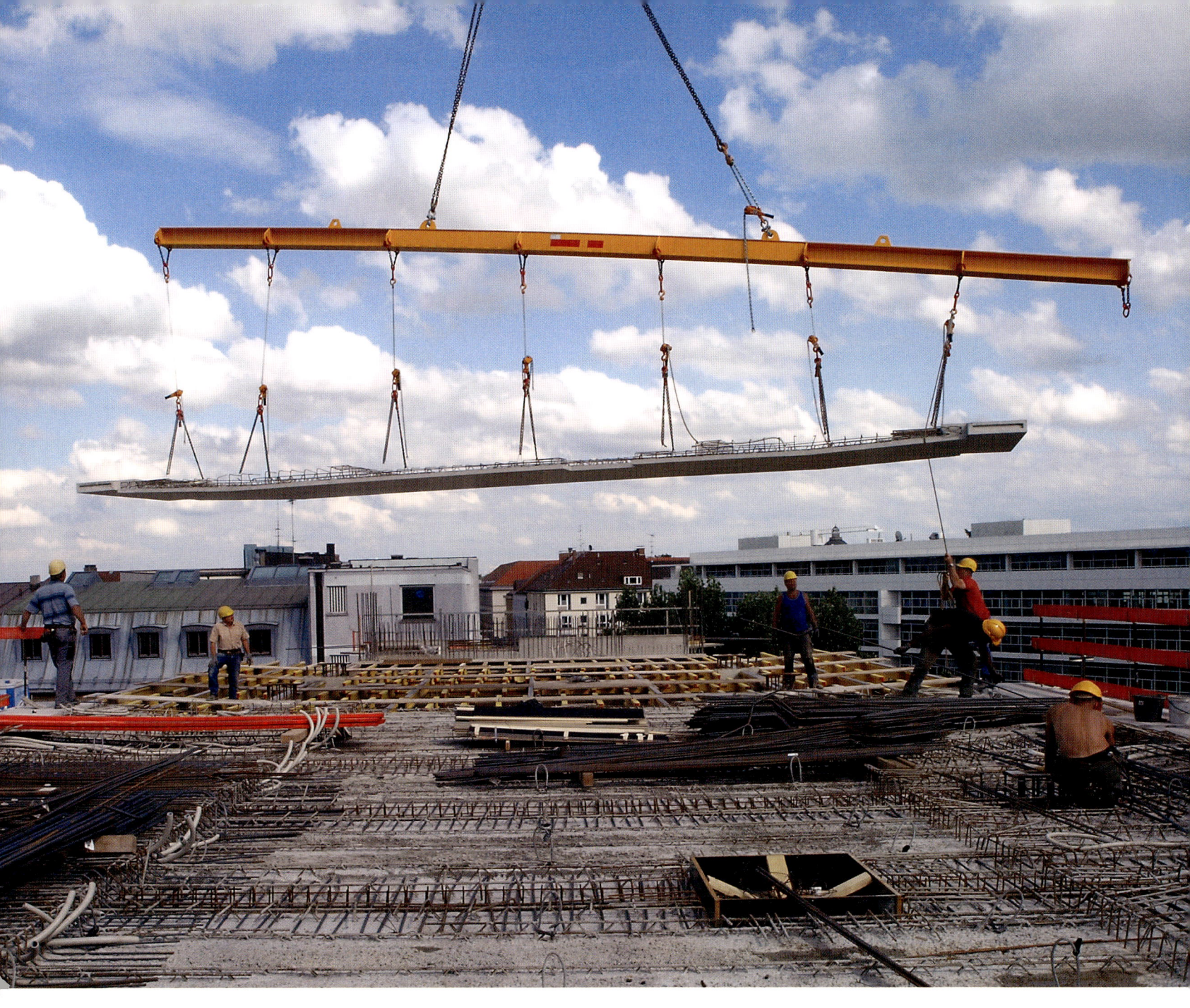

Strukturbestimmende Subsysteme, Räume und Bauteile
Isometrische Darstellung, Ansicht von Süden

1 Stahlbetontragwerk mit Aussteifung
2 Stahlkonstruktion mit beidseitiger Aufhängung in den äußeren Fassadenebenen
3 Stützen aus Fertigteilen als Halbrahmen
4 Decke aus „Filigran"-Elementen
5 Installationsschächte
6 Dreh-Falttüren
7 Gläserne Vorfassade
8 Thermische Röhrenkollektoren
9 Erdgeschoss und Obergeschosse
10 Untergeschosse
11 Tiefgarage
12 Sanitäranlage
13 Partykeller, zweigeschossig
14 Lagerräume

Principal Structural Subsystems, Rooms and Building Elements
Isometric diagram, south view

1 reinforced concrete structure with bracing
2 reinforced concrete structure with suspension of outer facade skin on both sides
3 pre-cast concrete columns as half frames
4 floor slab, consisting of filigree concrete elements
5 service shafts
6 pivoting, folding doors
7 glazed outer facade layer
8 tubular thermal collectors
9 ground and upper floors
10 basement storeys
11 basement garage
12 sanitary installation
13 two-storey basement party space
14 storerooms

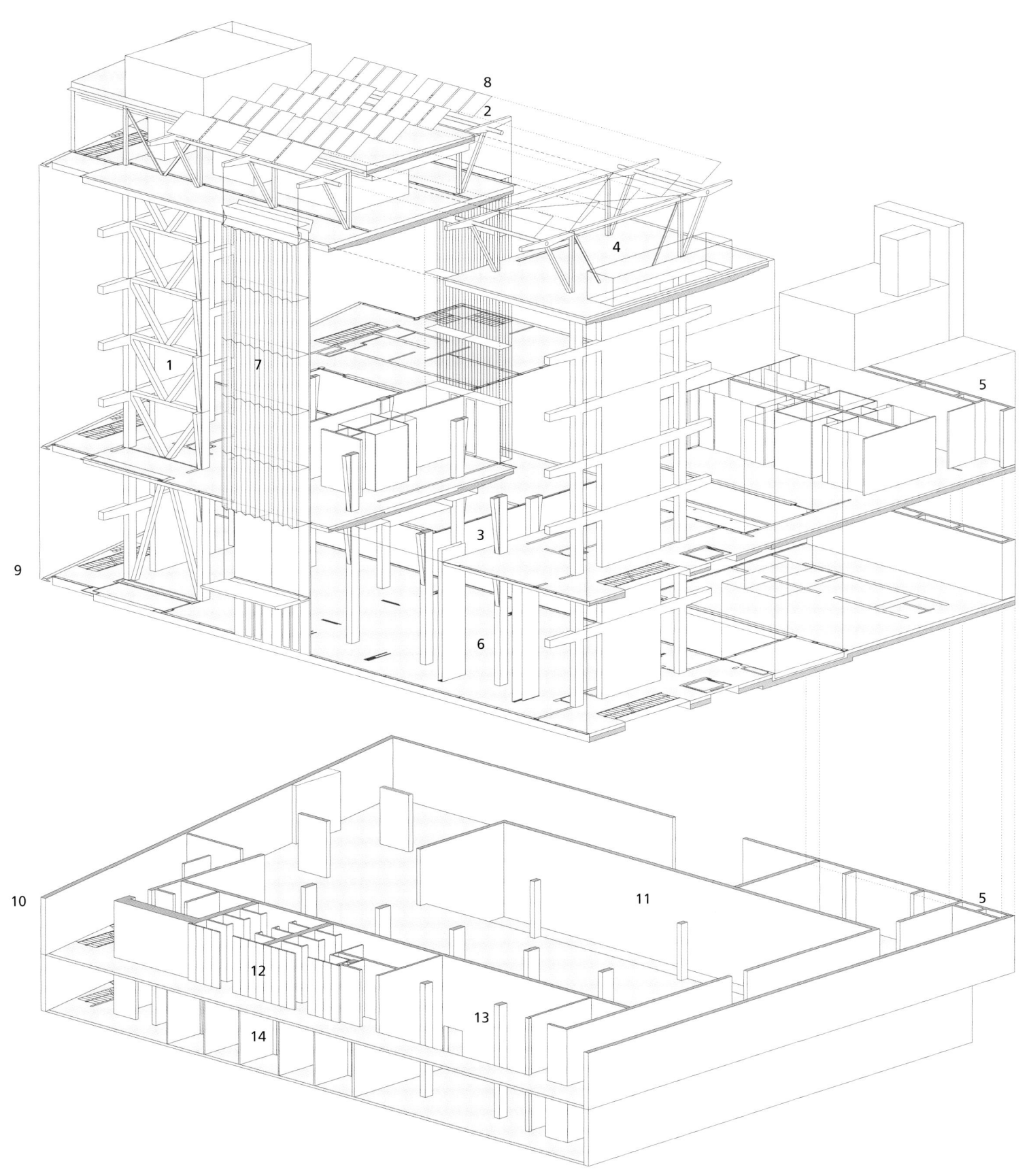

Zeichnung/Drawing: Herzog + Partner

Natürliche Lüftung und Entrauchung der Obergeschosse im Südbau

Thomas Herzog, Roland Schneider
Untersuchungen/Simulationen Rolf-Dieter Lieb

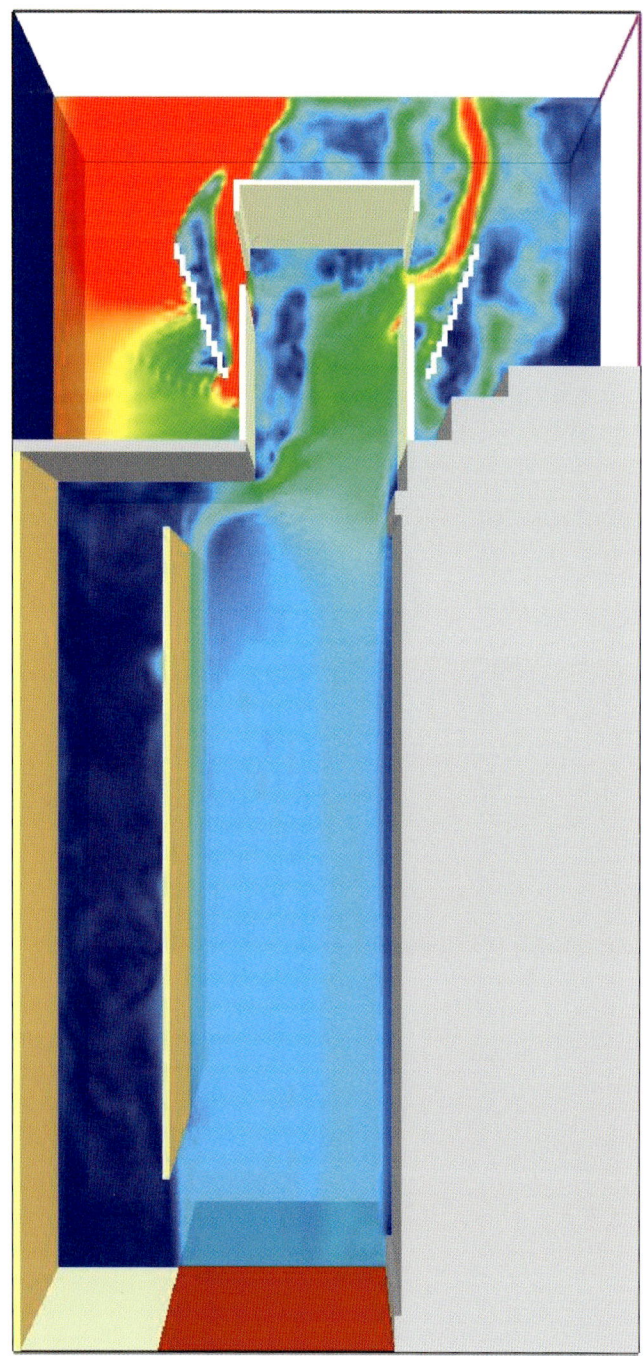

Im Zuge der Entwicklung der mehrfunktionalen, südlichen Doppelfassade wurden von Dipl.-Ing. Rolf-Dieter Lieb, Institut für Industrieaerodynamik GmbH an der Fachhochschule Aachen Simulationen zur Wirkungsweise und Funktionalität des Systems durchgeführt und für die konstruktive Ausarbeitung zugrunde gelegt. Die Abbildungen zeigen eine beschränkte Auswahl der Simulationen. Aus der Zusammenfassung der Resultate:

„Die Ergebnisse der zuerst berechneten Durchströmungssimulationen des Hauses zeigen, dass der Grundgedanke der unterstützenden natürlichen Lüftung durch die Lage der Treppenhäuser bereits mit wenigen Grundelementen und überwiegend manuell realisiert werden kann. Bereits mit normalen Öffnungsgrößen können sowohl im Sommer- wie auch im Winterfall auch für eine denkbare Party ausreichende Luftwechsel erreicht werden.

Die Abströmung in der doppelschaligen Fassade und vor allem die Gestaltung ihres oberen Abschlusses wurden darauf aufbauend in einer zweiten Strömungssimulation drei-

Variante 4: 70 cm Gitterbreite von Geschoss zu Geschoss, Analyse des Seitenwindeinflusses mit 5 m/s von Süden (im Bild links), **Strömungsgeschwindigkeiten** im obersten Geschoss der doppelschaligen Fassade

Simulation 4: 70-cm-wide grating from floor to floor; analysis of effects of side wind at 5 m/s from south (ill. left); **airflow speeds** in double-skin facade at top-storey level

dimensional instationär untersucht. Es zeigt sich, dass die aus dem Industriebau abgeleitete Form des oberen Abschlusses noch in Details optimiert werden kann, insgesamt aber auch mit nur 50 cm lichter Weite bereits eine günstige Abströmung erreicht werden kann, die sicher auch für einen Brandfall ausreichen würde und insbesondere windunabhängig ihre Funktion erfüllt."

Interessanterweise kommt der Autor in einer weiteren Untersuchung zur Entrauchung des Gebäudes im Brandfall nach Auswertung der Ergebnisse am dreidimensionalen, instationären Feldmodell zu folgendem Ergebnis: „Die Simulation der sommerlichen Lüftung hatte bereits gezeigt, dass die doppelschalige Fassade vorteilhaft von unten nach oben belüftet werden sollte und nicht durch frontale Öffnung, da sonst eventuell auftretende Winde (Exposition nach S/SW entspricht einer Hauptwindrichtung mit 25 % Jahresanteil in München!) die Lüftung und ebenso die Entrauchung stören könnten."
Unabhängig davon wurde eine zusätzliche Fassadensprinkleranlage gefordert.

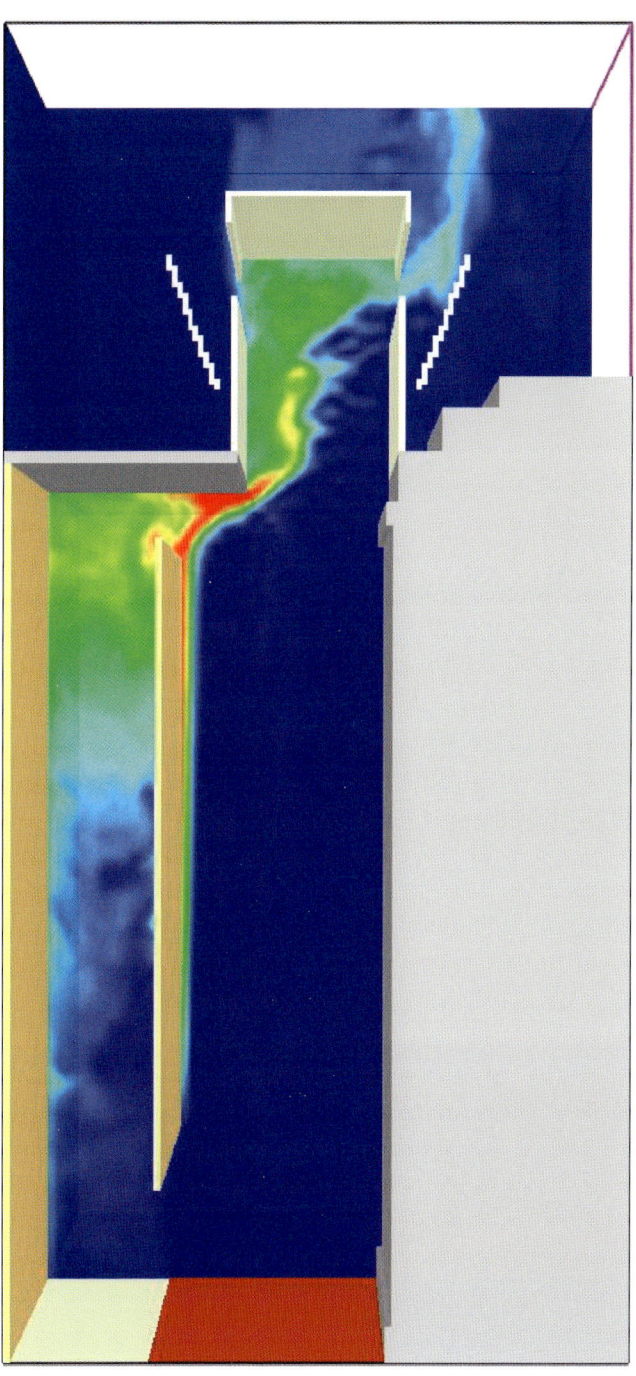

Variante 4: 70 cm Gitterbreite von Geschoss zu Geschoss, Analyse des Seitenwindeinflusses mit 5 m/s von Süden (im Bild links), **Temperaturentwicklung** im obersten Geschoss der doppelschaligen Fassade

Simulation 4: 70-cm-wide grating from floor to floor; analysis of effects of side wind at 5 m/s from south (ill. left); **temperature change** in double-skin facade at top-storey level

Natural Ventilation and Smoke Extract on the Upper Floors of the South Tract

Thomas Herzog, Roland Schneider
Tests / Simulations Rolf-Dieter Lieb

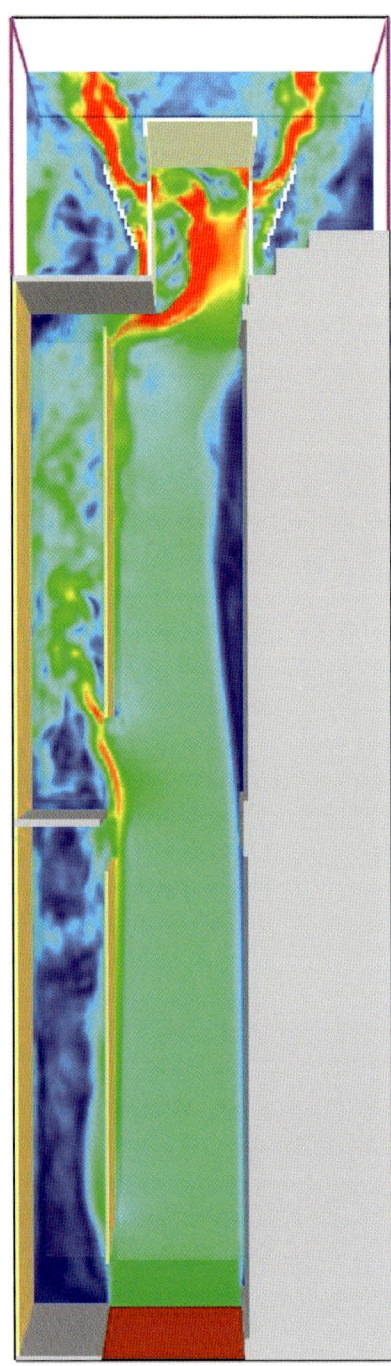

In developing the multifunctional double-skin facade construction for the south front of the building, simulations were carried out by Dipl.-Ing. Rolf-Dieter Lieb of the Institut for Industriedynamik GmbH at the University of Applied Sciences, Aachen. The aim was to investigate the way the system functioned as well as its efficiency. The development of the construction was based on the results of the simulations. A limited selection of these are shown in the illustrations. The following details are taken from a summary of the findings.

"The findings of the first airflow simulation for the building show that, in view of the position of the staircases, the underlying idea of a supportive system of natural ventilation can be implemented with relatively few basic elements and largely in a manual form. Even with normal-sized openings, it would be possible to provide adequate air changes both in summer and in winter, as well as for celebrations that may be held here from time to time...

"Based on this, the outflow of air from the double-skin facade and in particular the detailing at the top were investigated in a second airflow simulation in the form of three-dimensional computational fluid

Variante 6: 70 cm Gitterbreite von Geschoss zu Geschoss, Analyse des Einflusses der Geschosse untereinander, **Luftgeschwindigkeiten** in den beiden obersten Geschossen der doppelschaligen Fassade

Simulation 6: 70-cm-wide grating from floor to floor; analysis of mutual influence of different storeys; **air speed** in double-skin facade at level of top two floors

dynamics (CFD) with turbulent flow. It was shown that the construction at the top – based on industrial forms – could be optimized in the detailing. Nevertheless, with a clear width of only 50 cm, an efficient outflow can be achieved, and this would certainly be adequate in the event of fire. In addition, it would fulfil its function regardless of wind conditions."

Interestingly enough, in a further investigation of smoke extraction from the building in the event of fire, the author comes to the conclusion, after evaluating the results of three-dimensional CFD (turbulent flow), that: "The simulation of summer ventilation had already shown that the double-skin facade should be ventilated to best advantage from bottom to top and not by creating opening sections in the front face, because in the latter case the occurrence of wind could interfere with the ventilation as well as with smoke extract operations. (The south to south-west orientation of the facade means that in Munich, it would be subject to direct winds for 25 per cent of the time in the course of the year.)"

Independently of this, an additional facade sprinkler system was deemed necessary.

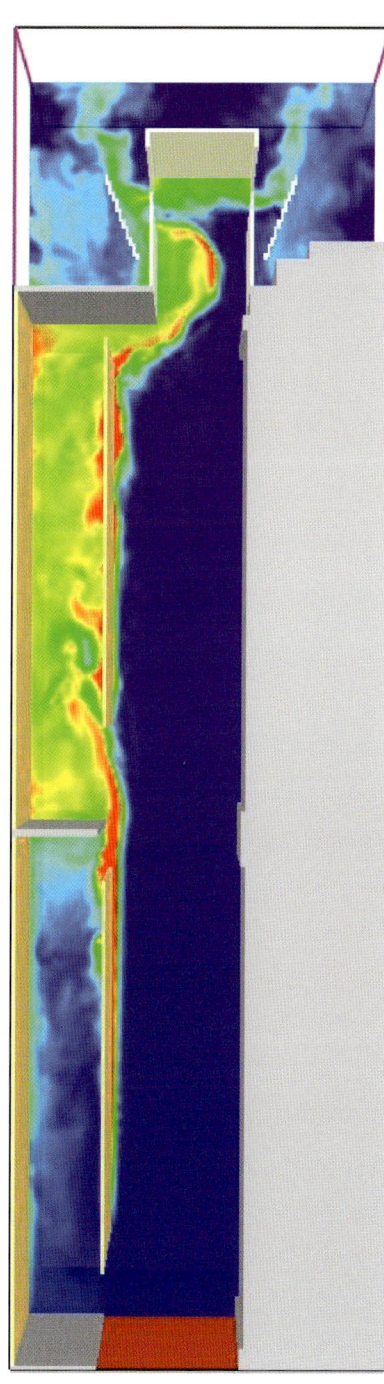

Variante 6: 70 cm Gitterbreite von Geschoss zu Geschoss, Analyse des Einflusses der Geschosse untereinander, **Temperaturentwicklung** in den beiden obersten Geschossen der doppelschaligen Fassade

Simulation 6: 70-cm-wide grating from floor to floor; analysis of mutual influence of different storeys; **temperature change** in double-skin facade at level of top two floors

Systeme der Gebäudetechnik

Christian Dotzauer

Planungsziel war die Realisierung eines sehr leistungsfähigen, energieeffizienten und ressourcenschonenden Gebäudes. Durch innovative Gebäudetechnik und moderne Anlagen entstand ein Gebäude mit geringem Verbrauch an Primärenergie. Zur Erreichung dieses Ziels kamen zum Einsatz:
– Solarwärmenutzung für Warmwasserbereitung, solare Kühlung und Heizungsunterstützung
– Mechanische Wohnraumlüftung mit hocheffizienter Wärmerückgewinnung
– Schaltung der Allgemeinbeleuchtung in Anhängigkeit von Außenhelligkeits- und Bewegungsmeldern
– Tageslichtabhängige Regelung in den Arbeitsplatzbereichen
– Sonnenstandsabhängige Steuerung der Jalousieanlagen in Veranstaltungsbereichen
– Natürliche Lüftung über Ansteuerung von Fassadenlamellen
– Wassersparende Sanitärarmaturen

Wärmeversorgung

Entsprechend der Auflage von Seiten der Stadtwerke München erfolgt die Wärmeversorgung über einen Anschluss an das städtische Fernwärmenetz Dampf. (Die eingebauten Hybridwärmetauscher sind sowohl für Dampf- als auch für Heißwasserversorgung geeignet.)

Wärmeerzeugung

Die bivalente Wärmeerzeugung wird zu rund 80 % des Wärmeenergiebedarfs von städtischer Fernwärme und zu rund 20 % durch die eingebaute Solarthermie gedeckt.
Die Heizzentrale des gesamten Gebäudes befindet sich im Untergeschoss. Die Wärmeleistung aller Heizkreise beträgt insgesamt 400 kW.
Die Versorgung der einzelnen Bereiche mit Wärme geschieht wie folgt:
Statische Heizflächen in Zimmern, Treppenbereichen und WCs.
Raumlufttechnik-Anlagen im Westbau (EG bis 3. OG), im Ostbau (1. bis 4. OG) und im Bistro, in den Wohnbereichen im Südbau mit Veranstaltungsraum im 7. OG und in der Halle sowie in den Lager- und Technikbereichen (UG).
Fußbodenheizung (FBH):
– Hallenbereich EG Südbau
– Öffentlicher Bereich EG West- und Ostbau
– Office im 1. Obergeschoss Westbau
– Zum Innenhof orientierte Räume des 2. OG und Dachgeschoss des Westbaus
– Öffentliche Bereiche vor den Zimmern und Dozentenappartements
– Zimmern und Dozentenappartements im Süd- und Ostbau
– Öffentlicher Bereich im Dachgeschoss Südbau

Warmwassererzeugung

Die Warmwassererzeugung mit Speicherladesystem im UG 2 versorgt die Verbraucher über Zwischenspeicherung in zwei 750 Liter-Pufferspeichern mit Steig- und Verteilleitungen sowie Zirkulationsleitungen.

Regelanlagen für Wärmetechnik

Die Mess-, Steuer- und Regelanlagen (MSR) sind in DDC-Technik ausgeführt.
In der Zentrale versorgt eine BUS-Verbindung den Hauptserver der Gebäudeleittechnik (GLT), die Folgendes leistet:
– Zentrale außentemperaturabhängige Regelung der Heizvorlauftemperaturen
– Raumtemperaturabhängige Nachregelung über thermostatische Heizkörperregulierventile an allen stationären Heizflächen
– Betrieb der Heizungsumwälzpumpen mit Stör- und Zeitumschaltung für Doppelpumpen
– Differenzdruckabhängige Drehzahlregelung der Heizungsumwälzpumpen
– Verbrauchserfassung über busfähige Zähler

Folgende Regelgruppen einschließlich zugehöriger Pumpenmotorsteuerungen werden hiermit bedient:
– Wärmetauscher – Fernwärme, bedarfsgeführte Vorlauftemperatur mit Rücklauftemperatur/Maximalbegrenzung
– Wärmetauscher – Solarthermie/Absorptionskälte, konstante Vorlauftemperatur mit Rücklauftemperatur – Maximalbegrenzung, variable Volumenregelung durch geräteinternen Leistungsregler
– Differenzdruckabhängige Regelung der Pumpenleistung an Wärmehauptverteilern
– Mengenabhängige Regelung der Pumpenleistung für Heizkreis – Raumlufttechnik
– Mengenabhängige Regelung der Pumpenleistung für Heizkreis – statische Heizung
– Außentemperaturabhängige Vorlauftemperaturregelung für Heizkreis statische Heizung
– Wärmetauscher Niedertemperaturkreis, konstante Vorlauftemperatur mit Rücklauftemperatur/Maximalbegrenzung
– Differenzdruckabhängige Regelung der Pumpenleistung am Niedertemperaturverteiler
– Mengenabhängige Regelung der Pumpenleistung der Niedertemperaturkreise (Halle, öffentliche Bereiche, Veranstaltung 7. OG, Westbau, Ostbau)
– Außentemperaturabhängige Regelung der Vorlauftemperatur von den Niedertemperaturkreisen mit Aufschaltung der Führungsgrößen durch Referenzfühler (Halle, öffentliche Bereiche, Veranstaltung 7. OG, Westbau, Ostbau)
– Wärmetauscher – Brauchwasser – Speicherladesystem, konstante Vorlauftemperatur, mit Rücklauftemperatur/Maximalbegrenzung
– Zeitoptimierte, temperaturgeregelte Steuerung der Zirkulationspumpen
– Freigabe der Fußbodenheizungskreise in Abhängigkeit von der Außentemperatur und der Temperatur des Referenzraumes
– Überwachung der Druckhalte- und Entgasungsstationen im HT- und NT-Kreis
– Überwachung der Schmutzwasserhebeanlage (Technikzentralen)
– Überwachung der Fettabscheider einschließlich Hebeanlage

Kältetechnische Anlagen

Die Kälteenergieerzeugung wurde in folgende drei Bereiche aufgeteilt:
„Freie Kühlung": Deckung von knapp 70 % des Kälteenergiebedarfes durch einen Kühlturm.
Die Verdunstungskälte gewährleistet kostengünstig auch bei hohen Außenlufttemperaturen die notwendigen Rückkühltemperaturen.
„Solare Kühlung": Solarkollektoren auf dem Dach decken 16 % des Kälteenergiebedarfes. Dabei wird Heißwasser erzeugt, welches eine Absorptionskältemaschine im zweiten UG antreibt.
„Kompressions-Kältetechnik": Eine Standardkompressionskältemaschine deckt bei Spitzenlasten 15 % des Kälteenergiebedarfes. Kälteenergie wird für folgende Bereiche benötigt:
– Raumlufttechnische (RLT)-Anlagen (Westbau EG – 3. OG, Ostbau 1.– 4. OG, Ober-

geschosse Südbau mit Veranstaltung im 7. OG, Halle Südbau sowie Bistro im EG Ostbau)

Fußbodenkühlung, wobei die Wassertemperatur nicht mehr als 2–3 °C unter der Raumlufttemperatur liegt in den Bereichen:
– Halle im EG Südbau
– Öffentliche Bereiche EG West- und Ostbau
– „Office" im 1. Obergeschoss Westbau
– In zum Innenhof orientierten Zimmern des 2. OG sowie Dachgeschoss des Westbaus
– Öffentliche Bereiche vor den Zimmern und Dozentenappartements im Süd- und Ostbau
– Zimmer und Dozentenappartements im Süd- und Ostbau
– Öffentlicher Bereich Dachgeschoss Südbau

Die maximale Gesamtkälteleistung beträgt 160 kW.

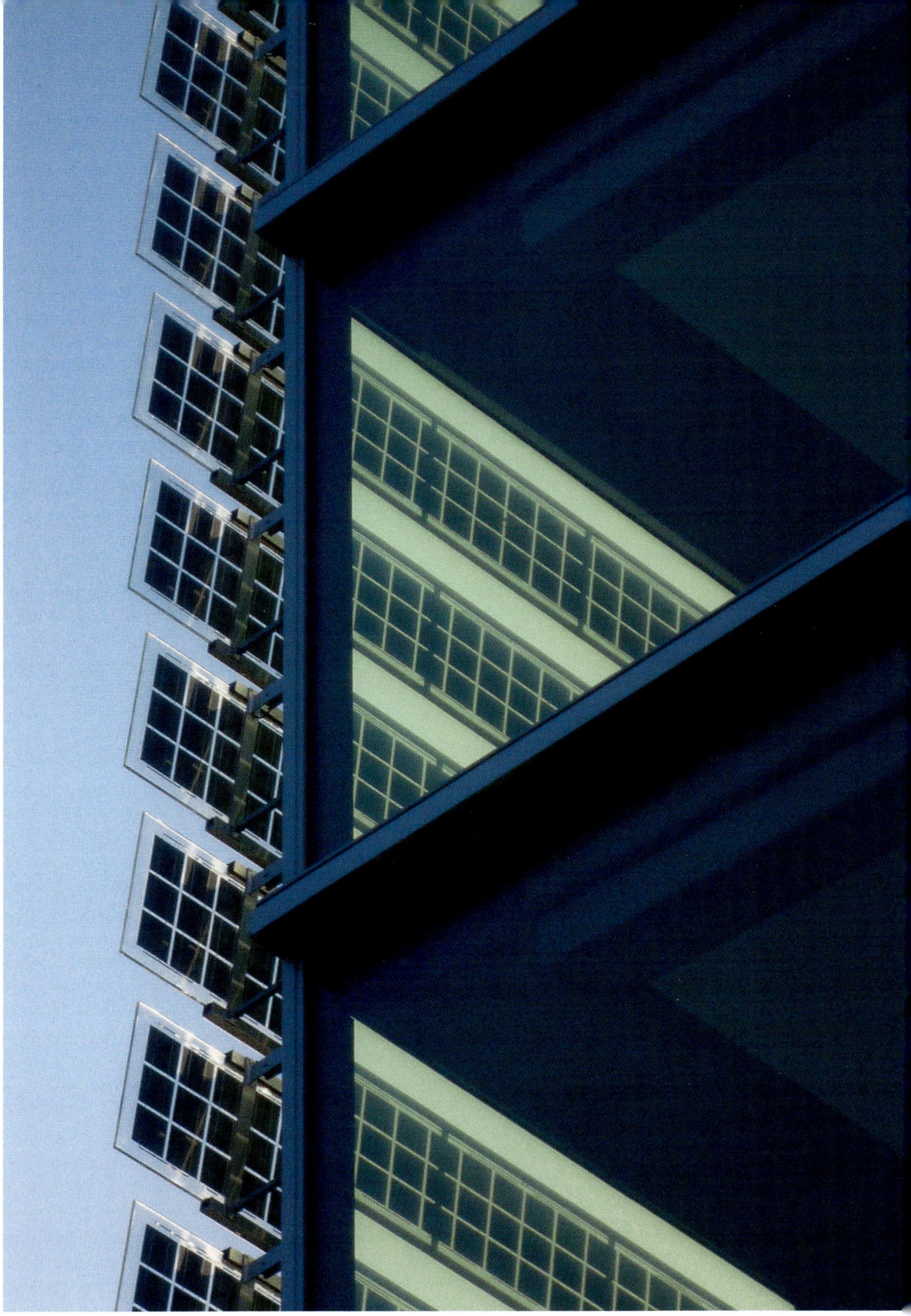

Regelanlagen für Kältetechnik

Die gesamten Mess-, Steuer- und Regelanlagen sind in DDC-Technik ausgeführt. Der Informationsschwerpunkt ist in der Zentrale mit den Heizungsanlagen gekoppelt:
– Kälteumwälzpumpen mit Stör- und Zeitumschaltung für Doppelpumpen
– Differenzdruckabhängige Drehzahlregelung der Kälteumwälzpumpen
– Betriebszeitoptimierung der Absorptionskältemaschine in Abhängigkeit von den Witterungsverhältnissen und vom Ladezustand des Kältespeichers
– Bedarfsgeführte Umschaltung der Fußbodenheizung auf Fußbodenkühlung
– Nutzung der Solarwärme zur Gebäudeheizung an kalten Tagen

Folgende Regelgruppen einschließlich zugehöriger Pumpenmotorsteuerungen werden bedient:
– Absorptionskältemaschine mit nachgeschalteten Pumpen (Lade- und Entladepumpe) in Abhängigkeit von Außentemperatur, Referenzraumtemperatur sowie Speicherbevorratung
– Wärmetauscher – Speicherentladung, konstante Vorlauftemperatur
– Mengenabhängige Pumpenleistungsregelung der Speicherentladepumpe
– Differenzdruckabhängige Pumpenleistungsregelung am Kältehauptverteiler
– Wärmetauscher Niedertemperaturkreis, konstante Vorlauftemperatur
– Freigabe der Fußbodenkühlkreise in Abhängigkeit von der Außentemperatur und der Temperatur des Referenzraumes
– Mengenabhängige Pumpenleistungsregelung für Kältekreis/RLT
– Wärmetauscher – freie Kühlung, konstante Vorlauftemperatur, Vereisungsschutz, außen-enthalpieabhängige Freigabe
– Differenzdruckabhängige Pumpenleistungsregelung am Hauptverteiler
– Kühlturmregelung (geräteinterne Regelung der Absorptionskältemaschine)
– Mengenabhängige Pumpenleistungsregelung für Kältekreis, Umluftkühlgeräte
– Überwachung/Druckhalte- und Entgasungsstation
– Überwachung der Dosierung des Biozids für die Kühlturmanlage
– Überwachung der Kühlturmheizung
– Steuerung der Kühlturmbefüllung/Entleerung
– Abschaltung/Kälteversorgung unter Berücksichtigung der Abfahrmechanismen der Absorptionskältemaschine
– Überwachung des Kältemittelverlusts

Entsprechend ergeben sich **rechnerisch** für das Gebäude nachfolgend aufgeführte Jahresenergieverbräuche:
Calculations for the building show the following annual energy consumption:

Lüftungskonzept Dachgeschoss
Regelgeschoss
Erdgeschoss
Querschnitt

Ventilation concept roof storey
standard floor
ground floor
cross-section

Deckungsgrade des Jahresenergieverbrauchs gesamt (Heizen und Kühlen)
Coverage of total annual energy consumption (heating and cooling)

Jahreskühlenergie Freie Kühlung (TauL < 18 °C) 116 kWh 27%
Cooling energy per annum free cooling (temp. external air <18 °C) 116 kWh 27%
Jahreskühlenergie Kompressionskältemaschine 26 kWh 6%
Cooling energy per annum compression cooling plant 26 kWh 6%

Jahresenergie Solar Cooling Wärme/Kälte 76 kWh 18%
Solar cooling energy per annum heating/cooling energy 76 kWh 18%
Jahresheizenergie Fernwärme 210 kWh 49%
Heating energy per annum district heating 210 kWh 49%

Deckungsgrade des Jahresenergieverbrauchs gesamt (Heizen und Kühlen ohne freie Kühlung)
Coverage of total annual energy consumption (heating and cooling, excluding free cooling)

Jahreskühlenergie Kompressionskältemaschine 26 kWh 8%
Cooling energy per annum compression cooling plant 26 kWh 8%

Jahresenergie 68% Solar Cooling Wärme/Kälte 76 kWh 24%
Solar cooling energy per annum 68% solar cooling heating/cooling energy 76 kWh 24%
Jahresheizenergie Fernwärme 210 kWh 68%
Heating energy per annum district heating 210 kWh 68%

Deckungsgrade des Jahresheizenergieverbrauchs gesamt
Coverage of total annual heating-energy consumption

Jahresheizenergie Solar Cooling Wärme 50 kWh 19%
Heating energy per annum solar cooling heating energy 50 kWh 19%
Jahresheizenergie Fernwärme 210 kWh 81%
Heating energy per annum district heating 210 kWh 81%

Deckungsgrade des Jahreskälteenergieverbrauchs gesamt
Coverage of total annual cooling-energy consumption

Jahreskühlenergie Freie Kühlung (TauL < 18 °C) 116 kWh 69%
Cooling energy per annum free cooling (temp. external air < 18 °C) 116 kWh 69%
Jahreskühlenergie Kompressionskältemaschine 25,5 kWh 15%
Cooling energy per annum compression cooling plant 25.5 kWh 15%

Jahreskühlenergie Solar Cooling Kälte 26 kWh 16%
Cooling energy per annum solar cooling cooling energy 26 kWh 16%

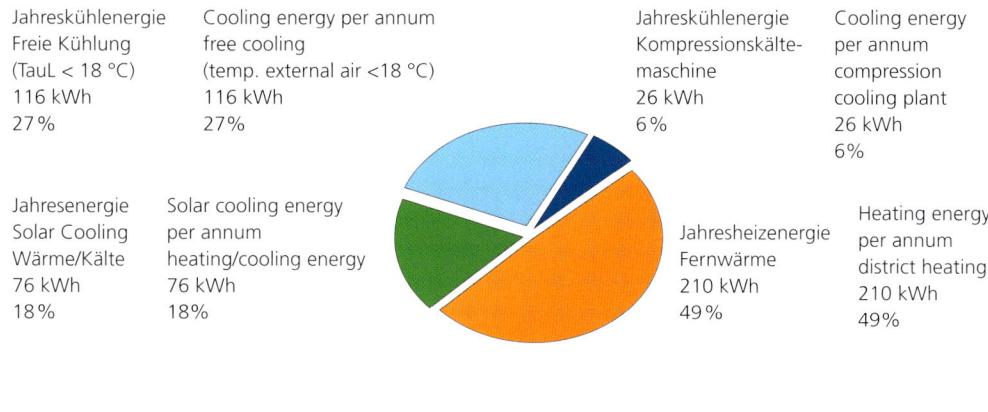
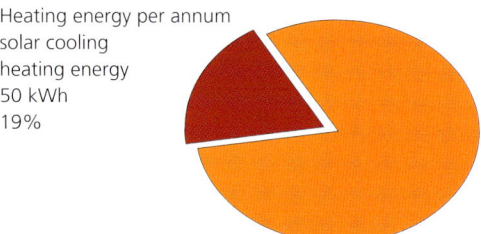

Raumlufttechnik

Mechanische Lüftungsanlagen versorgen folgende Bereiche mit Frischluft:

Südbau: Obergeschosse
Die Arbeits- und Schlafbereiche der Studenten, der öffentliche Gemeinschaftsbereich sowie das 7. Obergeschoss des Südbaus werden mechanisch be- und entlüftet. Die Luftkonditionierung der beiden Bereiche erfolgt getrennt mittels Zonenköpfen. Die Raumlufttechnik (RLT)-Anlage mit Wärme- und Kälterückgewinnung sowie Befeuchtungsfunktion liegt auf dem Dach des Südbaus.
Die Luftbefeuchtung erhöht in den Wintermonaten die Aufenthaltsqualität sowie die Behaglichkeit und reduziert das Infektionsrisiko speziell im Bereich der oberen Luftwege. Durch die individuelle Fensteröffnung ist ein hybrides Lüftungssystem für alle Bereiche möglich.
West- und Ostbau
Die öffentlichen Bereiche im EG und 1. OG sowie die Wohnung im 2. und 3. Obergeschoss des Westbaus und die 8 Dozentenappartements werden mechanisch be- und entlüftet.
Halle EG/Südbau
Ein zentrales Kastengerät mit Wärme-/Kälterückgewinnung und Außenluftansaugung im Untergeschoss sorgt in der großen Erdgeschosshalle über Luftqualitätsfühler mit variablem Volumenstrom bedarfsgerecht für kontrollierte Lufterneuerung.
Bistro EG Ostbau
Das Bistro für ca. 60 Personen im EG des Ostbaus ist ohne Befeuchtungsfunktion mechanisch be- und entlüftbar.
Lager- und Technikbereiche UG
Die Lager- und Technikbereiche werden mit zentraler Wärmerückgewinnung, jedoch ohne Befeuchtung mechanisch be- und entlüftet.
Tiefgaragenab- und -zuluft
Die über das Nachbargrundstück erschlossene Tiefgarage erhält die Außenluft durch einen separaten Nachströmkanal über die gemeinsame Außenluftansaugung. Die Fortluft wird über das Dach abgeführt. Für die Entrauchung der Tiefgarage ist ein 10-facher Luftwechsel erforderlich.

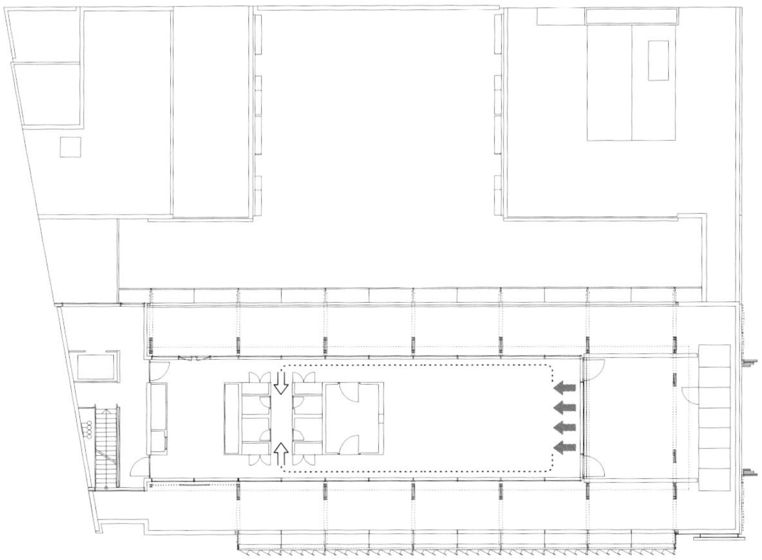

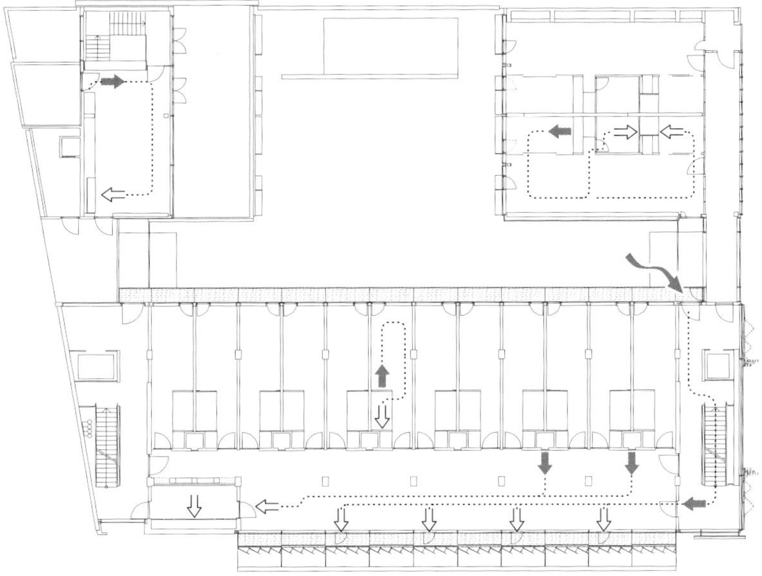

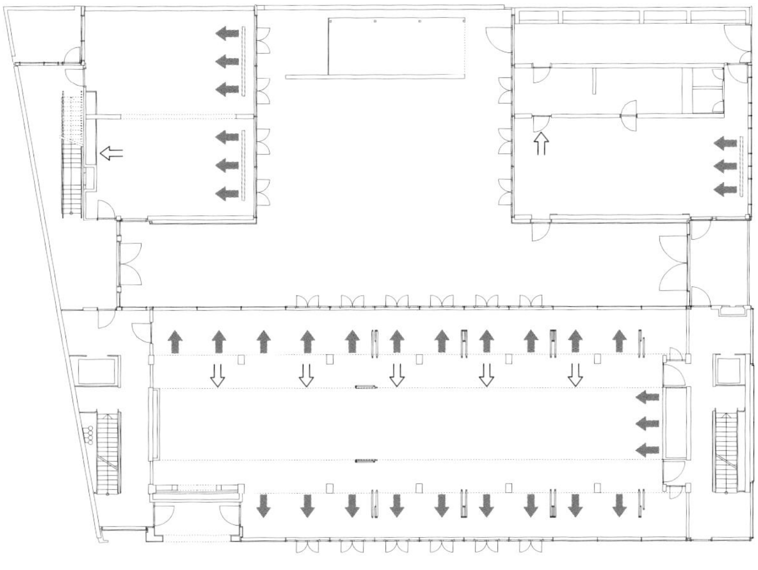

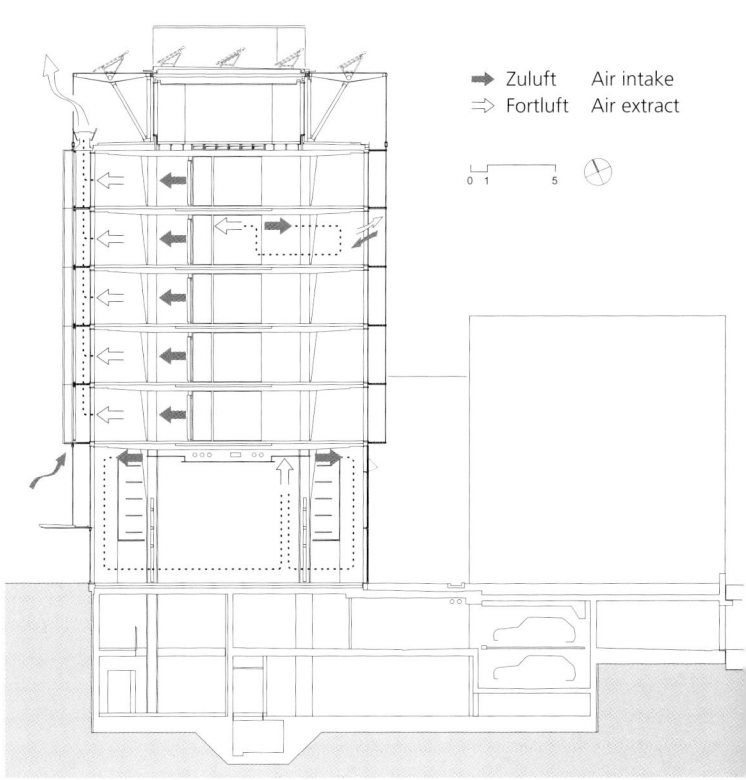

Müllraum
Der Müllraum wird durch einen Dachventilator entlüftet. Über eine freie Nachströmung aus dem Innenhof strömt frische Luft nach.
Batterieraum
Die verbrauchte und gegebenenfalls schadstoffbelastete Luft des Batterieraums im 1. UG wird über einen Dachventilator auf dem Ostbau entlüftet.

Die **Regelanlagen** für die Lüftungstechnik in DDC-Technik sind mit eigenständigen Informationsschwerpunkten in 4 Zentralen mit BUS-Verbindung zur zentralen Station verbunden. Sie leisten:
- Luftmengenregelung für gleichbleibende oder bedarfsgeführte Luftversorgung
- Kanaldruckabhängige Leistungsregelung der Zu- und Abluftventilatoren

Alle Obergeschosse des Südbaus
- Bedarfsabhängige Vorsteuerung der zentralen Heizungs- und Kälteversorgung

Folgende Regelgruppen mit Pumpenmotorsteuerungen betreffen:
In allen Bereichen:
- Luftkonditionierung mit Wärme-/Kälterückgewinnung und Vorerhitzer, einschließlich Vereisungs- und Frostschutzsteuerung
- Rauchüberwachung im Zuluftkanalsystem mit Gesamtabschaltung bei Raucheintrag
- Luftnachkonditionierung für Zonenkopf – Wohnbereich mit konstanter Zulufttemperatur – Luftnachkonditionierung für Zonenkopf des Veranstaltungsbereichs mit bedarfsgeführter Zulufttemperaturregelung in Abhängigkeit der Raum- bzw. Ablufttemperatur
- Anlage im täglichen Dauerbetrieb

Im Westbau und Ostbau:
- Luftnachkonditionierung mit konstanter Zulufttemperatur – Anlage im täglichen Dauerbetrieb

Halle EG/1. OG Südbau/Bistro EG Ostbau:
- Luftnachkonditionierung mit bedarfsgeführter Zulufttemperaturregelung, abhängig von Raum- bzw. Ablufttemperatur
- Bedarfsgeführte Luftmengenregelung in Abhängigkeit von der Luftqualität in der Halle
- Anlagenbetrieb über Zeitprogramm

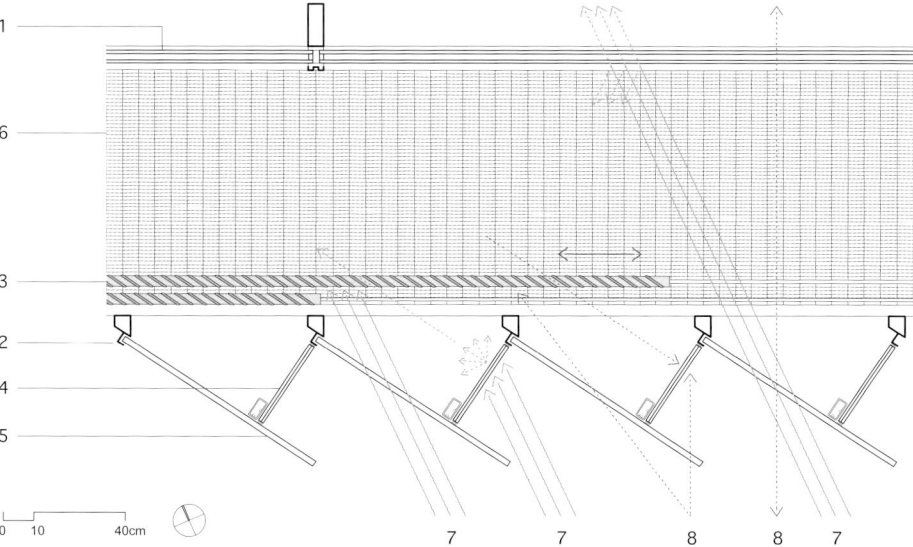

Vorfassade   Outer facade layer

——> Licht   Light path
······> Sichtlinie   Sight line

Doppelfassade

1. Innere Fassade als thermische Hülle mit Wärmeschutz-Isolierverglasung, öffenbare Fenster in dem Fassadenzwischenraum zur natürlichen Belüftung der Innenräume
2. Vorfassade, von der Dachkonstruktion über alle Geschosse abgehängte Metall-/Glaskonstruktion, als Schutz gegen äußere Witterungseinflüsse und Schallimmissionen
3. Hölzerne Läden, horizontal verschieblich, mit Lamellen als Sonnen-, Blend- und Sichtschutz, automatisch und manuell steuerbar
4. Einfachverglasung, transluzent
5. Einfachverglasung, transparent
6. Metallgitterrost als horizontaler Sonnenschutz, begehbar zu Wartungs- und Reinigungsarbeiten
7. Sonnen- und Blendschutz, direkte Sonneneinstrahlung auf die innere Fassade wird durch die Holzlamellen und die transluzente Verglasung weitestgehend vermieden. Die Geometrie der Holzlamellen lässt partiellen Tageslichteintriff zu. Reflektionen hellen die Rückseite der Lamellen zum Innenraum hin auf
8. Sichtschutz, durch die horizontal verschieblichen Läden und die transluzente Verglasung ergeben sich regelbare Ein- und Ausblicke

Double-skin facade

1. Inner facade layer, forming a thermal envelope: thermally insulating double glazing; openable windows to facade cavity for natural ventilation of internal spaces
2. Outermost facade layer: metal-and-glass construction suspended from roof structure as protection against external weather influences and noise immissions
3. Wood louvred shutters, horizontally sliding as protection against insolation and glare and as a means of visual screening; automatically and manually operable
4. Single glazing, translucent
5. Single glazing, transparent
6. Horizontal metal grating as sunscreen, capable of bearing foot traffic for maintenance and cleaning
7. Screening against solar radiation and glare: direct exposure of the inner facade skin to sunlight is prevented to a very high degree by the wood louvres and translucent glazing. The geometry of the louvres nevertheless permits the partial ingress of daylight. Light in the form of reflections is cast on the back of the louvres facing the internal spaces.
8. Visual screening: the horizontally sliding shutters and the translucent glazing allow views into and out of the building to be controlled.

In Lager- und Technikbereichen:
– Konstante Zulufttemperatur im Winter ca. 19 °C
Tiefgaragenab- und -zuluft
– Anlagenbetrieb ohne thermische Luftkonditionierung, zweistufig über Zeitprogramm und CO-Warnanlage
– Erste Betriebsstufe zeitgesteuert und bei CO-Alarm
– Zweite Betriebsstufe bei Auslösung des CO-Hauptalarms

Entrauchung Tiefgarage und 2. Untergeschoss

– Anlagenbetrieb wird durch Schlagtaster im Angriffsweg der Feuerwehr und durch Testschalter in der Brandmeldezentrale sowie automatisch durch die Brandmeldezentrale (BMZ) ausgelöst
– Durch Rauchmelder der BMZ werden einzelne Entrauchungsbereiche signalisiert, es erfolgt eine Vorsteuerung von Entrauchungsklappen der einzelnen Alarmbereiche (Zentralen, Flure, Räume)
Im Müll- und im Batterieraum werden die Anlagen dauerbetrieben.

Gebäudeleittechnik GLT-Netzwerk

Die Automatisierungsschwerpunkte werden über das hausinterne IT-Netzwerk miteinander kommunikativ verbunden. Dadurch können sämtliche Möglichkeiten des Datenaustauschs der Stationen untereinander und mit einem übergeordneten Managementsystem zum optimierten energiewirtschaftlichen Betrieb der gesamten Gebäudetechnik genutzt werden durch:
– Bedarfserfassung der Verbraucherkreise aus den Bereichen Heizung, Kälte, Raumlufttechnik und optimierte Vorsteuerung der energieerzeugenden Geräte
– Betriebszustandserfassung der Fassadensteuerung
– Raumtemperaturüberwachung in Server-/Netzwerkräumen
– Zentrale Betriebsführung mit Langzeitarchivierung von Messwerten und Betriebszuständen
– Fernalarmierung bei Störungen hoher Priorität über SMS/Fax
– Bedienungs-/Eingriffsmöglichkeit sämtlicher Haustechnikanlagen vor Ort oder von Ferne über Internet/Intranet mit Standardbrowserfenster

Wasserversorgung

Eine vorhandene Trinkwasserleitung DN 150 der Stadtwerke München mündet mit einer Hausanschlussleitung DN 65 von der Amalienstraße aus in das erste Untergeschoss.
Ein **Kalkschutzgerät** wandelt auf natürlichem Weg chemiefrei im Trinkwasser gelöste kalkbildende Ionen zu Kalkkristallen um, der feine Kalkstaub wird bei Wasserentnahme ausgespült.
Ein **Gerät zur Trinkwasserdesinfektion** tötet u.a. im Warmwasser temperaturresistente Legionellenstämme ab, die in kritischen Stagnationszeiten bei leerstehenden Einheiten auftreten können; gezielte Dosierung eines Desinfektionsmittels gegen Keime und Bakterien.
Die **Warmwasserbereitung** erfolgt zentral mittels Speicherladesystem und Warmwasserbevorratung. Die Verteilung geht über Zirkulationsleitungen.
Im Hausanschlussraum des 1. Untergeschosses erfolgt die Wasserzählung und die Verteilung auf das Hausnetz.

Abwasser- und Regenwasserentsorgung

Die Abwasserleitungen unter der Kellerdecke des 1. und 2. Untergeschosses münden in den öffentlichen Kanal der Stadt München. Die Steigstränge in den Montageschächten werden über Dach entlüftet.
Die Entwässerung unter der Rückstauebene im 1. und 2. Untergeschoss wird mittels einer Doppel-Hebeanlage entleert. Das Abwasser der Küche des Bistros wird über einen Fettabscheider entwässert.
Da das anfallende Regenwasser auf dem Grundstück nicht versickert werden kann,

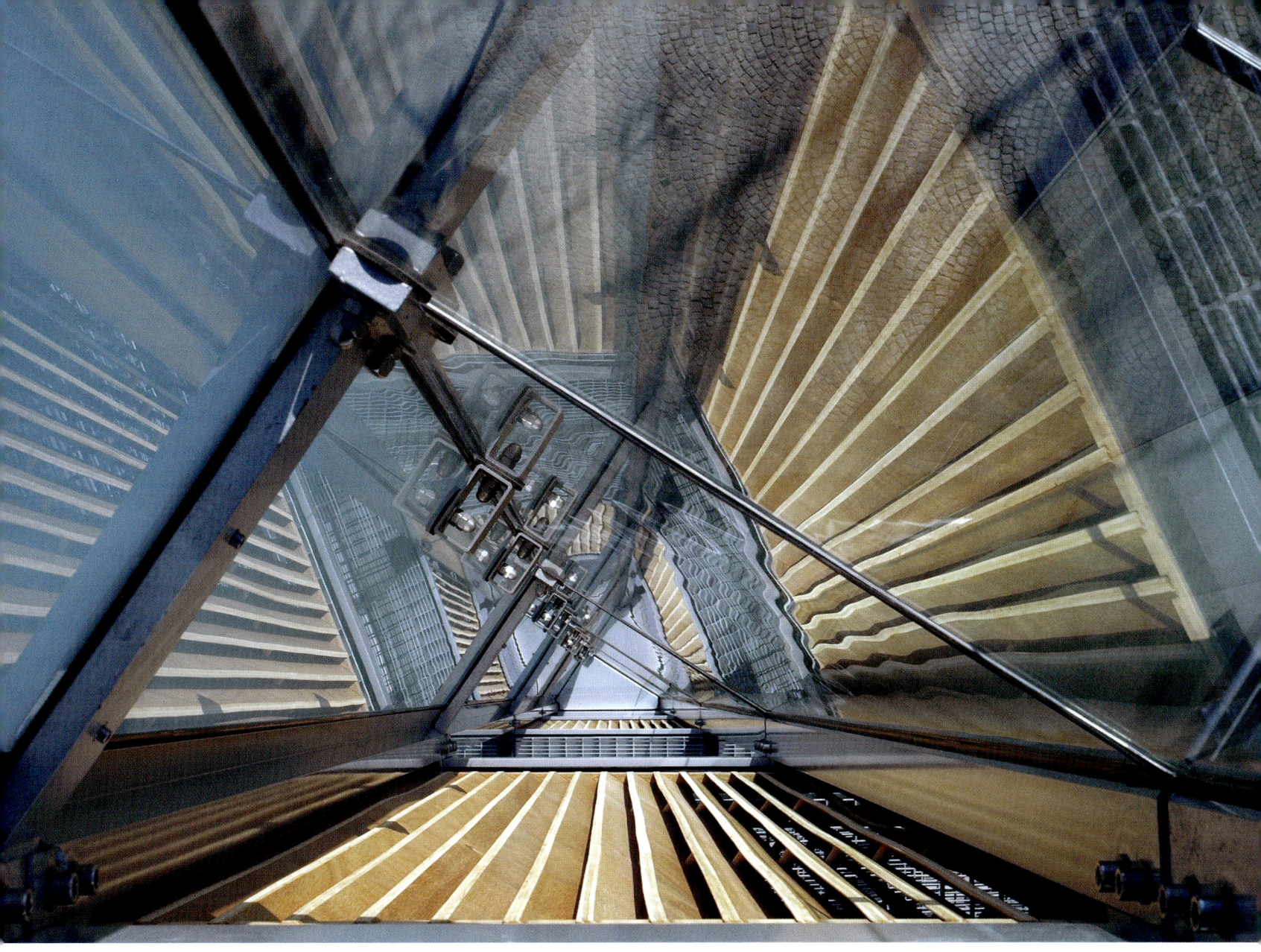

wird es im Mischsystem über einen Siphon mit dem anfallenden Schmutzwasser in die öffentliche Kanalentwässerung abgeleitet.

Sprinkleranlage/Löschwasser

Eine Hochdruckwassernebel-Löschanlage schützt die Hallenbereiche im EG sowie die Gemeinschaftsbereiche in den Obergeschossen. Die beiden Haupttreppenhausbereiche sind mit „trockenen" Feuerlöschleitungen ausgestattet.

Im Straßenbereich befinden sich Unterflurhydranten der öffentlichen Wasserversorgungsleitung.

Das Brandschutzkonzept macht besondere Vorkehrungen erforderlich um eine Brandausbreitung innerhalb der Doppelfassade zu verhindern. Als Sprinkler werden spezielle Wassernebelsprinkler eingesetzt. Die Vorteile dieser Wassernebelsprinkler sind:
– Geringer Platzbedarf für die Zentralentechnik
– Geringe Wasserbevorratung (ca. 10 % von normalen Anlagen)
– Kleine Leitungsquerschnitte, damit eine leichte Integration in die bauliche Situation
– Rauchauswaschung und Rauchunterdrückung

Als Löschmittel wird Wassernebel genutzt, der Brände durch die Nutzung von drei physikalischen Mechanismen löscht und unterdrückt:
– Kühlung: Wasser bietet als Wirkstoff zur Brandbekämpfung eine hervorragende Kühleigenschaft
– Verdrängung von Sauerstoff: Die schlagartige Verdampfung verdrängt lokal den Sauerstoff
– Abschirmung von Hitzestrahlung: Die große Dichte kleinster Wassertropfen absorbiert effizient die Hitzestrahlung

Die Sprinklerzentrale im 2. Untergeschoss am westlichen Treppenhaus bietet einen direkten Zugang für die Feuerwehr.

Die Löschwasserverteilung führt im Südbau über einen Sanitärschacht in die Geschosse 2–6. In der Halle sind die Sprinkler in dem abgehängten Deckenhohlraum angeordnet. In den Obergeschossen sind die Sprinkler entlang der Fassade in Sichtinstallation angeordnet.

Eine geschossweise Alarmunterteilung mit Strömungsmelder ermöglicht eine schnelle Branderkennung.

GWA – Gas-, Wasser-, Abwasser- und Feuerlöschtechnik
SPR – Sprinkleranlagen
WBR – Wärmeversorgungs-, Brauchwassererwärmungs- und Raumlufttechnik
MSR – Mess-, Steuer- und Regelungstechnik
RLT – Raumlufttechnik
DDC-Technik – digital data technik, in Texten immer mit DDC abgekürzt
HT- und NT-Kreis – Hochtemperatur- und Niedertemperaturkreis
BMZ – Brandmeldezentrale
GLT-Netzwerk – Gebäudeleittechnik-Netzwerk
OH1 – VdS (Verband deutscher Sachversicherer) – spezifische Bezeichnung für eine Brandgefahrenklasse bei einer Sprinklerung

Services Systems

Christian Dotzauer

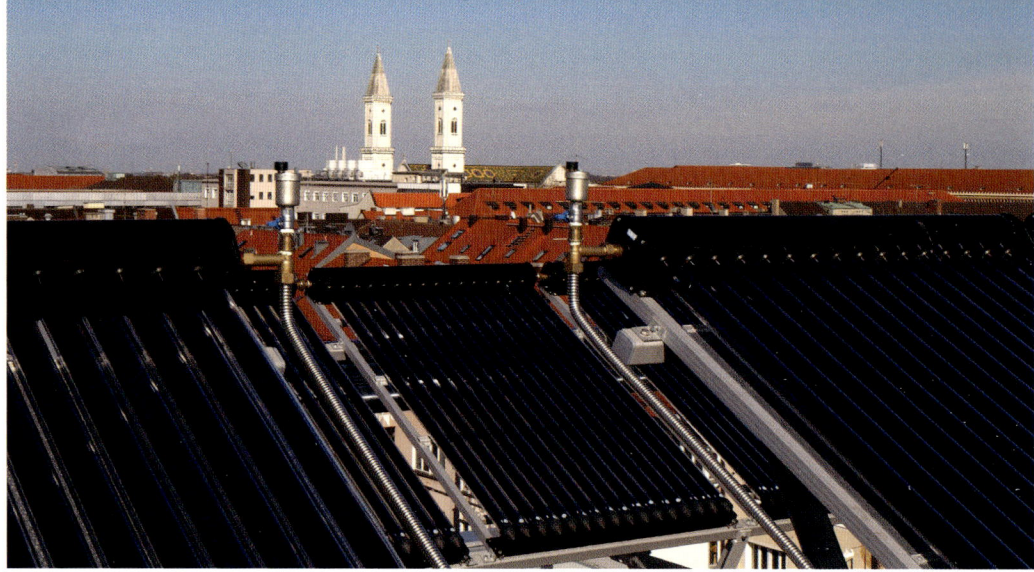

The aim of the planning was to implement a high-performance, energy-efficient building that would conserve resources. With the use of innovative constructional technology and modern plant and equipment, a structure was realized that has a low consumption of primary energy.
To achieve this goal, the following systems were used:
– exploitation of solar energy for the hot-water supply, solar cooling and heating backup;
– mechanical ventilation of the living spaces with highly efficient heat-recovery system;
– general lighting control in accordance with daylight levels and movement detectors;
– control in working areas in accordance with daylighting;
– regulation of blinds in events spaces in accordance with position of sun;
– natural ventilation through control of facade louvres;
– water-saving sanitary fittings.

Heating supply

In accordance with regulations imposed by the Munich public utility authority, the heating supply is provided by a connection to the municipal steam district-heating network. (The hybrid heat-exchange units that were installed are suitable for both steam and hot-water operation.)

Heat generation

In a bivalent heat-generation system, approximately 80 per cent of the heating-energy needs are covered by the municipal district-heating supply and about 20 per cent by solar thermal energy. The central-heating plant for the entire building is situated in the basement. The overall thermal output of all heating circuits is 400 kW.
The heating supply to individual parts of the building is as follows:
– static heating areas in the rooms, staircase areas and WCs;
– ventilation and air-conditioning plant in the west tract (ground to third floors); in the east tract (first to fourth floors) and in the bistro; in the south tract (living areas and the seventh floor events space as well as the hall; stores and mechanical services areas in the basement);
Underfloor heating:
– hall area on ground floor of south tract;
– public areas on ground floor of west and east tracts;
– office on first floor of west tract;
– rooms oriented to the internal courtyard on the second floor and the roof storey of the west tract;
– communal areas adjoining the private rooms and the lecturers' apartments;
– rooms and lecturers' apartments in the south and east tracts;
– communal area in the roof storey of the south tract.

Hot water plant

The hot-water plant on the second basement level with intermediate storage facilities (two 750-litre reserve tanks) supplies users via risers and distribution and circulation runs.

Automatic control systems for heating technology

The measurement, control and regulation plant was executed in direct digital control (DDC) technology.
In the central plant room for heating, a bus connection supplies the primary server for the control system in the building, which has the following functions:
– central control of heating supply temperatures in accordance with external temperatures;
– adjustment of room temperatures by means of thermostatically operated radiator valves fixed to all static heating surfaces;
– operation of heating-circulation pumps with default and time switching for twin pumps;
– speed regulation of heating-circulation pumps in accordance with differential pressure;
– monitoring of consumption by means of bus-compatible meters.
The following monitoring groups, including relevant pump-motor controls, are served in this way:
– heat-exchange units – district heating: supply temperature according to needs, with return-flow temperature/maximum limit;
– heat-exchange units – solar thermal energy/absorption cooling, constant supply temperature, with return temperature/maximum limits; variable volume control by means of output regulator within plant;
– control of pump output of main heating-supply distributors according to differential pressure;
– control of pump output for heating circuit in accordance with volume – air-conditioning installation;
– control of pump output for heating circuit, in accordance with volume – static heating;
– control of heating-supply temperature for static heating, in accordance with external temperature;
– heat-exchange units in low-temperature circuit; constant supply temperature with return-flow temperature/maximum limit;
– control of pump output for low-temperature distributor, in accordance with differential pressure;
– control of pumping output of low-temperature circuit in accordance with volume (hall, communal areas, events space on 7th floor, west and east tracts);
– control of supply temperature in low-temperature circuit in accordance with external temperatures, with activation of reference values by means of sensors (hall, communal areas, events space on 7th floor, west and east tracts);
– heat-exchange unit – non-potable water – water-storage tanks; constant supply temperature, with return-flow temperature/maximum limit;

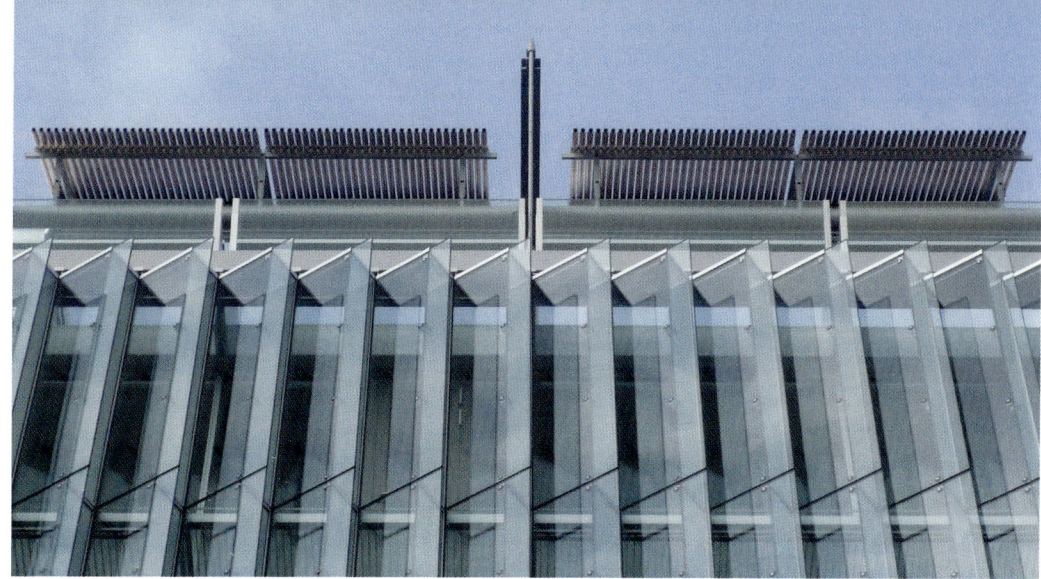

- time-optimized, temperature-controlled regulation of circulation pumps;
- opening of underfloor heating circuits in accordance with external temperature and temperature of reference space;
- monitoring of pressure-maintenance and degassing stations in high- and low-temperature circuits;
- monitoring of waste-water pumping plant (main services centres);
- monitoring of fat/grease trap, including raising plant.

Cooling plant

The generation of cooling energy was divided into the three following categories:
- "free cooling" – this covers almost 70 per cent of cooling-energy needs with the aid of a cooling tower. Evaporative cooling ensures the requisite return cooling temperatures in a cost-efficient form, even with high external air temperatures;
- "solar cooling" – solar collectors on the roof cover 16 per cent of cooling-energy needs. The hot water produced in the process is used to operate an absorption-cooling machine on the second basement level;
- "compression-cooling technology" – a standard compression cooling machine covers 15 per cent of the peak cooling-energy needs.

Cooling energy is required for the following purposes and in the following areas:
- ventilation and air-conditioning plant (west tract, ground– 3rd floor; east tract, 1st– 4th floors; upper floors in south tract with events space on 7th floor; hall in south tract, and ground floor bistro in east tract)
- underfloor cooling, whereby the water temperature is not more than 2–3 °C below room temperature in the following areas:
- ground floor hall, south tract;
- ground floor communal areas, west and east tracts;
- first floor "office", west tract;
- second floor rooms oriented to courtyard, and roof storey, west tract;
- communal areas outside students' rooms and lecturers' apartments, south and east tracts;
- students' rooms and lecturers' apartments, south and east tracts;
- communal areas, roof storey, south tract.

The maximum overall cooling capacity is 160 kW.

Control plant for cooling system

The whole of the measurement, control and regulation plant was executed in DDC technology. The information centre is coupled with the main heating plant:
- cooling circulation pumps with default and time switching for twin pumps;
- speed regulation of cooling-circulation pumps in accordance with differential pressure;
- optimization of absorption cooling plant operating time in accordance with weather conditions and the degree to which the cooling-energy accumulator is charged;
- switching of underfloor heating to underfloor cooling in accordance with needs;
- use of solar heat for heating building on cold days.

The following monitoring groups, including related pump-motor controls, are served:
- absorption cooling plant with control (charge and discharge) pumps in accordance with external temperature, indoor reference temperature and reserve supply;
- heat-exchange units – discharge from reserve supply, constant flow temperature;
- regulation of pump output for discharge from reserve supply in accordance with volume required;
- regulation of pump output of main cooling-energy distributors in accordance with differential pressure;
- heat-exchange units in low-temperature circuit, supply temperature;
- opening of underfloor cooling circuits in accordance with external temperature and temperature of reference space;
- control of pump output for cooling circuit in accordance with volume required – air-conditioning installation;
- heat-exchange units for "free cooling", constant supply temperature, protection against icing; opening dependent on external enthalpy;
- regulation of pump output of main cooling-supply distributors in accordance with differential pressure;
- regulation of cooling tower (internal controls within absorption cooling plant);
- control of pump output for cooling circuit, air-cooling unit;
- monitoring of pressure-maintenance and degassing station;
- monitoring of biocide dosage for cooling-tower plant;
- monitoring of cooling-tower heating;
- regulation of filling/evacuation of cooling tower;
- switching off cooling supply, taking account of the shut-down mechanisms of the absorption-cooling plant;
- observation of coolant loss.

Ventilation and air conditioning

Mechanical ventilation plant supplies the following areas with fresh air:

South tract – upper floors
The students' working and bedroom areas, the communal spaces and the 7th floor of the south tract are mechanically ventilated (air supply and extract). The air conditioning of these two realms functions separately by means of zone distribution units.
The air-conditioning plant, with recovery of heating and cooling energy and with a humidifying function, is situated on the roof of the south tract.
By humidifying the air, the habitable quality/comfort of the internal spaces is improved in the winter months, and the risk of infection

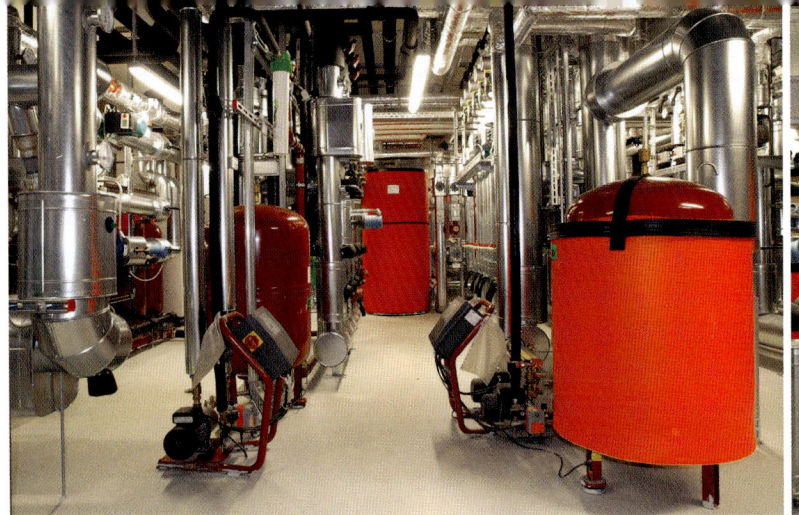
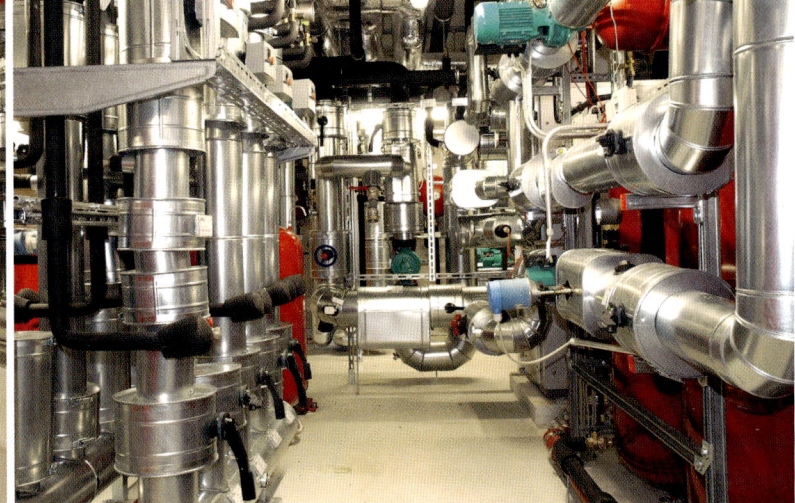

is reduced, especially in respect of the upper respiratory tracts.
The scope provided for opening windows individually allowed a hybrid ventilation system to be implemented in all areas.
West and east tracts
The communal areas on the ground and first floors, as well as the dwellings on the 2nd and 3rd floors of the west tract and the eight lecturers' apartments, are mechanically ventilated (air supply and extract).
Ground floor hall, south tract
A central air-handling unit (AHU) with recovery of heating and cooling energy and an air intake at basement level provides a controlled system of air renewal in the large hall on the ground floor via air-quality sensors, with a variable rate of flow in accordance with needs.
Ground floor bistro, east tract
The ground floor bistro in the east tract can accommodate 60 people and is mechanically ventilated without a humidifying installation.
Storage and services areas in basement
The storage and services areas are mechanically ventilated without a humidifying installation.
Basement garage: air extract and supply
The basement garage, access to which is via the adjoining site, has a fresh-air intake through a separate duct combined with the general air intake. Extract air is emitted above roof level. For the smoke-extract system in the basement garage, a tenfold air change is required.
Refuse room
The refuse room is ventilated by means of a roof fan.
Battery room
Exhaust air from the battery room on the first basement level may on occasion contain pollutants. The air is removed by a roof fan at the top of the east tract.

Automatic control systems

The automatic ventilation control systems were executed in direct digital control (DDC) technology and are linked with independent information points in four switching centres by means of bus interfaces to the central plant. They ensure:
– regulation of the amount of air to ensure a constant fresh-air supply or one that is regulated according to needs;
– regulation of air supply in conjunction with intake and extract fans, in accordance with duct pressure.

All upper floors of the south tract have pilot control of the central-heating and cooling supply, according to needs.
The following control groups with motor-pump operation function in all areas:
– air conditioning with recovery of heating and cooling energy, plus preheating, including regulation of ice and frost protection;
– monitoring of the presence of smoke in air-supply ducts with complete shutdown in the event of the entry of smoke;
– further conditioning of air for zone distribution unit – living realm with constant air-supply temperature; further conditioning of air for zone distribution unit in events area, with temperature regulation of air supply in accordance with indoor and air-extract temperatures.
– plant in daily (permanent) operation.
West and east tracts:
– further conditioning of air with constant air-supply temperature – plant in daily (permanent) use; ground floor hall/1st floor, south tract/ground floor bistro, east tract;
– further conditioning of air with regulation of air-supply temperature according to needs and dependent on indoor and air-extract temperatures;
– regulation of air-supply volume according to needs and dependent on air quality in hall;
– operation of plant according to time schedule.
Storage and services areas:
– constant air-supply temperature in winter, approx. 19 °C.

Basement garage air extract and supply:
– operation of plant without thermal air conditioning in two-phase modus by means of time schedule and with carbon monoxide (CO) warning system;
– first operating stage, time controlled and with CO alarm;
– second operating stage when main CO alarm set off.

Smoke extract from basement garage and second basement level

– The plant is activated by push-buttons in firefighting access routes and by a test switch at the central fire-alarm control point, as well as automatically from this point.
– Smoke-warning devices of the fire-alarm system show individual smoke-extract areas; an advance operation of smoke-extract flaps occurs in the individual alarm zones (plant rooms, corridors and other spaces).
In the refuse and battery rooms, the system is in permanent operation.

Central building control system – networks

The automated centres are linked with each other by a communications system via the internal IT network. As a result, every possible form of data exchange between stations and with an overall management system can be exploited to ensure an optimized energy-efficient operation of the entire systems technology in the building. This is achieved through:
– assessment of needs of load circuits in the fields of heating, cooling, air conditioning, and an optimized pilot control of energy-generating plant;
– assessment of the operating conditions of facade controls;
– monitoring of indoor temperatures in server and network spaces;
– central control of operations with long-term archiving of measurement values and operational conditions;

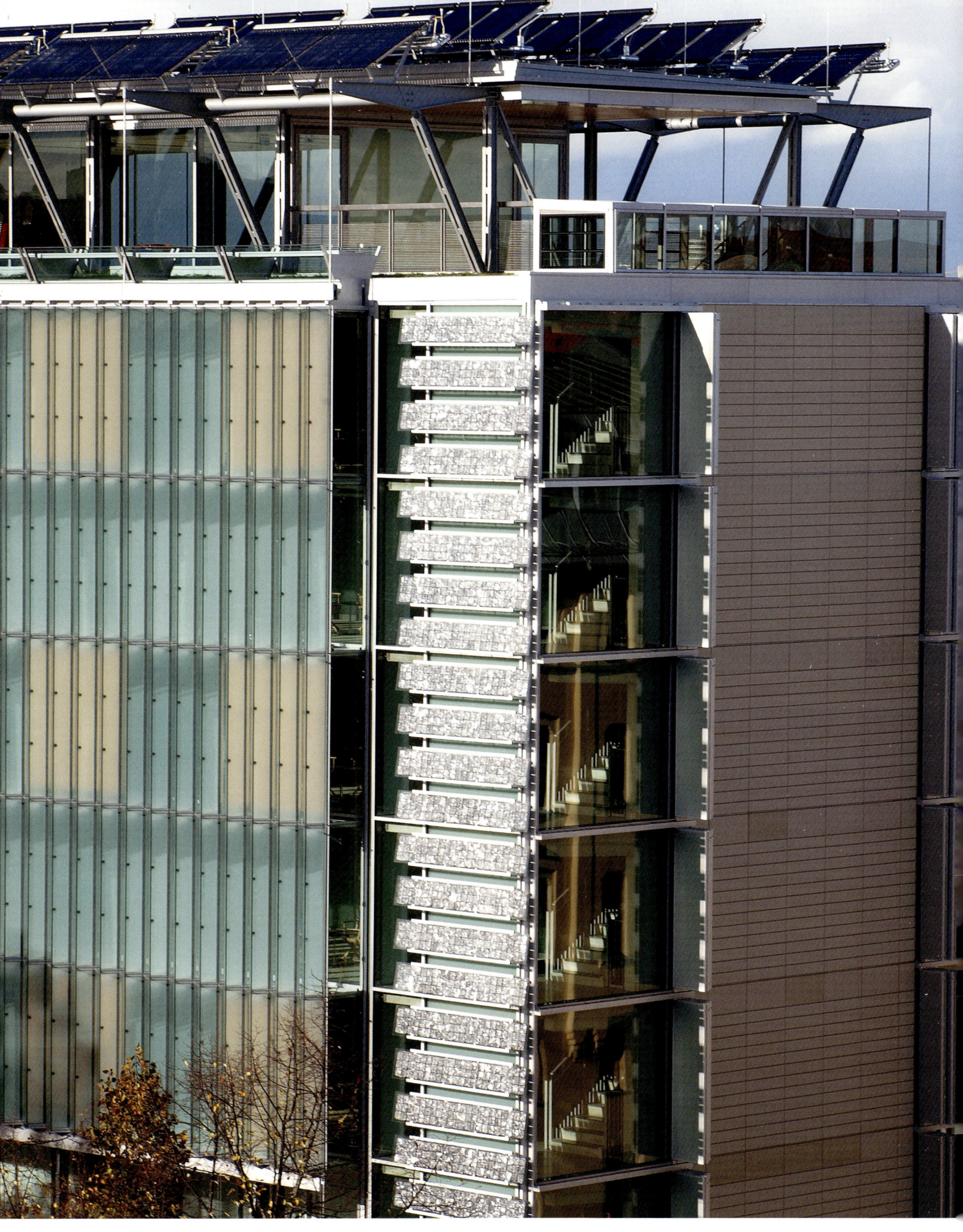

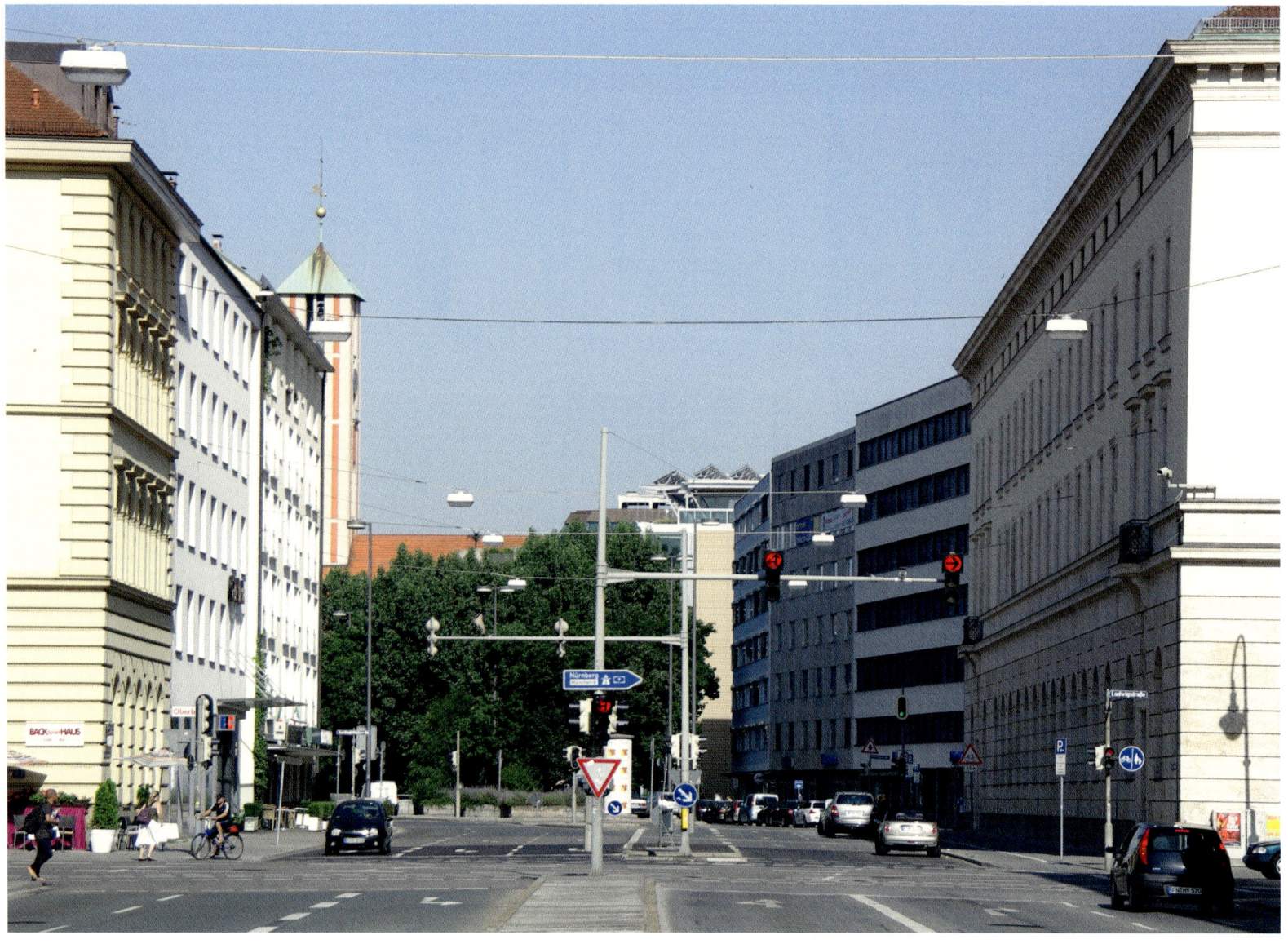

- remote alarm system in the case of defects requiring urgent treatment via SMS/fax;
- provision for operation of all service plant within the building/scope for intervention on site or by remote control via internet/intranet with standard browser window.

Water supply

An existing drinking-water supply pipe (Ø 150 mm nom.) branches off from the main run of the Munich municipal works in Amalienstrasse, entering the forum building (Ø 65 mm nom.) at first basement level.
An installation that provides **protection against lime and calcium deposits** in water transforms calcium-forming ions dissolved in the water into crystals in a natural process without the use of chemicals. The fine calcium grains are washed out when water is drawn off.
An **installation to disinfect drinking water** destroys, among other things, temperature-resistant legionellae in hot water. These can occur in empty units in critical periods of stagnation. The disinfection is achieved through a specific dosage of disinfectant against germs and bacteria.

Water is heated and stored centrally. Distribution is via circulation runs. Installed in the room for service connections on the first basement level are the water meters and the distribution to the internal runs within the building.

Waste-water and rainwater drainage

Waste-water drainpipes beneath the ceilings on the first and second basement levels flow into the municipal sewage network. Vertical runs in the pipe ducts are ventilated above roof level.
Drainage of waste and soil water below the back-pressure level on the first and second basement floors is removed by means of a dual pumping plant. Waste water from the bistro kitchen is removed through a grease trap.
Since rain that falls on the site cannot seep away, it is drained off in a combined system via a trap, together with waste water, into the public sewers.

Sprinkler plant and water for firefighting

A high-pressure water-vapour fire-extinguishing plant protects the hall areas on the ground floor and the communal areas on the upper floors. The two main staircases are equipped with "dry" fire mains.
Underfloor hydrants of the public water-supply system were installed along the adjoining roads.

The special fire protection concept prevents fire spreading within the double-skin facade. Special water-vapour sprinklers were used here. The advantages of this form of installation are:
- little space is required for the central plant;
- only a small amount of water has to be stored in reserve (approx. 10 per cent of that required for normal systems);
- only small-diameter pipe runs are required, which eases their integration into the construction;
- smoke is washed out and suppressed.

Water vapour is used as a means of firefighting; this extinguishes and suppresses fires

through the use of three physical mechanisms:
– cooling – water possesses an outstanding cooling property when used in firefighting;
– displacement of oxygen: the sudden moisturizing effect displaces oxygen locally;
– protection against heat radiation: the great density of tiny water droplets effectively absorbs heat radiation.

The sprinkler plant room on the second basement level in the western staircase area allows direct access for the fire brigade. In the south tract, the fire-extinguishing water is conducted via a sanitary installation shaft to floors 2–6. In the hall, the sprinklers are fitted in the cavity behind the suspended soffit. On the upper floors, the sprinklers are visibly located along the facade. A floor-by-floor division of the alarm system with a flow-warning device allows a rapid identification of the location of a fire.

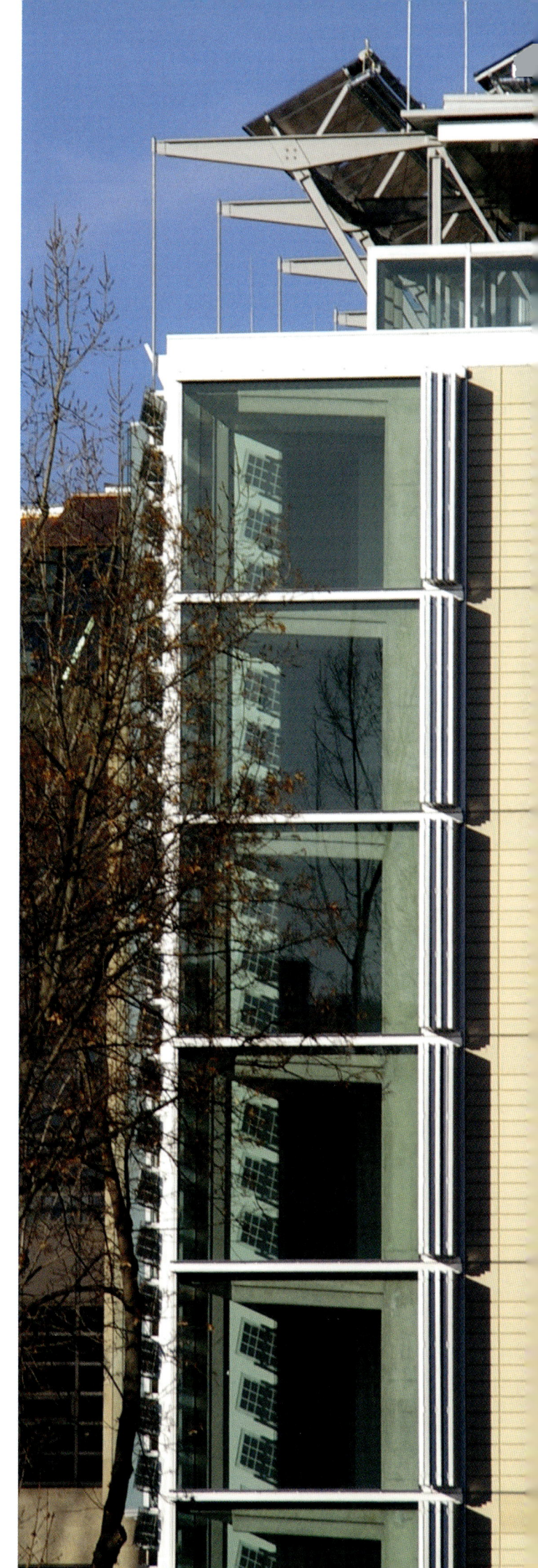

Gebäudetechnische Subsysteme

Isometrische Darstellung, Ansicht von Norden

1 Zuluft Zimmer Studierende
2 Abluft Zimmer Studierende
3 Zuluft Gemeinschaftsräume
4 Abluft Gemeinschaftsräume über Küche
5 Zuluft (Quellluft) Dachgeschoss
6 Abluft Dachgeschoss
7 Zuluft Halle EG
8 Zuluft (Quellluft) Halle EG
9 Abluft Halle EG
10 Fortluft Lüftungszentrale Südgebäude
11 Außenluft
12 Rückkühlwerk
13 Lüftungszentrale Südgebäude mit Wärmerückgewinnung
14 Vorlauf/Rücklauf Rückkühlwerk
15 Vor- und Rücklauf der thermischen Solarkollektoren
    Solare Kühlung und Heizung
16 Thermische Röhrenkollektoren
17 Zuluft Appartement
18 Abluft Appartement
19 Zuluft (Quellluft) Bistro
20 Abluft Bistro/Küche
21 Fortluft
22 Kühlturm/freie Kühlung/Rückkühlwerk
23 Vor- und Rücklauf freie Kühlung/Rückkühlwerk
24 Außenluft Lüftungszentrale 2. Untergeschoss
25 Fortluft Lüftungszentrale 2. Untergeschoss
26 Zuluft Partyraum
27 Abluft Partyraum
28 Lüftungsgeräte mit Wärmerückgewinnung
    Saal und Bistro in EG, Partyraum im 1./2. Untergeschoss
29 Wärmetauscher Absorber (Solar)
30 Wärmetauscher freie Kühlung (Rückkühlwerk)
31 Absorbtionskältemaschine
32 Kompressionskältemaschine
33 Verteiler Kälte
34 Verteiler Heizung
35 Kältepufferspeicher
36 Wärmepufferspeicher
37 Fernwärme Übergabestation
38 Einspeisung Fernwärmenetz

39 Wärme-/Kältezentrale 2. Untergeschoss
40 Lüftungszentrale 2. Untergeschoss
41 Lüftungszentrale Ostgebäude
42 Lüftungszentrale Südgebäude
43 Lüftungszentrale Westgebäude

Subsystems for technical services

Isometric diagram, north view

1 Air supply student rooms
2 Air extract student rooms
3 Air supply common areas
4 Air extract common area above kitchen
5 Air supply (air well) roof storey
6 Air extract roof storey
7 Air supply in ground floor hall
8 Air supply (air well) in ground floor hall
9 Air extract in ground floor hall
10 Exhaust air from ventilation plant: south tract
11 Fresh air
12 Recooling plant
13 Ventilation plant with heat recovery: south tract
14 Supply and return runs recooling plant
15 Supply and return runs for solar thermal collectors/
    solar cooling and heating
16 Thermal tube collectors
17 Air supply in apartment
18 Air extract in apartment
19 Air supply (air well) in bistro
20 Air extract in bistro/kitchen
21 Exhaust air
22 Cooling tower/free cooling/recooling plant
23 Supply and return runs/recooling plant
24 Fresh air for ventilation plant in U2
25 Exhaust air from ventilation plant in U2
26 Air supply in party room
27 Air extract in party room
28 Ventilation installation with heat recovery for hall
    and bistro in ground floor and party room in U1/U2
29 Heat-exchange unit absorber (solar)
30 Heat-exchange unit free cooling (recooling plant)
31 Absorption chiller
32 Compression chiller
33 Distributor cooling
34 Distributor heating
35 Cold-water storage
36 Hot-water storage
37 District-heating network hub
38 Feed for district-heating network

39 Heating/cooling plant in U2
40 Ventilation plant: U2
41 Ventilation plant: east tract
42 Ventilation plant: south tract
43 Ventilation plant: west tract

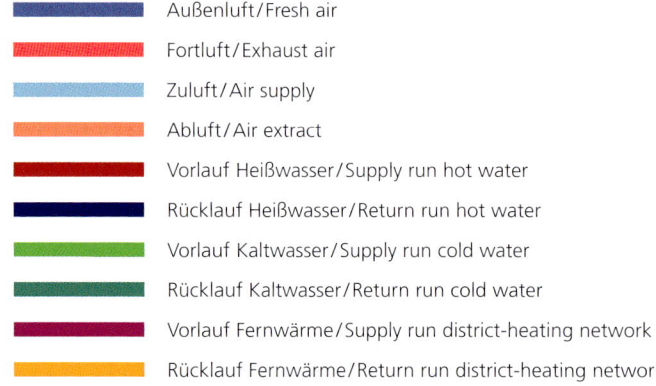

Außenluft/Fresh air
Fortluft/Exhaust air
Zuluft/Air supply
Abluft/Air extract
Vorlauf Heißwasser/Supply run hot water
Rücklauf Heißwasser/Return run hot water
Vorlauf Kaltwasser/Supply run cold water
Rücklauf Kaltwasser/Return run cold water
Vorlauf Fernwärme/Supply run district-heating network
Rücklauf Fernwärme/Return run district-heating network

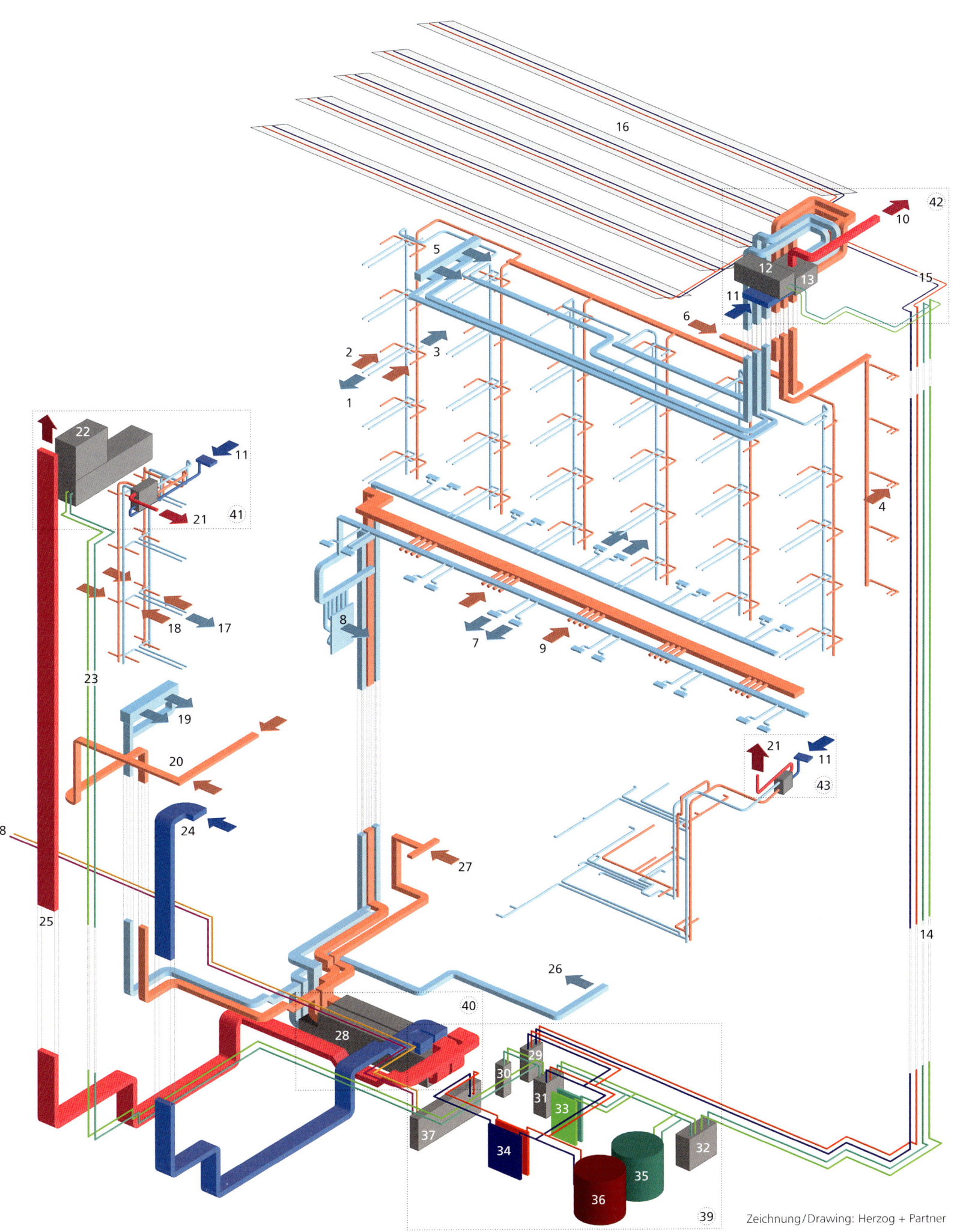

Zeichnung/Drawing: Herzog + Partner

63

Gebäudeautomation

Automation in the Building

Werner Rösener

Orientiert an ökonomischen Grundsätzen wurde zur Wärme- und Kälteversorgung sowie der Raumklimatisierung eine wasser- und lufthydraulische Vernetzung der versorgungstechnischen Anlagen eingebaut. Die auf dem Dach befindlichen Hochleistungs-Solarkollektoren liefern bei extern verursachter Kühllast Heißwasser an eine Absorptionskältemaschine. Durch dieses neuartige Prinzip der solaren Kühlung werden die sonst üblichen elektrischen Spitzenlasten zur Kälteerzeugung bei hoher sommerlicher Sonneneinstrahlung gänzlich vermieden.

Automationsnetzwerk

Die Steuerung der jeweils energetisch günstigsten Betriebsweise dieses Anlagenverbundes übernimmt ein Gebäudeautomationssystem mit zentralem Server im IT-Raum und rechnergestützten Automationseinheiten in den 5 Haustechnikzentralen. Der Informationsaustausch dieser Einheiten untereinander wird durch das hauseigene IT-Netzwerk sichergestellt. Ein Raumbussystem dient der exakten bedarfsgerechten Versorgung des gebäudeweiten Fußbodenheiz- bzw. kühlsystems. Im Gebäudeautomationsverbund werden standardisierte Übertragungsverfahren wie BACnet (**Data Communication Protocol for Building Automation and Control Networks**) und LON (**Local Operating Network**) verwendet.

Der Gebädeautomationsserver steht als OPC-Client (OLE for Process Control) im Verbund mit den Kommunikationssystemen des Elektrogewerks (Elektro Installations Bus – EIB). Hier werden die Messwerte der hauseigenen Wetterstation übermittelt und den Regelstrategien für wirtschaftlichen Betrieb der Heizungs- und Kälteversorgung sowie der Gebäudeklimatisierung zugeführt.

Fernalarmierung

Betriebsdaten aus allen haustechnischen Bereichen werden im Gebäudeautomationsserver gesammelt. Wichtige, betriebsrelevante Alarme aus den Bereichen Brandmelde-, Sprinkler-, Sanitärtechnik, Tiefgaragen-CO-Warnsystem werden über das integrierte Fernalarmierungssystem dem technischen Betriebsdienst via SMS und Telefax gemeldet.

Fernwartung

Zur Fehleranalyse und -behebung besteht die Einwahlmöglichkeit durch externe Wartungsdienste. Die grafisch-schematischen Darstellungen der haustechnischen Anlagen werden über WEB-Browser visualisiert und können von hier aus beobachtet und unter Voraussetzung entsprechender Zugriffsrechte bedient werden.

Besondere energiewirtschaftliche Aspekte, Regelungs- und Steuerstrategien:

Bedarfsgeführte Regelung/Steuerung

Der durch das Automationsnetzwerk realisierte Anlagen-Betriebsverbund ermöglicht die Bereitstellung der Versorgungsarten – Fernwärme, Solarwärme, Kompressionskälte und solare Kälte im jeweils betriebstechnisch optimalen Verhältnis. Die Lastzustände sämtlicher Verbrauchersysteme (Fußboden-Heiz-/Kühlkreise, Heizkörper- und Luftheizkreise) dienen in Kombination mit den Daten der Wetterstation den zentralen Regelkreisen als Sollwertvorgabe. Temperaturen der Heiz- und Kühlmedien werden jeweils nur auf lastbedingt notwendigem Niveau produziert. Bei hoher Sonneneinstrahlung wird die gesamte Wärmeproduktion des Solarkollektorfeldes der Absorptionskältemaschine zur Deckung von extern verursachten Spitzenkühllasten zugeführt. Bei geringerer Einstrahlung wird der solare Wärmeertrag zur Erzeugung von Brauchwarmwasser genutzt. Überschussleistungen können in dem Warmwasser-/Kaltwasser-Puffersystem „zwischengelagert" werden.

Natürliche Lüftung/natürliche Kühlung der Gemeinschaftsbereiche

Die durch den thermischen Auftrieb verursachte Sogwirkung der südlichen Doppelfassade dient der natürlichen Belüftung der Gemeinschaftsbereiche in den Obergeschossen. Manuell bedienbare Lüftungsklappen zum östlichen Treppenraum und die öffenbaren Türflügel hinter der Vorfassade ermöglichen ein Nachströmen von Außenluft aus dem Innenhof. Die im Osttreppenhaus im Bereich des 1. und 2. Obergeschosses eingebauten, motorisch betriebenen Lamellenfenster werden je nach Anzahl geöffneter Lüftungsklappen in den Etagen nach einer voreingestellten Steuermatrix mehr oder weniger weit geöffnet, um den Luftstrom zu kontrollieren. Die Steuerung wird erst dann aktiv, wenn hohe Kühllast anfällt und gleichzeitig ein Kühleffekt durch niedrige Temperaturen im Innenhof gewährleistet ist.

Natürliche Lüftung/Kühlung der Treppenhäuser

Gleichzeitig ist dieser manuell ausgelösten Art der Lüftung eine temperaturgesteuerte Lüftungsregelung beider Treppenhäuser (Ost und West) überlagert. Bei hohen Temperaturen in den Treppenhäusern wird durch Öffnen der Rauch- und Wärmeabzugsklappen und der unteren Lamellenfenster eine natürliche Durchströmung und Kühlung der Treppenräume bewirkt.

In accordance with economic principles, the heating and cooling system as well as the air conditioning are based on a water- and air-hydraulic network of service installations. In the event of cooling loads occurring, caused by external conditions, the high-performance solar collectors on the roof supply hot water to an absorption cooling plant. This innovative principle of solar cooling allows the complete avoidance of the usual peak electrical loads for the production of cooling energy in summer when there is a high degree of insolation.

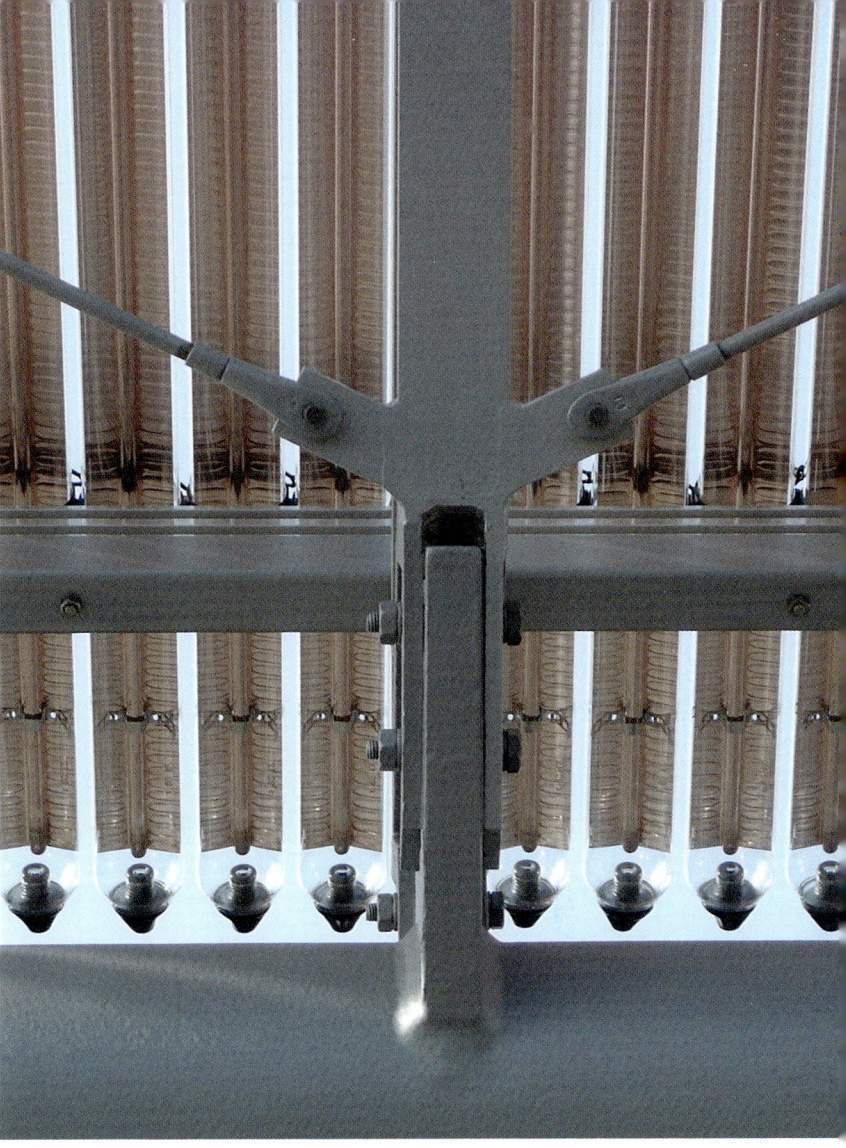

Automation network
The task of guaranteeing an optimum, energy-saving mode of operation in each particular situation within this combined installation network is assumed by a system of automation for the building with a central server in the IT room, as well as computer-supported automation units in the five central services spaces. The exchange of information between these units is ensured by an internal IT network within the building. A room bus system provides the underfloor heating/cooling supply throughout the forum precisely in accordance with needs. In the combined automation system, standardized transmission processes like BACnet (data communication protocol for building automation and control networks) and LON (local operating network) are used. The automation server for the building, an OPC-client (OLE for process control) is combined with the communications system of the electrical works (electrical installation bus EIB). Measurement data from the building's own weather station are transmitted here and used to determine the control strategies for an economic operation of the heating and cooling supply and the air conditioning.

Remote-controlled alarm system
Operating data from all internal service systems are collected in the automation server for the building. Important alarm signals that are of relevance in respect of fire protection, sprinkler plant, sanitary installation and basement garage carbon-monoxide (CO) warning are reported to the technical operating service via the integrated remote alarm system by means of SMS and telefax.

Remote-controlled maintenance
As a means of analysing and eliminating faults in the system, an option is provided for dialling into external maintenance services. A graphic-diagrammatic depiction of the various service installations in the building is drawn by a Web-browser. This allows problems to be observed from this point and remedied – given the appropriate rights of intervention, of course. Special economic aspects of energy production, regulation and control strategies are considered below.

Regulation and control according to needs
The combined plant-operating system made possible by the automation network serves to provide the following services: district heating, solar heating, compression cooling and solar cooling, each in an optimum operating relationship.

The states of loading in all user systems (underfloor heating/cooling circuits, radiator and warm-air heating circuits) serve – in combination with data from the weather station – as target values for the central control circuits. The temperatures of the heating and cooling media are generated only to the requisite level, in accordance with loading conditions.

With a high degree of insolation, the entire heating energy generated by the solar collectors is fed into the absorption cooling plant to meet peak cooling loads caused by external factors. With a lower level of insolation, the yield of solar heating energy is used to produce hot water for the rooms. Production in excess of requirements can be temporarily kept in the hot-/cold-water reserve storage system.

Natural ventilation/Natural cooling of communal zones
The suction effect in the south-facing double-skin facade caused by thermal uplift serves as a natural means of ventilating the communal areas on the upper floors. Manually operated ventilation flaps in the eastern staircase, together with the openable doors behind the outer facade layer, allow the intake of external air from the courtyard. The motor-operated louvred windows in the eastern staircase on first- and second-floor level are opened to a certain degree – not more and not less – taking account of the number of ventilation flaps open on the various floors. The operation is based on a control matrix with a default setting which regulates the flow of air. The controls take effect only when a high cooling load occurs and when a cooling effect is guaranteed by low temperatures in the courtyard.

Natural ventilation/Cooling of the staircases
Overlaid on this manually operated means of ventilation in the two staircases (east and west) is a temperature-based form of control. In the event of high temperatures in the staircases, the smoke-extract and heat-exhaust flaps and the lower louvred windows can be opened to ensure a natural throughflow of air and the cooling of these spaces.

Elektro- und Informationstechnik

Peter Hross

Bei der Elektrotechnik wurde versucht, unter dem Gesichtspunkt einer energieeffizienten und umweltorientierten Betriebsführung der Individualität Raum zu geben. Neben der Nutzung von Solarenergie für Kälte und Strom sorgen intelligente Steuerungssysteme für einen bedarfsgerechten automatischen Betrieb.
In den mit aktueller Medientechnik ausgestatteten Präsentations- und Veranstaltungsräumen auf drei Ebenen können Events jeglicher Art, von Ausstellungen bis zu Vorträgen, abgehalten werden.

Stromversorgung

Die Versorgung des Objekts mit elektrischer Energie erfolgt aus dem öffentlichen Niederspannungsnetz der Stadtwerke München (SWM).
Die im alten Haus vor seinem Abbruch vorhandene Station 5744 Amalienstraße wurde für die SWM erneuert und dient mit 50 % der Nennleistung zur Versorgung des Gebäudes.
Die Energieverteilung im Gebäude erfolgt vom eigenen Niederspannungshauptverteiler im 2. Untergeschoss über die Abspeisekabel in brandgeschützten Schächten zu den jeweiligen bereichsbezogenen Unterverteilungen in den einzelnen Etagen.
Die Haupt- und Submessungen für große Verbraucher, wie z.B. Kältetechnik, sind ebenfalls im Hauptverteilerraum untergebracht.

Beleuchtung

Mit architektonisch abgestimmten Leuchten werden durch direkte und indirekte Lichtverteilung die unterschiedlichen Bereiche individuell beleuchtet.
Die Allgemeinzonen und Innenhofbereiche sind mit tageslichtabhängiger Steuerung ausgestattet. Für die Effektbeleuchtung wurden LED-Leuchtmittel verwendet, um einen sparsamen Energieeinsatz gewährleisten zu können (ca. 1/10-tel gegenüber konventioneller Beleuchtung).

Notbeleuchtung

Die gesetzlich vorgeschriebene Mindestbeleuchtung der Flucht- und Rettungswege und die Sicherheitsbeleuchtung (mit Antipanikbeleuchtung) erfolgt durch eine zentralbatteriegestützte Notbeleuchtungsanlage. Durch eine Überwachung der Allgemeinlichtstromkreise werden die Sicherheitsleuchten im Normalfall auf Bereitschaft (also „aus") geschaltet. Dies trägt zur Verringerung der Betriebskosten bei.

Gebäudeautomation

Um eine kosteneffiziente Steuerung der Beleuchtung in Abhängigkeit von der Wirkung der Verschattungssysteme für die Allgemein- und Gemeinschaftsbereiche, wie z.B. bei ausreichendem Tageslicht oder bei geringem Nutzeraufkommen zu erreichen, ist das Objekt mit einem zentral gesteuerten Bussystem NETxEIB basierend auf KNX ausgestattet. Die medientechnische Creston-Steuerung ist mittels Schnittstelle ebenfalls in das System eingebunden.
Das Bussystem nützt das lokale Netzwerk als leistungsstarkes Rückrat (Backbone) und zur Kommunikation mit den zentralen Steuerungen und der Wetterstation.
Eine Visualisierung und Verknüpfung mit relevanten Datenpunkten der MSR (Steuerung von Heizung, Klima und Lüftung) wurde über den KNX-OPC-Server realisiert. Dort wird die über Helligkeit und Außentemperatur geregelte Jalousiesteuerung am OPC-Server umgesetzt und visualisiert, kann aber auch für ein bestimmtes Zeitintervall manuell bedient werden. Einzelne Verbrauchergruppen können zeit- und lastabhängig geschaltet werden.

Photovoltaik-Anlage

An der Südfassade des östlichen Treppenhauses ist eine teiltransparente PV-Anlage mit Rückeinspeisung ins öffentliche Netz der SWM installiert. Trotz der senkrechten Montage wurde hier durch lamellenförmige, schräg geneigte Paneele eine optimale Ausrichtung zur Sonne erreicht, welche zudem durch eine gewollte Teilverschattung des Innenraums einen deutlich verringerten Wärmeeintrag bewirkt.

Brandmeldeanlage

Für das gesamte Objekt ist eine vollautomatische Brandmeldeanlage in bidirektionaler Ringnetztechnik (Loop) installiert, um einen maximalen Schutz für Personen und Gebäude zu gewährleisten. Im Bereich des großen Veranstaltungssaales im EG wurde ein Rauchansaugsystem eingesetzt, das die variable Nutzung in Teilzonen problemlos möglich macht.
Die Ansteuerungen für Lüftung, Brandrauchentlüftung und Notbeleuchtung funktionieren automatisch. Im Alarmfall erfolgt eine sofortige Information über eine spezielle Telefonleitung an die Feuerwehr München.

Zugangskontrolle

Mit der Kombination von On- und Offlinesystem und programmierbarem Schlüssel werden die Zimmertüröffner mit fix kodierten, batteriebetrieben Türschlössern, die Gebäudezugänge und Garagenzufahrt mittels fest verdrahteten berührungslosen Lesern überwacht.
Vorteil der Kombination gegenüber einem reinen Offline-System ist die automatische Vergabe für neue Zugangsberechtigungen beim Betreten des Gebäudes am Onlineleser (wird immer nur für einen begrenzten Zeitraum vergeben – Vorteil bei Diebstahl oder Verlust). Außerdem können Berechtigungszonen über Softwareunterstützung neu vergeben werden. Zusätzlich können damit auch die Abrechnungssysteme für Kopierer und Getränkeautomaten angebunden werden. Das heißt also: Ein Schlüssel für alles.

Videoüberwachung

Eine Videoüberwachung in der Tiefgarage mit 3 Kameras und Videosprechstellen an den Eingangsbereichen kann wahlweise von der Verwaltung oder beim Empfang über die Visualisierung der Gebäudeleittechnik erfolgen.

Sprechanlage

Eine vandalensichere Displaysprechanlage (editierbare Namensliste für 100 Einträge) mit Telefonanlagenaufschaltung und Videokamera ist an den beiden Hauptzugängen errichtet. An den Innenstellen in den Appartements, Gemeinschaftsbereichen und der Verwaltung kann der Ruf signalisiert in Bild und Ton angenommen werden.

Informationstechnologie (IT)

Passives Netzwerk (Strukturierte Verkabelung)
Die passive Verkabelung ist hier unter Verzicht auf die Sekundärverkabelung ausgeführt, da die größte Länge vom Gebäudeverteiler zum Endgerät unter den zulässigen 90 m liegt.
Tertiärleitungen in Kupfer CAT 6+. Wegen der großen Kabelmenge liegt der EDV-Hauptverteiler des IT-Raums direkt unter dem Hauptsteigschacht.

TK-Anlage
Die digitale Telefonanlage mit Verknüpfung an die Türsprechanlage kann für Einzelabrechnung erweitert werden.

Aktives Netzwerk
Als universitätsnahe Einrichtung ist die IT-Infrastruktur an das Leibniz-Rechenzentrum als Provider für Internet und E-Maildienste über eine neu errichtete LWL-Leitung in der Amalienstraße 17 angebunden. Für die einzelnen Sicherheitsbereiche wie Verwaltung, Studentenzimmer und Gebäudetechnik wurden sogenannte selbstverwaltete aktive Komponenten mit V-LANs (mehrere virtuelle Netze) installiert.

Firewall/LAN Security
Durch den Provider wird die Sicherung des Netzwerkes gegen Angriffe von Innen und Außen inklusive Anti-Spamsystem und Sperrfilter für ungesetzliche Internetseiten durchgeführt.

W-LAN
In den Veranstaltungs- und Gemeinschaftsbereichen wird durch eine Nutzung der WLAN-Versorgung für Gäste und Veranstalter der Zugang zum Internet ermöglicht.

TV-Anlage
Eine flexible TV-Versorgung mit beliebiger Beschaltung der IT-Enddosen wurde mit passiver LAN-Verkabelung umgesetzt. An zentraler Stelle im IT-Raum wird das Kabelfernsehsignal für die Übertragung über das LAN aufbereitet und mittels spezieller Demodulierer (Balloons) für konventionelle Fernsehgeräte zurückgewandelt.

Medientechnik
Für die Veranstaltungsbereiche sind hochwertige Beschallungsanlagen mit Lautsprecher, Funkmikrophonen und Einspielmöglichkeit von PC und Audio-Mischpult sowie ein Projektionssystem mit leistungsstarkem Beamer und Leinwänden an der Decke befestigt, die vom Laptop angesteuert werden. Die Mediensteuerung mit fixen und mobilen Bedieneinheiten (Creston Touchpanel) für Bild, Ton, Licht- und Verdunkelungssysteme und zur Matrixsteuerung sind in Zukunft bei Bedarf erweiterbar.

OLE = Object Linking and Embedding
OPC = Object Linking and Embedding Process Control
KNX = Feldbus zur Gebäudeautomation, neuer Name für EIB (European Installation Bus)

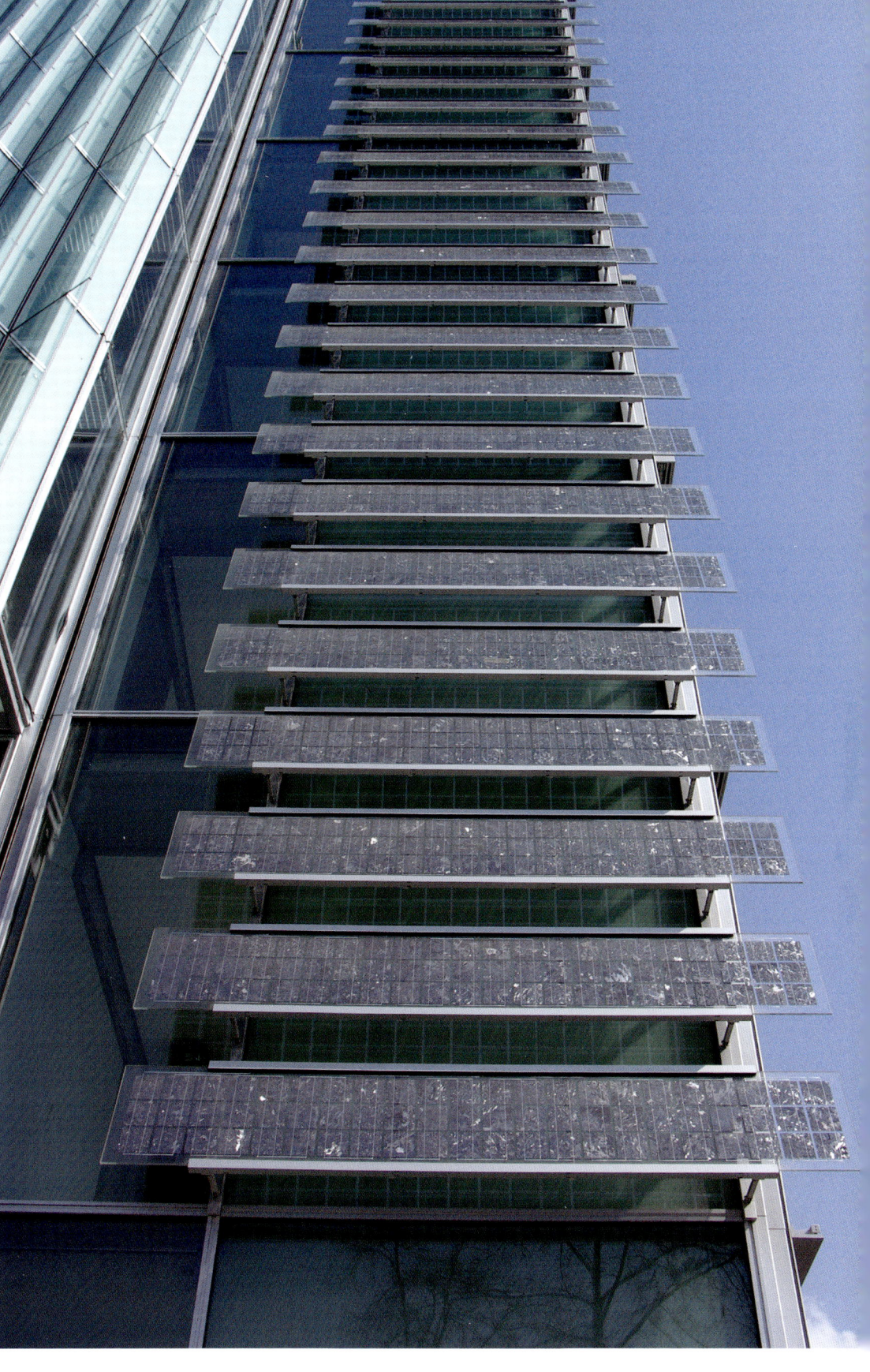

Electrical and Information Technology

Peter Hross

As part of the electrical engineering, an attempt was made to allow scope for individuality in the context of energy-efficient and environmentally sustainable operations. In addition to the exploitation of solar energy for the cooling and the electrical supply, intelligent control systems ensure automatic operations to meet the various needs within the building.
The presentation and events spaces are laid out over three levels and are equipped with modern media technology. Here, exhibitions, lectures and many other events can be staged.

Electrical supply
The electrical supply for the building is provided from the public low-voltage municipal power distribution network of the Stadtwerke Munich (SWM). The station 5744 Amalienstrasse, which existed in the previous building prior to its demolition, was renewed for the SWM and provides the forum with 50 per cent of the nominal capacity.
Energy distribution within the building comes from a low-voltage main distributor on the second basement level via a cable run in fire-resisting shafts to the subdistribution installations for the various areas on individual floors of the building.
Basic and secondary measurement facilities for large-scale consumer plant (e.g. cooling technology) are also housed in the main distribution room.

Lighting
The light fittings are coordinated with the architecture. The various areas of the building are individually illuminated by direct and indirect forms of lighting distribution.
The general zones and the courtyard areas are fitted with controls that are dependent on daylight conditions. For decorative and display effects, LED lighting was installed to ensure an economic use of energy (approximately 1/10 compared with conventional forms of lighting).

Emergency lighting
The legally required minimum level of lighting for escape and evacuation routes and the emergency lighting (with anti-panic illumination) is provided by a central, battery-supported emergency lighting system. Monitoring of the general lighting circuits means that the safety lighting is normally switched to standby mode (i.e. turned off), which helps to reduce operating costs.

Automation in the building
To achieve cost-efficient control of the lighting, while at the same time taking account of the effects of the shading systems for general and communal areas (for example in conjunction with adequate daylighting or when only a few users are present), a centrally controlled bus system NETxEIB was installed based on KNX technology.
The Creston control system with its media technology is also integrated via an interface. The bus system uses the local network as a high-powered backbone and as a means of communication with the central controls and the weather station. A visualization system and links with relevant data points of the instrumentation and control (heating, air conditioning and ventilation control) were implemented via the KNX-OPC server. There, the shutters are controlled in accordance with the degree of brightness and external temperatures by an OPC server. For a specific period of time, they can also be regulated by hand. Individual user groups can be switched according to a particular time or loading.

Photovoltaic installation
On the south face of the eastern staircase is a partially transparent photovoltaic installation. The return-flow energy that is generated is fed into the public network of the city of Munich. In spite of the vertical form of assembly, an optimal inclination to the sun was achieved through angled strip-like panels. Here, the partial shading of the internal spaces provided by the panels means that they also reduce heat gains significantly, in accordance with plans.

Fire-alarm system
A fully automatic fire-alarm system was installed for the entire building in bidirectional ring-network (loop) technology. This guarantees maximum protection for people within the forum and the building itself.
In the large hall for special events on the ground floor, a smoke-extract system was also foreseen. As a result, the space can be used in distinct zones for various purposes without any problem. Ventilation, smoke removal and emergency lighting are activated automatically. In case of an alarm, information is immediately passed to the Munich fire brigade via a special telephone link.

Controlled access
The access control system works with a combination of on- and offline systems. The battery-operated locks of the room doors can be opened with programmable keys. The points of entry to the building and the garage access are monitored by hard-wired, non-contact scanners.
One advantage of this combination over a purely offline system is the automatic allocation of new rights of access on entering the building via the online scanner. (These are granted only for a limited period of time, which is also of advantage in respect of theft or loss.) In addition, rights of access to certain zones can be granted with software support. Furthermore, billing systems for the use of photocopying and drink-vending machines can be coupled with these facilities. In other words, this system is the key to everything.

Closed-circuit television (CCTV)
Closed-circuit television monitoring of the basement garage by means of three cameras and videophones in the entrance area can be operated from the administration or the reception with a visualization of central control systems in the building.

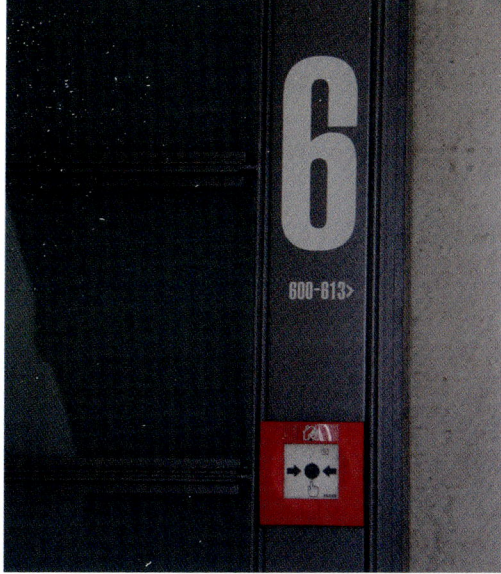

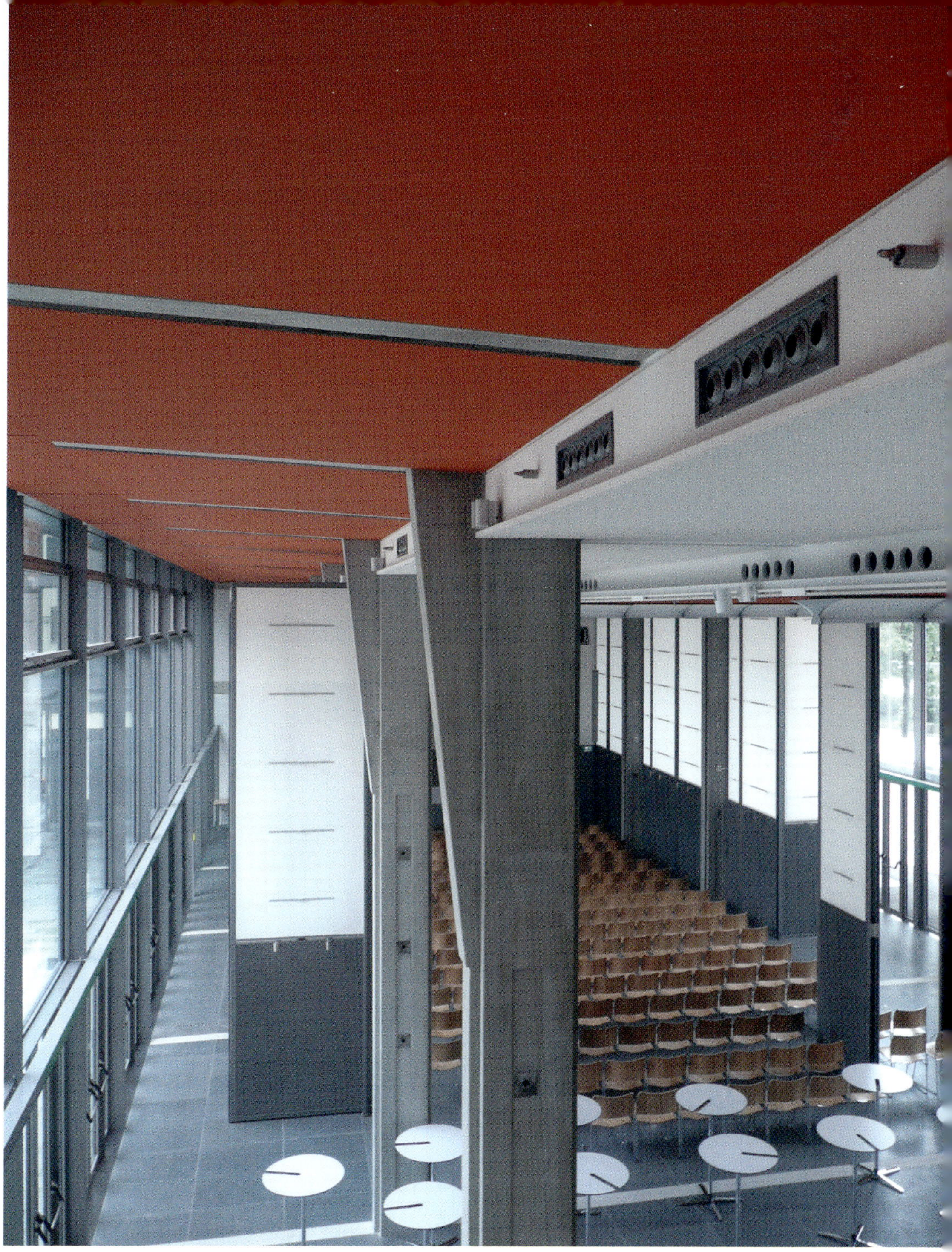

Intercom

A vandalproof display intercom system (editable list of names with up to 100 entries) with a telephone intrusion system and video camera has been installed at the two main entrances to the building.
At various internal points – in the apartments, in the communal areas and the administration – sound and visual signals can be received.

Information technology (IT)

Passive network (structured cable networks)

Passive cable runs were installed here without a secondary cable system, since the greatest distance between the distribution board and an outlet is less than the permitted maximum of 90 metres. Tertiary runs are in copper CAT 6+. In view of the large amount of cabling, the EDP main distributor in the IT room is situated immediately beneath the principal vertical distribution shaft.

Telecommunications system

The digital telephone installation, with links to the door interphone system, can be extended for individual accounting.

Active network

As a system in close proximity to the university, the IT infrastructure is linked to the Leibniz data-processing centre as a provider for internet and e-mail services via a newly installed fibre-optic cable at Amalienstrasse 17. For individual security areas like administration, students' rooms and building services autonomous, active components with VLANs (virtual local-area networks) were installed.

Firewall / LAN security

Safeguarding the network against internal and external attack is carried out by the provider and includes an anti-spam system and a band-elimination filter for illegal internet pages.

WLAN

In the events space and communal areas, a WLAN system of internet access is available to guests and the organizers of various activities.

TV installation

A flexible TV system with free switching of the IT terminal boxes was installed using the passive LAN cable system.
At a central point, in the IT room, the cable TV signal is provided for transmissions via the LAN and converted back by means of special demodulators (balloons) for conventional TV sets.

Media technology

High-quality public-address systems with loudspeakers and radio microphones as well as scope for PC input and an audio mixing console were installed for the events areas, as well as a high-performance projection system with screens fixed to the ceiling. These can be operated from a laptop.
Media control, with both fixed and mobile operating units (Creston touchpanel) for visual images, sound, lighting and darkening systems and for matrix control, can be extended as the need arises in the future.

EIB = European installation bus, a communications protocol that is now part of the KNX standard
KNX = a standardized network communications protocol for intelligent buildings
OLE = object linking and embedding
OPC = object linking and embedding process control

Schallschutz und Raumakustik

Sound Insulation and Spatial Acoustics

Gerhard Hilz

Schallschutz gegen Außenlärm

Durch die Lage des Gebäudes an dem Kreuzungsbereich der großen innerstädtischen Straßen entsteht eine erhebliche Schallbelastung der Südfassade.
Im Entwurf wurde der Situation durch die Grundrissgestaltung begegnet sowie durch bauliche Maßnahmen in Form einer dafür entwickelten multifunktional wirksamen Schallschutzblende vor der eigentlichen wärme- und schalldämmenden Hauptfassade.
Die Anordnung der Gebäude bietet zum Innenhof hin Nutzungsbereiche mit geringer Schallbelastung für die dahin orientierten Fassaden.
Für die Veranstaltungsbereiche im Erdgeschoss wurde der erforderliche Schallschutz durch eine schall- und wärmedämmende Einfachfassade sichergestellt und für hochwertigere Veranstaltungen wie Vorträge, Tagungen und dergleichen wurden im Innenraum der Halle durch schallschluckende schwenk- und faltbare Drehwandelemente zusätzlich pegelsenkende Maßnahmen realisiert.

Schallschutz innerhalb des Gebäudes

Bedingt durch die hohe Nutzungsdichte der drei Gebäudeteile war es nicht möglich, durch Zwischenschaltung von Räumen mit nur gemäßigten Ansprüchen ein direktes Angrenzen von lauten Räumen an hochwertige Aufenthaltsräume zu vermeiden. Prinzipiell wurde versucht, besonders laute Räume – wie den Partyraum –, in Geschossen unterzubringen, welche im Hinblick auf den Schutz der sensibleren Aufenthaltsräume, – wie Schlafraum und Studierzimmer –, alleine durch die räumliche Anordnung aufwändige bauliche Maßnahmen vermeiden.
Im Südbau grenzen die Veranstaltungsräume nach oben hin direkt an Aufenthaltsräume. Neben den schallschluckend detaillierten Bauteilen, in erster Linie den Trenndecken, wurde ein hoher Schallschutz durch eine vollständige Unterbrechung der flankierenden Außenbauteile erreicht. Die Fassadenkonstruktion im Erdgeschoss ist vollkommen von der Fassadenkonstruktion der Obergeschosse entkoppelt. Der Veranstaltungsraum im zurückspringenden Dachgeschoss weist durch den Flächenversatz keinerlei flankierende Bauteile zum darunter liegenden Geschoss auf. Insbesondere wurde dort ein Fußbodenaufbau mit möglichst hoher Trittschallminderung und gleichzeitiger Möglichkeit zur Aufnahme der Versorgungsleitungen für die Konditionierung des Raumes auf Basis von üblichen Bauweisen eingesetzt.
Für möglichst hohen Schallschutz zwischen den einzelnen Studentenzimmern wurde eine quasi Raum-in-Raum-Bauweise mit angepasster Grundrissgestaltung entwickelt.
Im Zugangsbereich der Studentenappartements vom Gemeinschaftsraum aus sind untergeordnete, Distanz schaffende Raumnutzungen angeordnet. Der anspruchsvolle Studier-/Schlafbereich ist zum ruhigen Innenhof hin orientiert. Durch nicht miteinander verbundene Doppelständer in Trockenbauweise wird neben der hohen Luftschalldämmung auch eine hohe Körperschallentkopplung zwischen den Appartements erreicht. Der Raumabschluss mittels Trockenbauschalen wird durch einen schwimmenden Estrich und die pro Einzelzimmer elementierte und damit von Nachbarbauteilen entkoppelte Innenhoffassade ergänzt.
Um die mit der Konstruktion erzielbaren hohen Dämmwerte nicht über durchdringende Installationsführungen zu verschlechtern, werden die Appartements über Stichleitungen aus dem Gemeinschaftsbereich versorgt.

Raumakustik

Die räumliche Verteilung von den absorbierenden Flächen gewährleist eine ausreichende Senkung von Geräuschpegeln und hohe Sprachverständlichkeit im Veranstaltungssaal des Erdgeschosses. Dadurch wurde der Gefahr von Flatterechos und zu geringer Diffusität entgegengewirkt.
Die absorbierenden und in geringem Maße schalldämmenden Falt- und Drehwände, die über Türhöhe aus transluzenten Membranen bestehen, stellen Sonderentwicklungen der Architekten mit schalltechnischer Beratung durch den Verfasser dar. Diese Konstruktionen wurden im unteren Teil durch Lochblechabsorber ergänzt. Ziel der Entwicklung war, neben der Schaffung eines Sicht- und eines eingeschränkten Schallschutzes effiziente Absorber mit geringen Gewichtsanteilen herzustellen. Durch die Wahl entsprechender mikroperforierter Membranen konnte in der begrenzten Wandstärke auch ohne Hohlraumbedämpfung eine entsprechend gute Schallabsorption entwickelt werden. Um auch im geschlossenen Zustand die Bereiche außerhalb der Veranstaltungszonen zu bedämpfen und hier insbesondere Störpegel herabzusetzen, weisen die Dreh-/Faltwände beidseitig absorbierende Oberflächen auf.
Die Wahl der Absorberkonstruktion im unteren Wandteil unterstützt zusätzlich eine geringe, jedoch im Fall der geschlossenen Wandflächen wirksame Schalldämmung.

Sound insulation against external noise

The location of the building at the intersection of major inner-city roads means that the south face is exposed to considerable noise disturbance. This was overcome in the design partly through the layout and partly by constructional measures in the form of an additional acoustic screen that functions in a number of ways and was specially developed for this purpose. The screen was set in front of the actual main facade, which has its own thermal and sound insulation.
The layout of the building also creates user areas that are oriented to the internal courtyard, where the facades are subject to relatively little noise disturbance.
For the areas on the ground floor that are used to stage various events, the requisite sound insulation is provided by a single-skin facade with acoustic and thermal insulation. For more demanding occasions, when lectures, conferences and the like are held, sound-absorbing pivoting and folding wall elements were installed inside the hall space as an additional means of reducing noise levels.

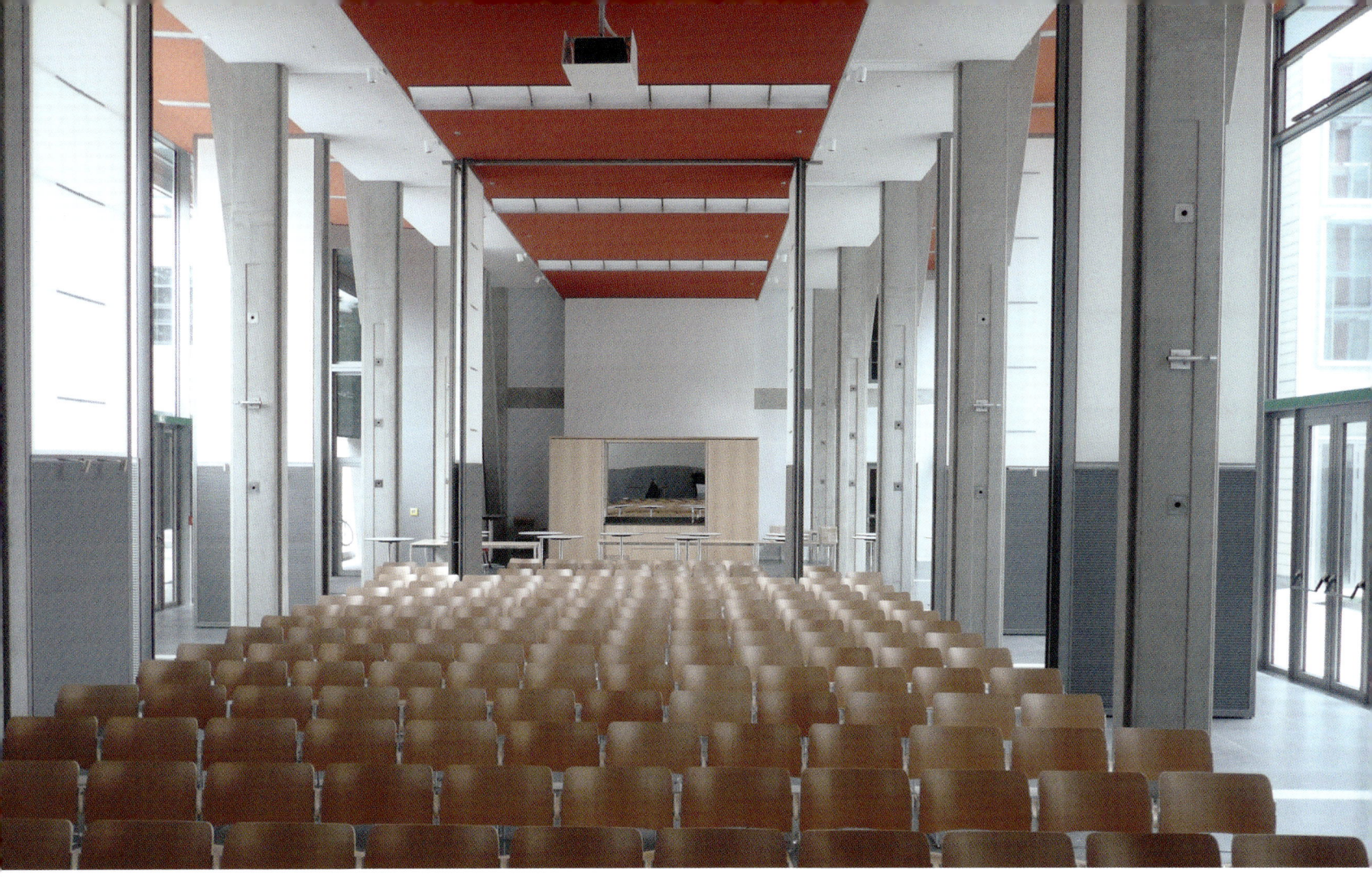

Sound insulation within the building

In view of the intense use to which the three tracts of the building are put, it was not entirely possible to avoid locating spaces with high noise levels alongside high-quality leisure areas by placing rooms with only moderate acoustic demands between the two. Nevertheless, it was a principle to avoid over-elaborate building measures by situating spaces with particularly high noise levels, like the party room, on different floors from more sensitive areas, such as the bedrooms and study spaces. In the southern tract, events spaces directly adjoin the recreational areas above. A high standard of noise protection was ensured by designing structural elements – first and foremost the floors between storeys – in a sound-absorbing form of construction, as well as by the high standard of acoustic protection achieved by a complete separation of flanking external elements. The ground floor facade, for example, is wholly isolated from that of the upper floors; and as a result of the set-back skin of the events space in the roof storey, no constructional facade elements immediately adjoin those on the floor below. Here in particular, the floor was constructed with a maximum possible reduction of impact-sound transmittance; at the same time, this provided scope for accommodating air-conditioning service runs for the space above in a similar way to that found in conventional forms of construction.

To achieve as high a level of sound insulation as possible between the individual student rooms, a kind of room-within-a-room solution was created with the appropriate layout design.

Secondary functions are located in the access zones to the student apartments where one enters from the communal space. In this way, it was possible to create a certain distance, with the more sensitive study/sleeping areas oriented to the quiet courtyard. Using a system of dry walling with double layers of studding that are not connected, a high degree of airborne-sound insulation was achieved, as well as insulation against structure-borne sound between apartments. The spatial enclosure, in the form of dry-construction elements, is complemented by floated screeds, and individual facade elements on the courtyard face of each room that are separated from each other.

In order not to reduce the high insulation values achieved through this form of construction by laying continuous service runs from room to room, the individual apartments are served by branch runs from the communal area.

Spatial acoustics

The spatial distribution of absorbent surfaces ensures an adequate reduction of noise levels and a high degree of intelligibility of speech in the events hall on the ground floor. This helps to avoid the danger of flutter echoes and poor sound diffusion. The absorbent and slightly sound-insulating folding and pivoting walls, which consist of translucent membranes above door height, are the outcome of special developments undertaken by the architects, with the author acting as a sound-engineering consultant. This form of construction was complemented by perforated sheet-metal absorbers in the lower sections of the walls. In addition to providing a visual screen and a limited amount of sound insulation, the aim of the design was to create efficient absorbers of low weight. By selecting the appropriate micro-perforated membranes, it was possible to achieve correspondingly good sound absorbency with a limited wall thickness and without acoustic insulation in the cavity. In order to dampen noise in the areas outside the events zones, even in a closed state, and to reduce the levels of noise disturbance, the pivoting/folding walls have absorbent surfaces on both sides. The choice of construction to achieve this absorbency in the lower part of the wall also contributes a small degree of sound insulation that is nevertheless effective in the closed wall surfaces.

Entstehung und Zielsetzung des Projekts

Thomas Herzog

In den zurückliegenden Jahren war in Verlautbarungen der Fakultät für Bauingenieur- und Vermessungswesen der Technischen Universität München immer wieder darauf verwiesen worden, dass es bei der Etablierung von neuen, insbesondere internationalen Masterkursen angesichts des knappen Wohnungsangebotes und hoher Mietpreise in München schwierig ist, Studierende unterzubringen.

In Kreisen der bayerischen Bauwirtschaft, wie auch in Leitungsgremien der Technischen Universität München (TUM) entstand unabhängig davon die Überlegung, dass für junge Ingenieure im Bereich des Bauwesens, für die ein hoher Bedarf besteht und die zudem in wachsender, internationaler Konkurrenz stehen, eine erhöhte Attraktivität der sie ausbildenden Institution geschaffen werden sollte, von der ihre berufliche Zukunft ja maßgeblich abhängig ist.

Das Bauen in Deutschland erlebt in den letzten Jahrzehnten grundlegende, zum Teil sehr dynamische Veränderungen. Eine sich ständig vergrößernde Komplexität der Baumaßnahmen, das Bewusstsein über Auswirkungen auf die Umwelt und die vielfältige Entwicklung neuer Materialien, Planungs- und Bautechniken rücken ein nachhaltiges Bauen als maßgebliche Bedingung für die Tätigkeit der Ingenieure im Bauwesen als einer weltweit tätigen High-Tech-Branche in die Mitte der Gesellschaft. Die erforderlichen Prozesse bei Forschung und Entwicklung, Planung, Realisierung und Betrieb von Bauvorhaben haben die Ingenieuraufgabe zu einer interdisziplinären Tätigkeit mit hoher Kommunikationsdichte werden lassen.

Dies zusammengenommen führte zur Überlegung, dass es erforderlich sei, an zentraler Stelle in München und in einer fußläufig möglichst kurzen Distanz sowohl zur Technischen Universität als auch zur Obersten Baubehörde und zum Zentrum der Stadt, eine „Adresse" entstehen zu lassen, welche die Unterbringung von ausgewählten Studierenden der Masterstudiengänge, und auch von einzuladenden Gastprofessoren und Gastdozenten sowie Doktoranden, jungen Wissenschaftlern und ausgezeichneten Meistern in Bauberufen ermöglicht. Wir waren der Meinung, dass eine Einrichtung dieser Art für die TU München – als einer auch nach international geltenden Kriterien als Spitzenhochschule zu bewertenden Institution – äußerst zuträglich sei. Ansonsten würde eine wesentliche Dimension fehlen, um zu den weltweit führenden Universitäten weiter aufzuschließen.

Die bayerische Bauwirtschaft legt ihrerseits Wert auf erstklassigen Nachwuchs. Durch die Investitionen, welche die Ausbildung an der TUM unterstützen, will man in unserem Land neue Spitzenkräfte der Bauberufe, auf die Wirtschaft und das Kulturleben angewiesen sind, für den globalen Wettbewerb und Leistungsexport fördern.

Mit dieser Zielsetzung konnte die Gemeinnützige Urlaubskasse des Bayerischen Baugewerbes e.V.* als Bauherr aktiv werden. Es gelang, das Anwesen am Oskar-von-Miller-Ring zu erwerben, um dort (nach Abriss des vorhandenen Bestandes von nicht umnutzbaren Büroflächen aus den 60er Jahren) Studentenwohnungen in einem entsprechenden Neubau zu errichten. Zur Absicherung dieses Vorhabens eingereichte Bauvoranfragen mussten von Seiten der Stadt München jedoch zunächst abgelehnt werden, weil der funktionale Zweck eines reinen Wohnheimes mit den Festlegungen des vor Ort rechtskräftigen Bebauungsplans nicht verträglich war. Es ist uns dann gelungen, in einem weiteren Anlauf von Seiten der Lokalbaukommission der Landeshauptstadt als Genehmigungsbehörde, des Bezirksausschusses Maxvorstadt und der Stadtgestaltungskommission, ausdrücklich Zustimmung zu einem sehr viel ambitionierteren Vorhaben der oben beschriebenen Art zu erlangen. Wesentlich hierfür war die Struktur der Grundrisse. Ein weiterer Grund für die Bereitschaft der Stadt, diverse Ausnahmegenehmigungen zu bewilligen war der Umstand, dass wir im Erdgeschossbereich anstelle von rein privater Nutzung einen großen, immer wieder auch für Publikum zugänglichen Bereich zu realisieren versprachen, in welchem Ausstellungen, Vorträge und weitere Veranstaltungen stattfinden können – dies auch in Wechselwirkung mit dem davor liegenden noch neu zu definierenden Freiraum und dem im Inneren liegenden, anspruchsvoll gestalteten Hof. So konnte das Vorhaben realisiert werden.

Das Leben im Haus selbst wird durch eine Mischung aus Privatsphäre und Gemeinschaft bestimmt. Jeder Studiengast hat einen akustisch gut abgeschirmten individuellen Rückzugsbereich für Entspannung, Arbeit und Ruhe. Auf der anderen Seite stehen großzügige Gemeinschaftsbereiche für die Begegnung mit den Mitbewohnern zur Verfügung.

Das Bistro sowie der Bereich Clubraum/Bibliothek dienen je nach Anlass als legerer oder anspruchsvoller Treffpunkt für die Begegnung der Studien- und sonstigen Hausgäste, mit den Mitgliedern der Stiftung, der Baufakultäten, den Alumni und einem noch zu bildenden Förderkreis.

Eigeninitiative, teilweise Selbstverwaltung im Hause werden unterstützt.

Ein disziplinübergreifendes Programm für Veranstaltungen, Kommunikation und Diskussion soll die Gesamtheit der baumeisterlichen Aufgaben bewusst machen sowie die langfristig positiven Zukunftsaussichten für die Ingenieure im Bauwesen fördern. Ganzheitliche Denkweise, interdisziplinäres Verständnis, Universalität der Ausbildung, integrative Fähigkeiten in Wahrnehmung und Kommunikation von Kundenanforderungen können entwickelt werden, unkomplizierte Begegnungen der Studiengäste mit maßgebenden Persönlichkeiten der Berufspraxis, der Wissenschaft, der Kultur, der Politik und wichtiger gesellschaftlicher Gruppen können stattfinden. Die Gäste des Hauses werden gebeten, ihrerseits für das Privileg ihres Aufenthaltes entsprechende Gegenleistungen in Form von Beiträgen für die akademische Gemeinschaft zu erbringen.

Erfreulicherweise bildete sich in dem für das Vorhaben entscheidenden Gremium, dem beschlussfassenden Vorstand der Bauherrschaft, ein durchgängiger Konsens über die Identität dieses anspruchsvollen Projekts, was auch die Handlungen und Entscheidungen der Beteiligten über die ganze Planungs- und Bauphase bestimmte.

* Die Gemeinnützige Urlaubskasse des Bayerischen Baugewerbes e.V. ist eine Einrichtung der Tarifvertragsparteien der bayerischen Bauwirtschaft. Mitglieder sind paritätisch die Industriegewerkschaft Bauen-Agrar-Umwelt und die Arbeitgeberverbände. Das Urlaubskassenverfahren in der Bauwirtschaft ermöglicht es, dass für die gewerblichen Arbeitnehmer Freizeit- und Vergütungsansprüche für einen zusammenhängenden Urlaub angespart werden können.

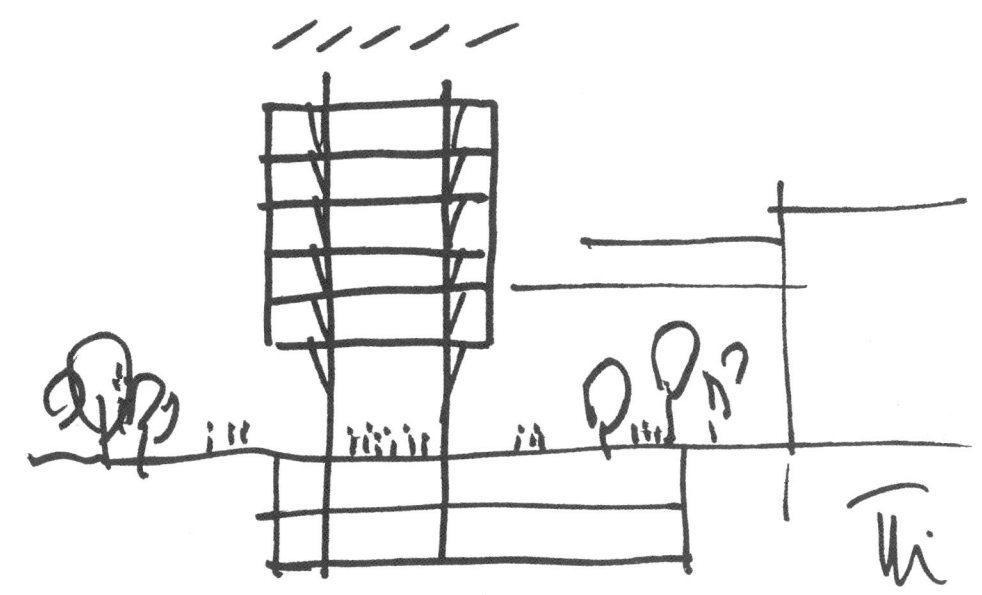

The Origins of the Project and its Aims

Thomas Herzog

Over the years, statements made by the faculty for civil engineering and surveying of the Technische Universität München (TUM) have repeatedly pointed out that it is difficult to establish new master courses – particularly international ones – and to accommodate students in view of the limited supply of accommodation and the high rents in Munich.

Independently of this, ideas were formulated in the Bavarian building sector, as well as in executive committees of the TUM, relating to young engineers and masters of building trades, for whom a great need exists, yet who find themselves exposed to growing international competition. The concepts that were outlined involved increasing the attractiveness of the educational institution on which the professional future of these young people largely depends.

In recent decades, construction in Germany has undergone changes that have been of a quite dynamic nature in part. The constantly increasing complexity of building measures, a growing awareness of the environmental implications of construction, and the development of new materials, planning and building technology on many different fronts make sustainable forms of construction a vital condition for the work of architects, engineers, and the like and place these professions – professions that are internationally active in a field of high technology – at the centre of society. The various processes involved in the realms of research, development and planning, as well as in the implementation and operation of buildings, have made the role of these professions an interdisciplinary one with a need for great communicational intensity.

All these considerations led to the conclusion that it was imperative to create an "address" in a central location in Munich – if possible within walking distance of the TUM, the Chief Building Authority of the State of Bavaria and the city centre. This institution would accommodate selected students participating in master courses, those studying for a doctorate, young scientists and outstanding masters from the building trades, as well as visiting professors and lecturers. In our opinion, an institution of this kind is essential for the TUM, which is a top-rank university according to international criteria. Otherwise a significant dimension would have been lacking in the bid to narrow the gap even further to the world's leading universities. The Bavarian building sector, for its part, attaches great importance to top up-and-coming talent.

Through investments made to further studies at the TUM, the state of Bavaria seeks to support outstanding ability in the building professions, on which both the economy and cultural life are dependent. These measures not only equip young people to face global competition; they also serve as a means of exporting high levels of achievement.

Once the objective was defined, the client, the "Gemeinnützige Urlaubskasse des Bayerischen Baugewerbes e. V."*, was able to act. It succeeded in acquiring the envisaged property on Oskar-von-Miller-Ring, where, after the demolition of an existing office building dating from the 1960s that it was not possible to convert, an appropriate new structure, containing student dwellings, could be erected. The outline building proposals for this scheme were, however, rejected by the city of Munich because a development exclusively for housing purposes was not compatible with the legally binding conditions laid down in the development plan for this site.

In a further application, we then succeeded in gaining approval from the city of Munich, from the civil committee for the Maxvorstadt district and from the commission for urban design to erect an even more ambitious scheme than that originally envisaged.

The structure of the floor plans was a decisive factor. Another reason for this readiness on the part of the municipal authorities to grant permission for various exceptional measures was the fact that instead of installing purely private uses on the ground floor, we promised to implement measures that would make this realm accessible to the public from time to time for various events, such as exhibitions, lectures and the like. The ground floor was also to be used in conjunction with the open space in front of it (to be newly defined) and with the internal courtyard with its impressive design. As a result, therefore, it proved possible to proceed with the scheme.

Life within the building is characterized by a mixture of private and communal spaces. All guests, whether students or visiting lecturers, have acoustically well screened individual realms at their disposal to which they may withdraw to work or simply to find some peace and relax.

At the same time, there are generous communal areas where one can meet fellow-residents. The bistro and the clubroom/library serve respectively as informal and more formal places where students and other guests can meet members of the foundation and the faculties for building studies, as well as former students and representatives of a society (yet to be formed) for the promotion of this institution. Initiative and an element of personal administration of the building are encouraged.

A programme of interdisciplinary communication, disussions and other events is designed to make people aware of the full range of activities a master builder has to cover and to promote a positive long-term perspective for architects and constructional engineers. In this way, holistic thinking, interdisciplinary understanding, a universal outlook in the education provided, and comprehensive, integrative abilities in the perception and communication of the needs of clients can be developed. Informal encounters between study guests and leading minds from the professional world and from the realms of science, culture and politics, as well as important groups in society, can also take place here. At the same time, one hopes that guests of this institution will contribute something in return for the privilege of being able to reside here: in the form of input to the academic community, for example.

Fortunately, general consensus was reached on the identity of this demanding project within the decisive body for the development, namely the clients' executive board. This helped to define the actions and decisions of all those involved in the scheme throughout the planning and construction phases.

*A non-profit organisation in which employers and employees of the Bavarian building sector bargain collectively to fund their holidays.

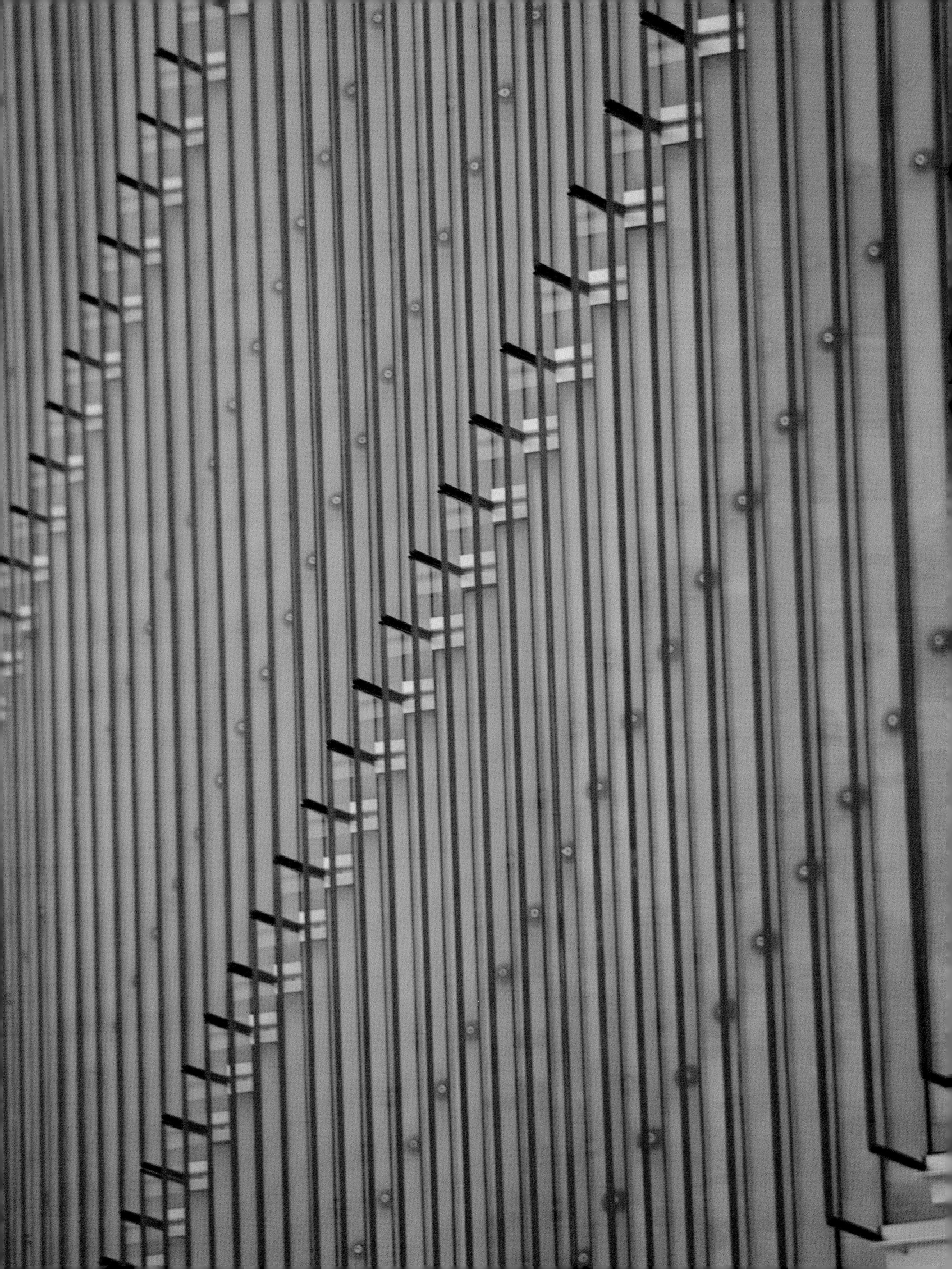

„Die Wahl des Systems entscheidet"
Hommage an Oskar von Miller

"The Choice of System is Decisive"
A Homage to Oskar von Miller

Sabine Kammerl

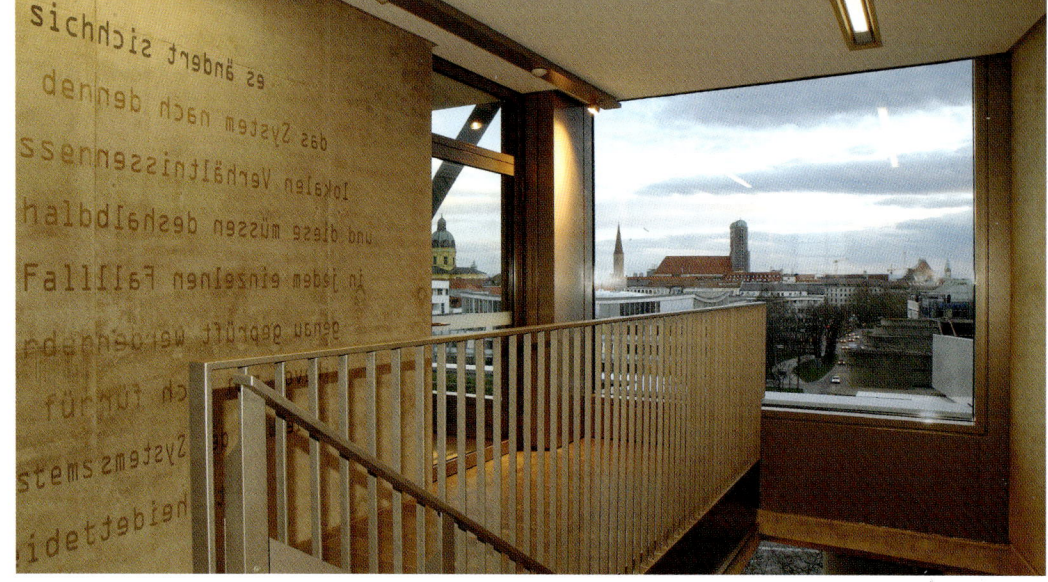

Bei den Recherchen stieß ich auf eine faszinierende Aussage Oskar von Millers aus dem Jahr 1891. Sie kann – auch wenn er sie in anderem Zusammenhang formulierte – als Quintessenz seiner persönlichen Haltung gelesen werden. Gleichzeitig ist sie von zeitloser Aktualität.

„Es ändert sich
das System
nach den lokalen Verhältnissen
und diese müssen deshalb
in jedem einzelnen Fall
genau geprüft werden
bevor man sich für
die Wahl des Systems entscheidet"

Oskar von Miller begeistern zeitlebens die verschiedensten technischen und wissenschaftlichen Disziplinen. Seine feste Überzeugung ist es, dass technischer Fortschritt allen zugute kommen soll und sich keiner Ideologie unterwerfen darf. Genaue und sorgfältige Betrachtung und Abwägung sind von Bedeutung, nicht ein absolutes oder gar totalitäres System, das anderen als gewissenhaften Begründungen folgt.
Konsequenterweise steht Oskar von Miller deshalb auch in offener Opposition zum Nationalsozialismus – der, kaum an der Macht, versucht alles und jeden zu instrumentalisieren und geht dabei keinerlei Kompromisse ein.

Für das Kunstprojekt wählte ich, analog zur inhaltlichen Orientierung, die diese außergewöhnliche Persönlichkeit bietet, das Haupttreppenhaus als räumliches Äquivalent.
Im Erdgeschoss wird man vom Zitat Oskar von Millers empfangen. Es erscheint in spiegelnder Edelstahlschrift – lesbar und gleichzeitig in Spiegelschrift.
In den Worten von 1891 erscheint das Heute, es spiegeln sich die Menschen, die im Forum arbeiten, leben, Kontakte knüpfen, Projekte entwickeln. In jedem Moment ist das Zitat im Jetzt.

Die mehrfache Spiegelung ist darüber hinaus Symbol für und Kommentar zur Offenheit und dem Nicht-Absolutheitsanspruch Oskar von Millers.

Von Stockwerk zu Stockwerk verändert der Text seine Erscheinung und seinen inhaltlichen Schwerpunkt. Beim Hinaufsteigen verschwindet Zeile um Zeile der spiegelnden Schrift. Die verschwundenen Spiegelzeilen bleiben als Schattenzeile und Erinnerung an das Ganze zurück. Beim Hinuntergehen erscheint Zeile für Zeile wieder. Der Hinauf- bzw. Hinabsteigende ist Motor dieser Veränderung. Im Zitat selbst liegt wiederum das Potential, zum Anlass für Überlegungen und Gedanken der Betrachter zu werden.

In the course of research work, I came across a fascinating statement made by Oskar von Miller in 1891. Even though it was formulated in a different context, it may be regarded as the quintessence of his personal belief. At the same time, it possesses an enduring relevance.

"The system
changes according
to local circumstances,
and these must therefore
be precisely investigated in
every single situation before
one decides in favour of
a particular system."

Throughout his life, Oskar von Miller was fascinated by all kinds of technical and scientific disciplines. It was his firm conviction that technical progress should be for the benefit of everyone and should not be subject to any ideology. Precise, careful observation and assessment are important, not an absolute or possibly totalitarian system that is followed by others as a means of appeasing one's conscience.

Oskar von Miller thus stood in open opposition to National Socialism, which, no sooner had it acceded to power, sought to instrumentalize everything and everybody. He, for his part, made no compromises.
In response to the orientation this exceptional personality provides for the content of the present artistic project, I chose the main staircase as an appropriate spatial counterpart.
On the ground floor, one is welcomed by the above quotation from Oskar von Miller: it is reproduced in reflecting stainless-steel lettering – readable, and also in mirror-image form. In these words, dating from 1891, one finds the present day as well: reflected in the lettering are the people who live, work and forge new contacts in the forum, and who develop projects there. At every instant, the quotation is part of the present.
These multiple reflections are a symbol of and a commentary on the candour and the absence of any claim to absoluteness on the part of Oskar von Miller.
From floor to floor, the text changes in appearance and in the emphasis placed on its contents.
As one ascends the stairs, the reflecting quotation disappears line by line. The words that have already gone remain only in the form of shadowy lines in remembrance of the whole. When one descends, they reappear line by line. People ascending and descending the stairs are, therefore, the motor of these changes. In the quotation itself, the observer finds a possible spur for new thoughts and ideas.

es ändert sich
das System nach denen
lokalen Verhältnissen
und diese müssen deshalb
in jedem einzelnen Fall
genau geprüft werden
bevor man sich für
die Wahl des Systems
entscheidet

Oskar von Miller

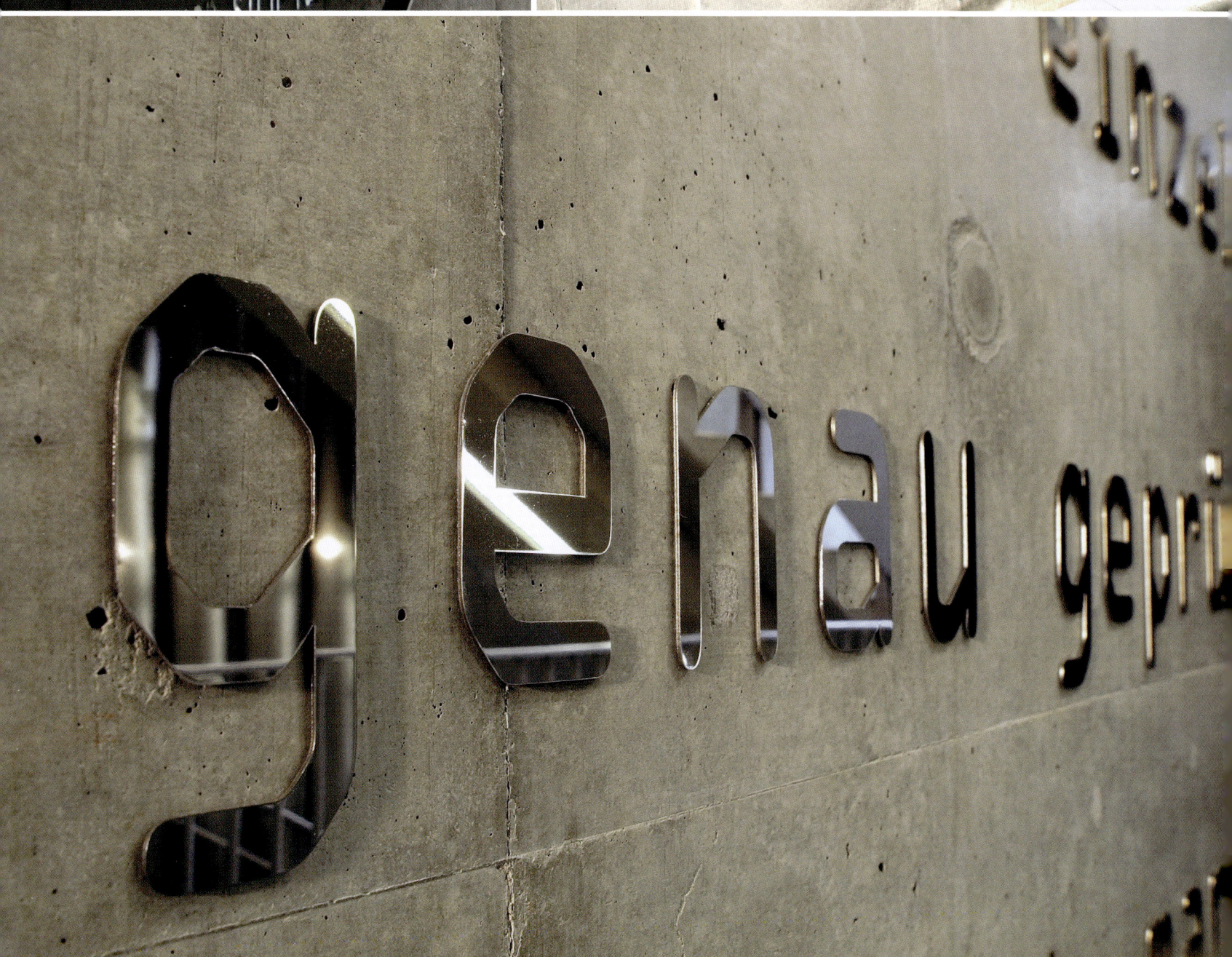

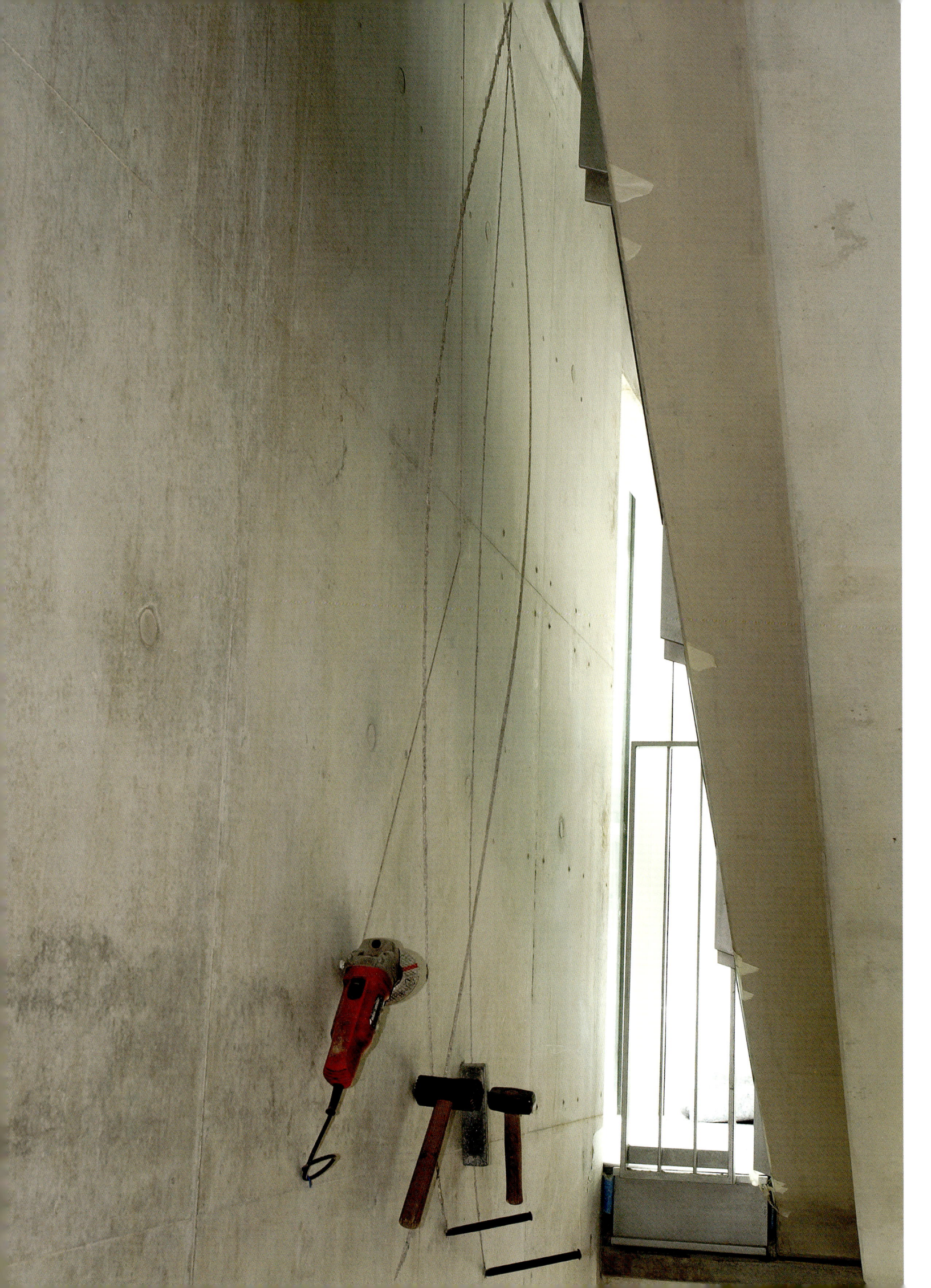

Gravuren
Engravings

Nikolaus Lang

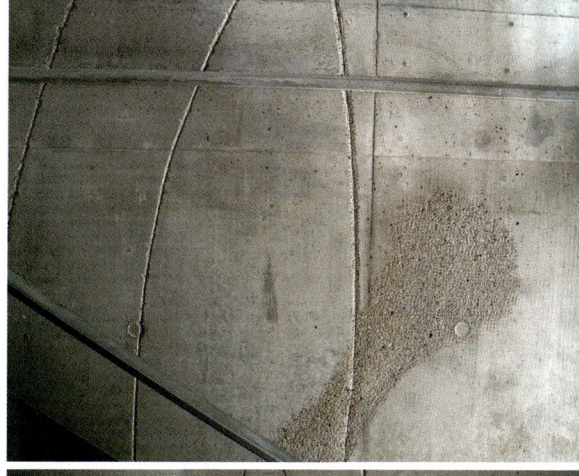

Innenbereich
Treppenhaus Ost – Arbeitsspuren

Arbeitsspuren durch Schneiden, Spitzen, Stocken, Schleifen und Polieren auf Betonwand.
Montierte Werkzeuge: Spitzeisen, Schlegel, Stockhammer, Schleifstein, Winkelschleifer. Die Werkspuren ziehen sich innen über die gesamte Wandfläche im östlichen Treppenhaus und über die gesamte Mauerfläche der Hofwand im Außenbereich. In ihren überlagernden, labilen Linienführungen stehen sie in direktem Gegensatz zu der Klarheit der Architektur.

Internal area
Eastern staircase – Work Traces

Work Traces: formed by cutting, point hacking, bush hammering, grinding and polishing a concrete wall
Tools mounted on the wall: pointing chisel, stonemason's hammer, bush hammer, grinding stone, angle grinder
The traces of work extend internally over the entire wall surface in the eastern staircase and across the whole area of the courtyard wall externally. The tentative, intersecting lines form a direct contrast to the clarity of the architecture.

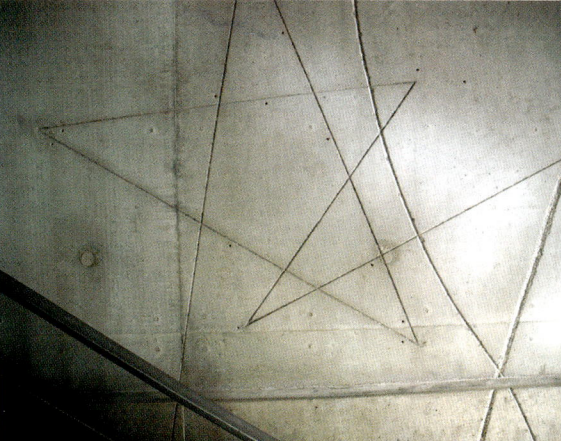

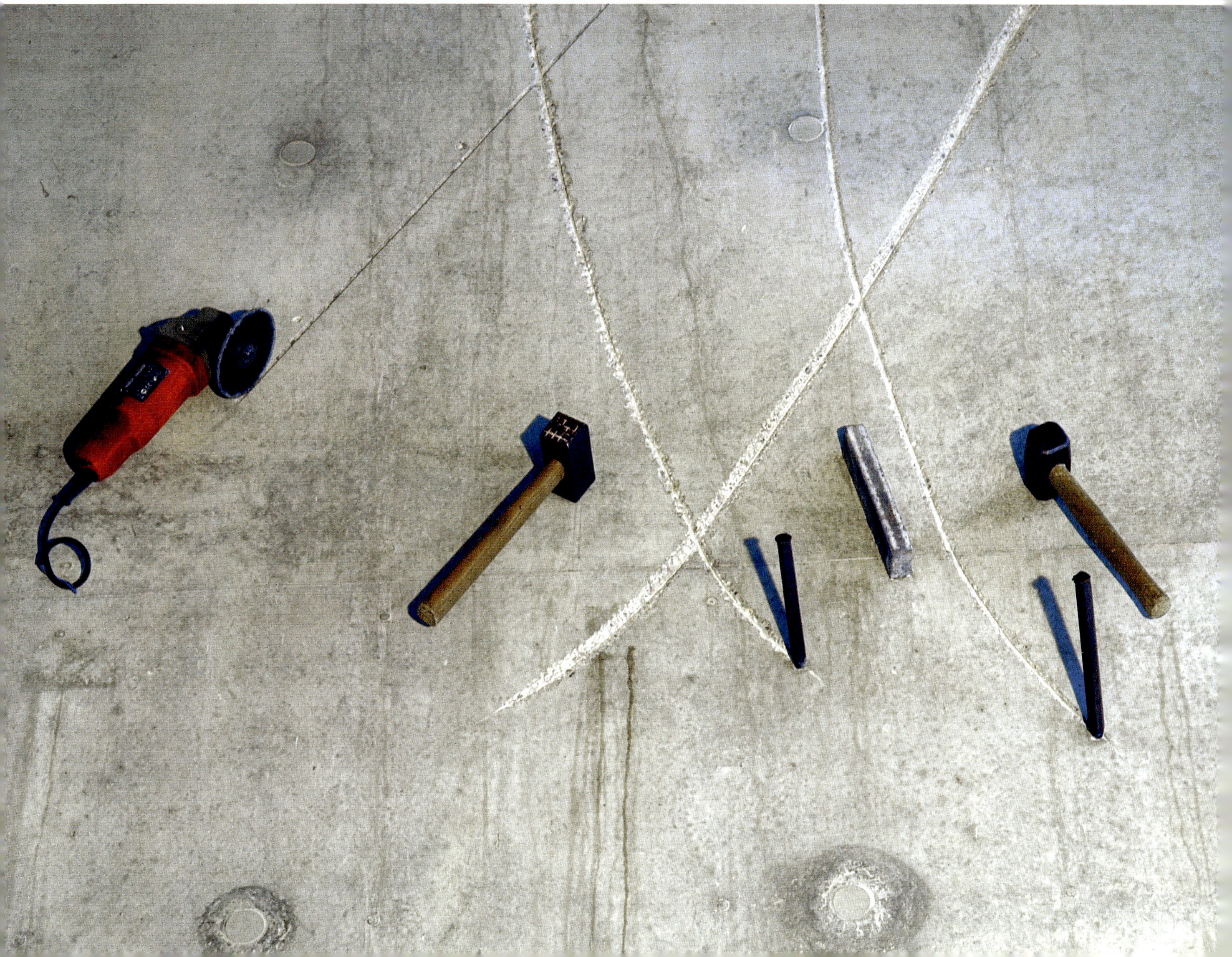

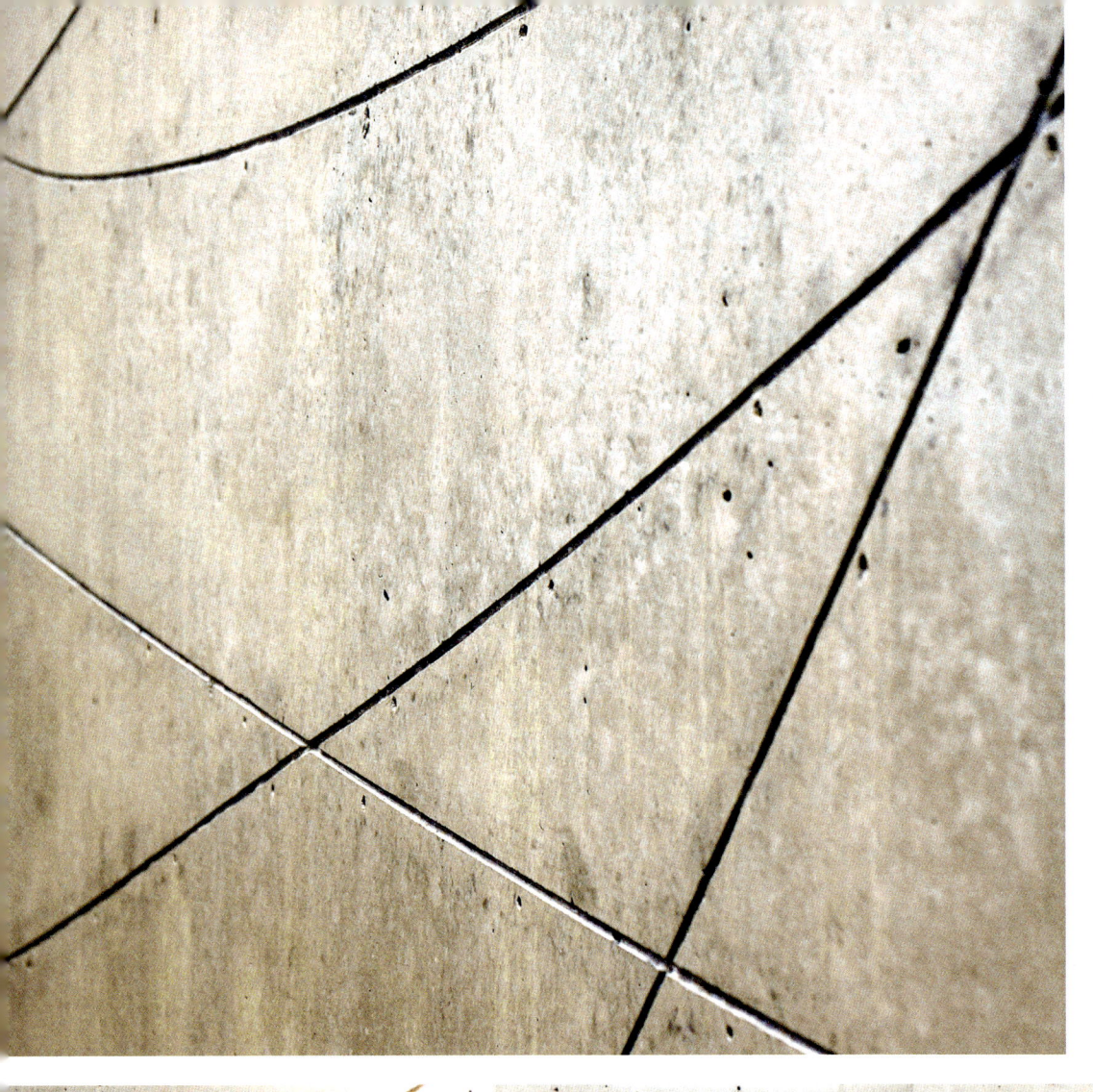

Außenbereich
Hof Nord – Arbeitsspuren

Arbeitsspuren durch Schneiden auf Betonwand. Montierte Werkzeuge: Winkelschleifer-Trennscheiben

External area:
Northern courtyard – Work Traces

Work Traces: incisions in a concrete wall
Tools fixed in wall: angle-grinder cutting discs

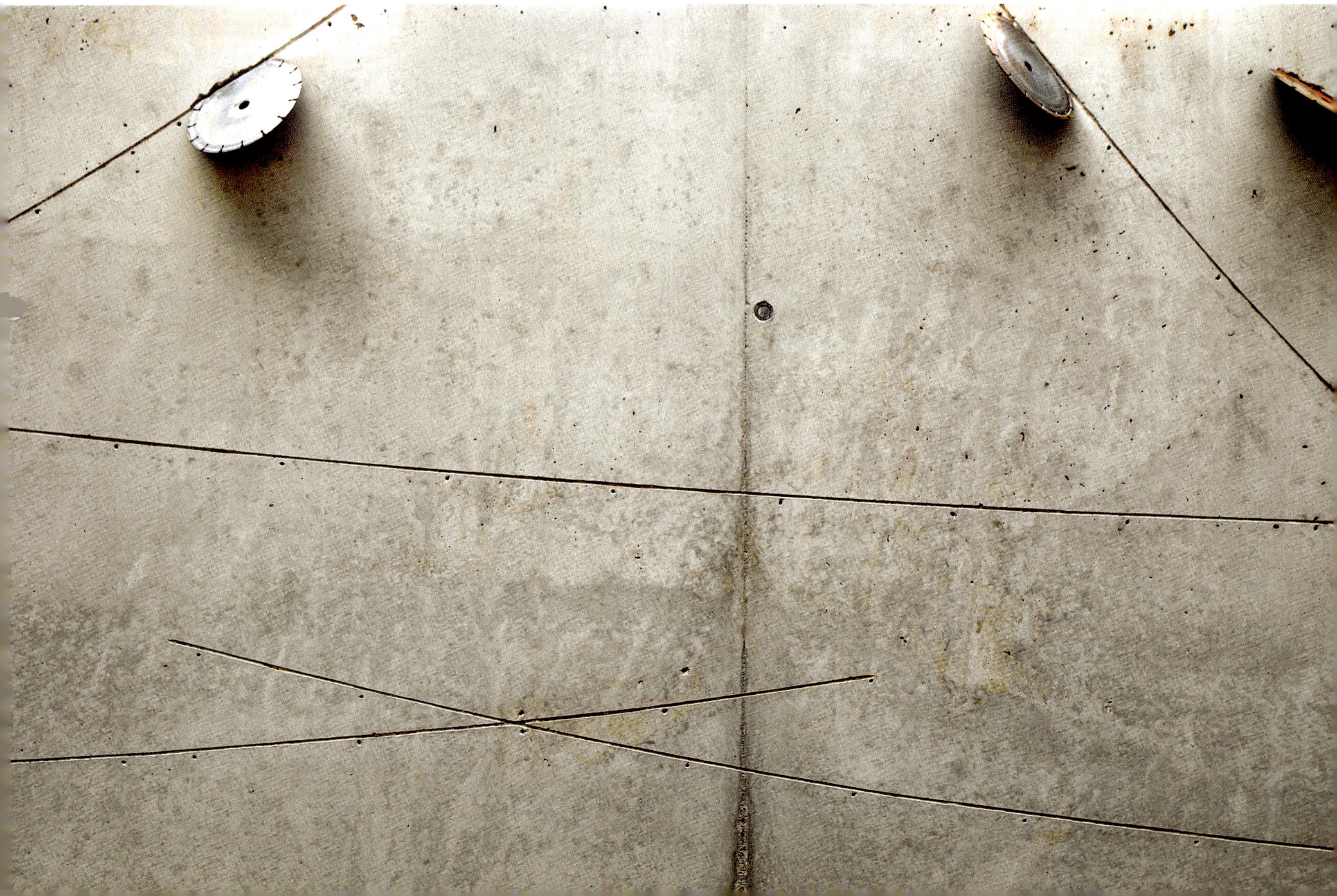

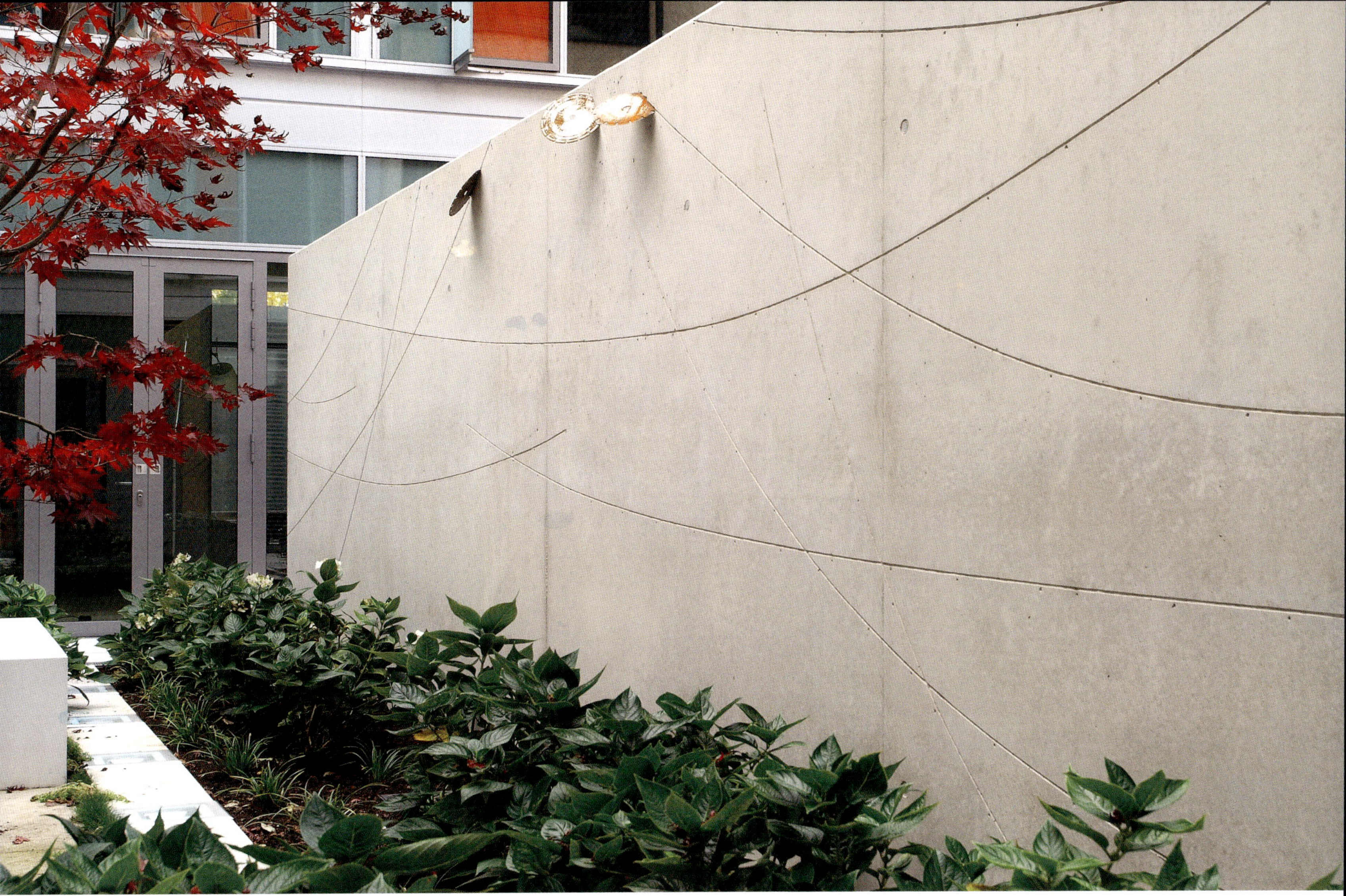

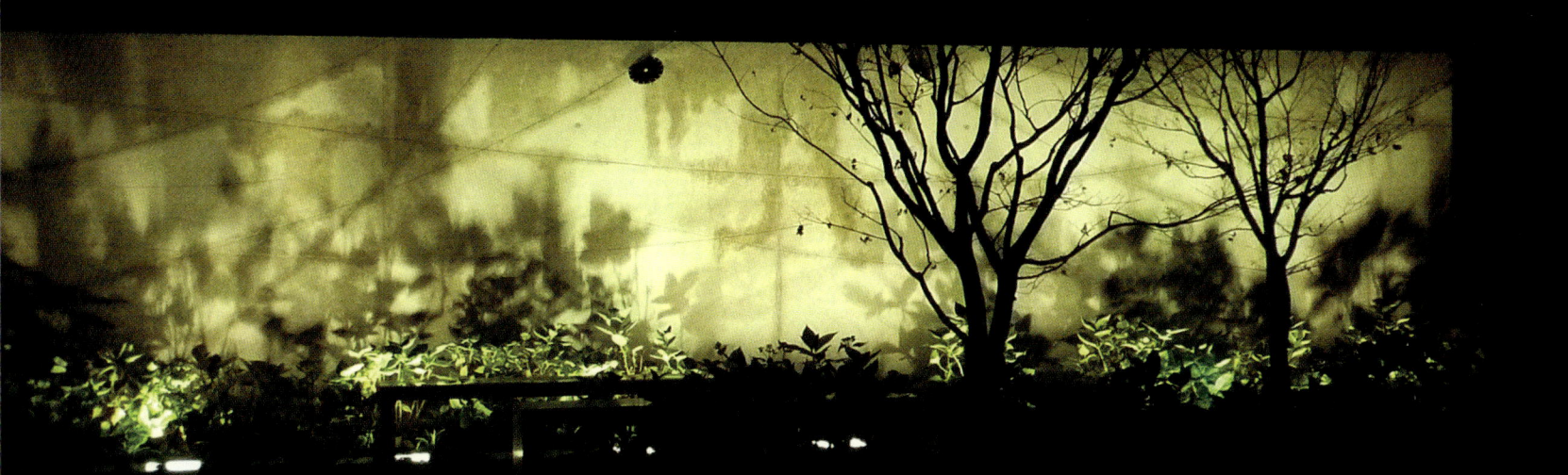

„L'artista e l'ingegnere"
Leonardo Da Vinci, Künstler, Ingenieur und Architekt
Glastafeln/Siebdruck, Keimfarbe, Acrylatdispersion
und Blattgold auf Sichtbetonwand West, 375 x 1720 cm

"L'artista e l'ingegnere"
Leonardo da Vinci, artist, engineer and architect
Screen printing on glass, mineral-based paint, acrylate emulsion paint
and gold leaf on west-facing exposed concrete wall, 375 x 1720 cm

Rainer Wittenborn

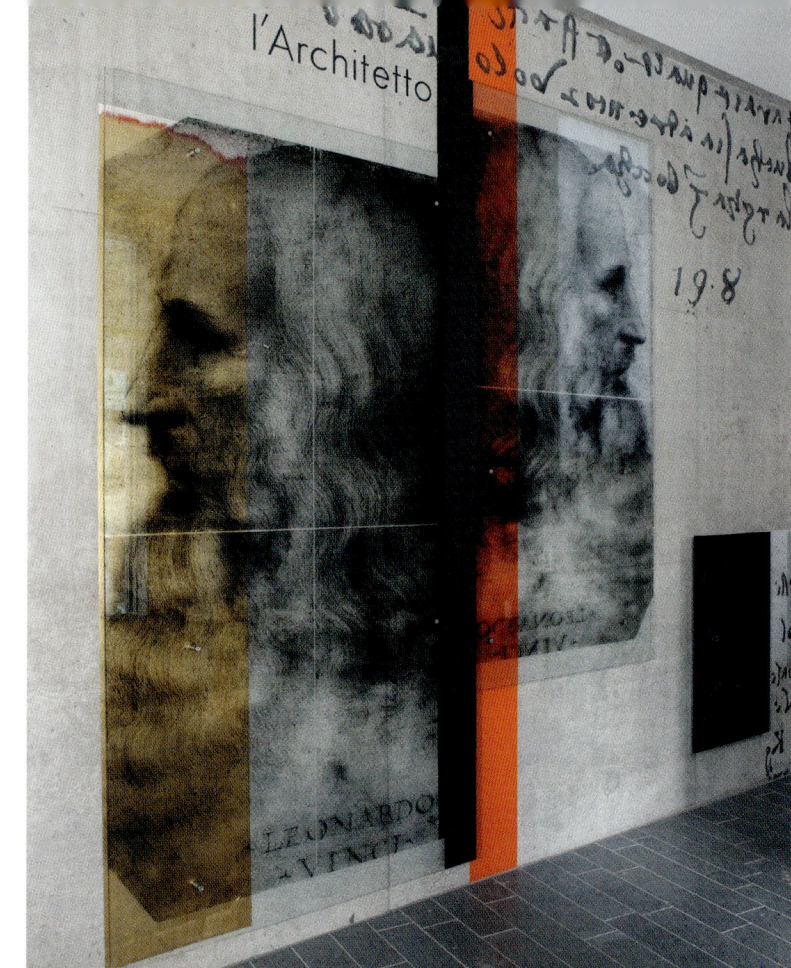

Im mehrgeschossigen westlichen Eingangsraum bietet die lange Wand Fläche für Annäherung und Berührungspunkte an die Person Leonardos als Künstler, Ingenieur und Architekt – also verschiedene Aspekte, Ausschnitte und Details, meist als Versatzstücke, aus drei Bereichen seiner äußerst breit gefächerten Interessen und seines immensen Schaffens.
Die auf großen Glastafeln gedruckten Profilzeichnungen des Leonardo Portraits sind nach Nord und Süd ausgerichtet und finden durch die hinter Glas gedruckten Zeichnungen Leonardos ihre thematische Entsprechung zu Kunst, Architektur und Ingenieurwerken. Partien handschriftlicher Notizen in der von Leonardo meist benutzten Spiegelschrift und ein wandfüllender Ausschnitt einer seiner technischen Zeichnungen sowie wechselnde farbige Partien bilden den Hintergrund zu dem Band schwarzer Glasplatten der ins negativ gesetzten Zeichnungsreihe.

The western entrance space extends over a number of storeys, and the long wall here provides an area where it is possible to converge and find points of contact with the person of Leonardo da Vinci as artist, engineer and architect: in other words, various aspects, extracts and details, largely in the form of set pieces from three areas of his extremely broad range of interests and his immense creative oeuvre.
Facing north and south are outline drawings of the Leonardo portrait printed on large sheets of glass. The fact that these drawings by Leonardo are printed on the rear face of the glass creates thematic parallels to works of art, architecture and engineering. The background to this strip of black glass sheets with the reverse-image series of drawings is formed by extracts from handwritten notes in the mirror-image manner commonly used by Leonardo, together with part of one of his technical drawings – which fills the entire wall – and areas in different colours.

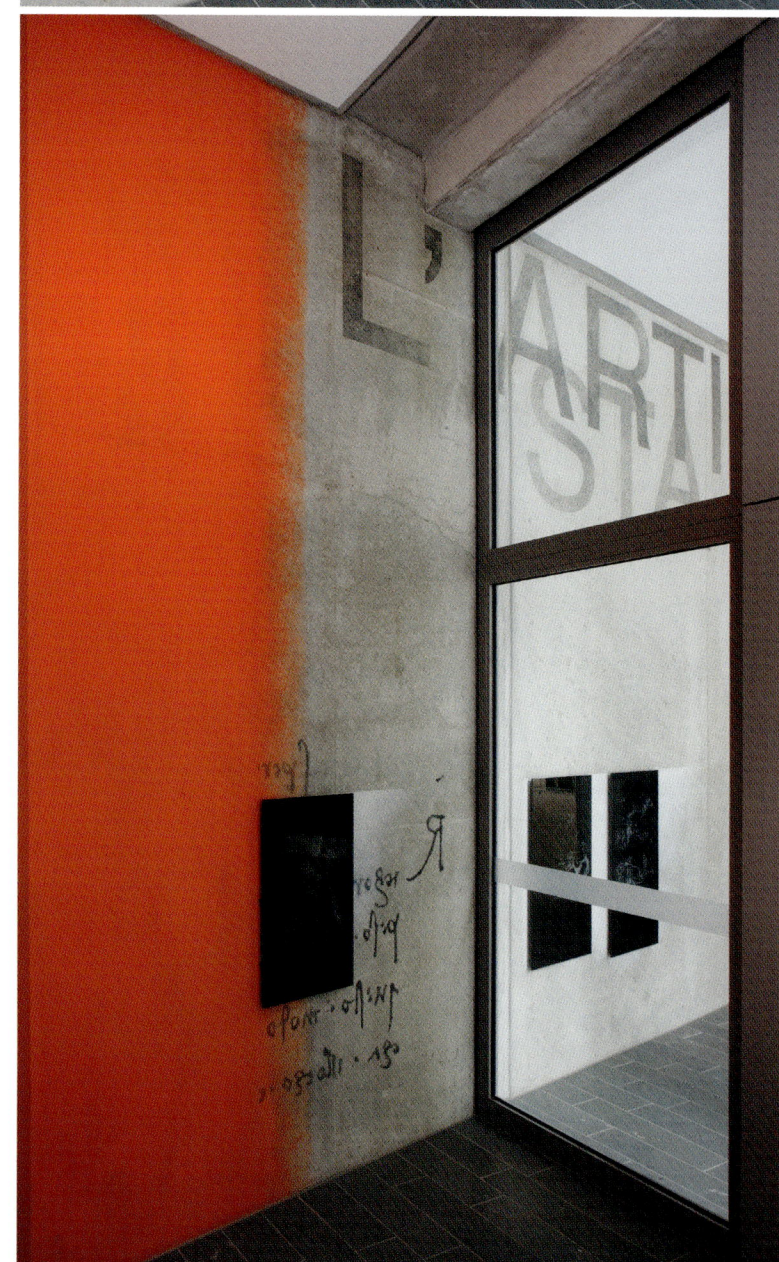

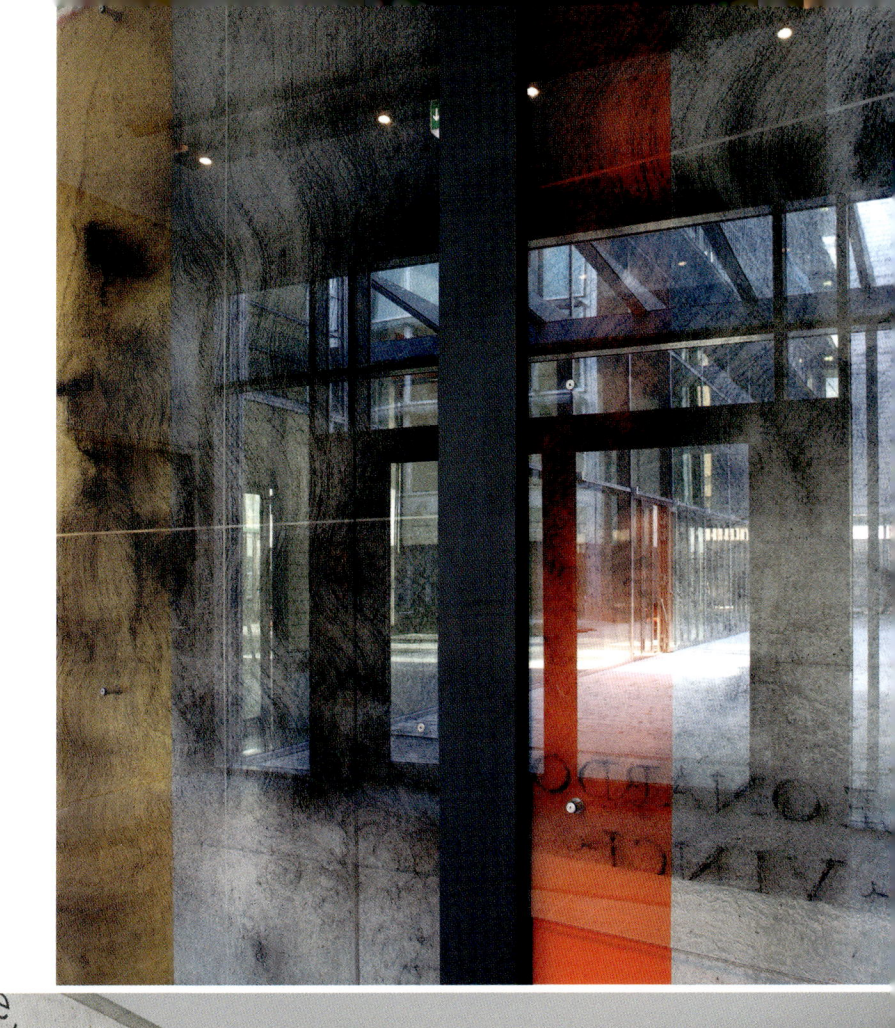

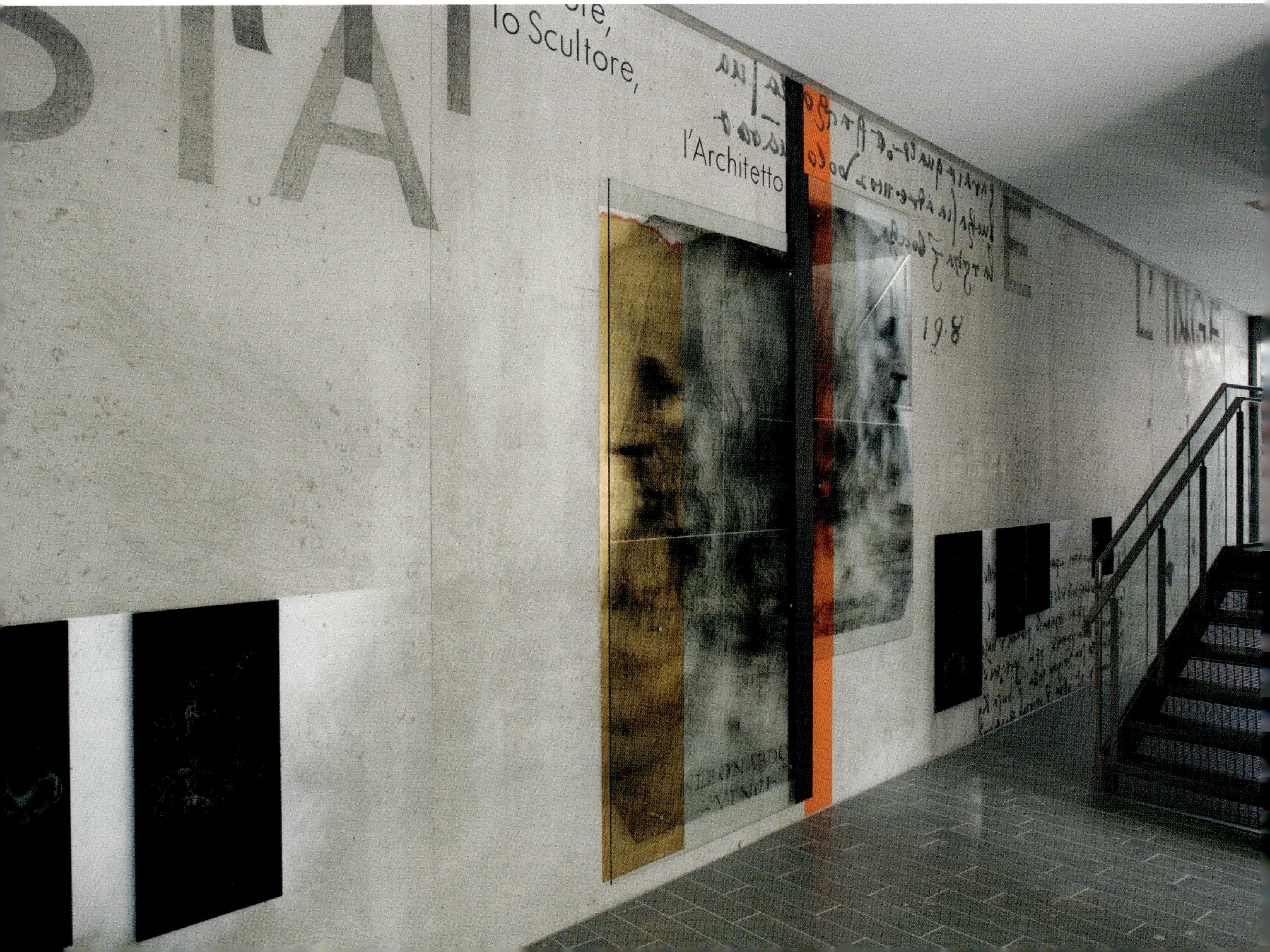

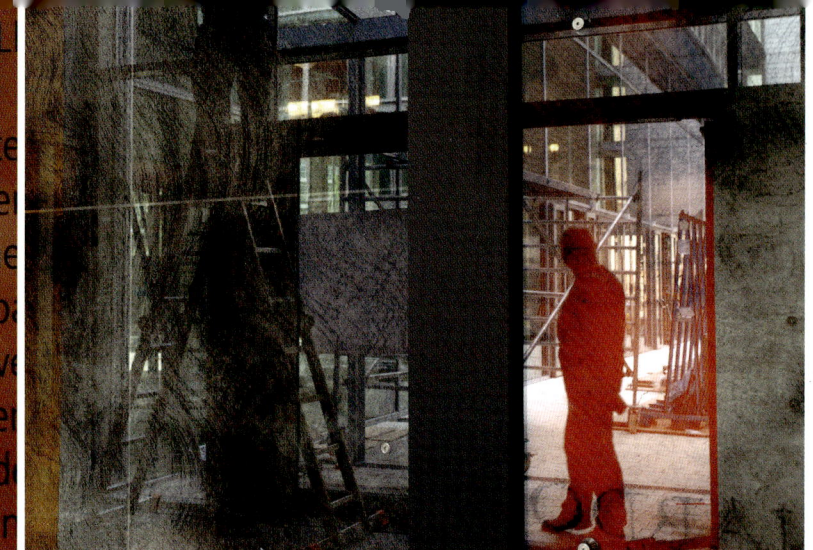

ART UND WEISE DEN GEIST ZU VERSCHIEDENERLEI ERFINDUNGEN ZU MEHREN UND ANZUREGEN.

Ich werde nicht unterlassen unter diesen Vorschriften eine neuerfundene Art des Schauens anzusprechen, die sich zwar klein und fast lächerlich ausnehmen mag, nichtsdestoweniger aber doch sehr brauchbar ist den Geist zu verschiedenerlei Erfindungen zu wecken. Sie besteht darin, dass du auf manche Mauern hinsiehst, die mit allerlei Flecken bedeckt sind, oder auf Gestein von verschiedener Art. Hast du irgend eine Situation zu erfinden, so kannst du da Dinge erblicken, die diversen Landschaften gleichen, geschmückt mit Gebirgen, Flüssen, Felsen, Bäumen, grossen Ebenen, Thal und Hügeln in mancherlei Art. Auch kannst du da allerlei Schlachten sehen, lebhafte Stellungen sonderbar fremdartiger Figuren, Gesichtsminen, Kleidung und unzählige Dinge, die du in vollkommene und gute Form bringen magst. Es tritt bei derlei Mauern das Aehnliche ein, wie beim Klang der Glocken, da wirst du in den Schlägen jeden Namen und jedes Wort wiederfinden können, die du dir einbildest. Achte diese meine Meinung nicht gering, in der ich dir rathe, es möge dir nicht lästig erscheinen manchmal stehen zu bleiben und auf die Mauerflecken hinzusehen oder in die Asche im Feuer, in die Wolken, oder in Schlamm und auf andere solche Stellen; du wirst, wenn du sie recht betrachtest, sehr wunderbare Erfindungen in ihnen entdecken. Denn des Malers Geist wird zu neuen Erfindungen angeregt, sei es in Compositionen von Schlachten von Thier und Menschen, oder auch zu verschiedenerlei Compositionen von Landschaften und von ungeheuerlichen Dingen, wie Teufeln u. dgl., die angethan sind, dir Ehre zu bringen. Durch verworrene und unbestimmte Dinge wird nämlich der Geist zu neuen Erfindungen wach. Sorge aber vorher, dass du alle die Glieder der Dinge, die du vorstellen willst, gut zu machen verstehest, so die Glieder der lebenden Wesen, wie auch die Gliedmaassen der Landschaft, nämlich die Steine, Bäume u. dgl.
Leonardo da Vinci (1452 – 1519) – aus: Trattato della Pittura

WAY TO AUGMENT AND STIMULATE THE MIND TOWARD VARIOUS DISCOVERIES.

I shall not fail to include these precepts a new discovery, and aid to reflection, which, although it seems a small thing and almost laughable, nevertheless is very useful in stimulating the mind to various discoveries. This is: look at walls splashed with a number of stains or stones of various mixed colors. If you have to invent some scene, you can see there resemblances to a number of landscapes, adorned in various ways with mountains, rivers, rocks, trees, great plaines, valleys and hills. Moreover, you can see various battles, and rapid actions of figures, strange expressions on faces, costumes, and an infinite number of things, which you can reduce to good, integrated form. This happens thus on walls and varicolored stones, as in the sound of bells, in whose pealing you can find every name and word you can imagine. Do not despise my opinion, when I remind you that it should not be hard for you to stop sometimes and look into the stains of walls, or the ashes of a fire, or clouds, or mud, or like things, in which, if you consider them well, you will find really marvelous ideas. The mind of the painter is stimulated to new discoveries, the composition of battles of animals and men, various compositions of landscapes and monstrous things, such as devils and similar creations, which may bring you honor, because the mind is stimulated to new inventions by obscure things. But be sure that you first know how to make all the parts of the objects that you wish to represent, such as the limbs of animals, and the elements of landscape, that is rocks, plants, and such things.
Leonardo da Vinci (1452 – 1519) – from: Trattato della Pittura

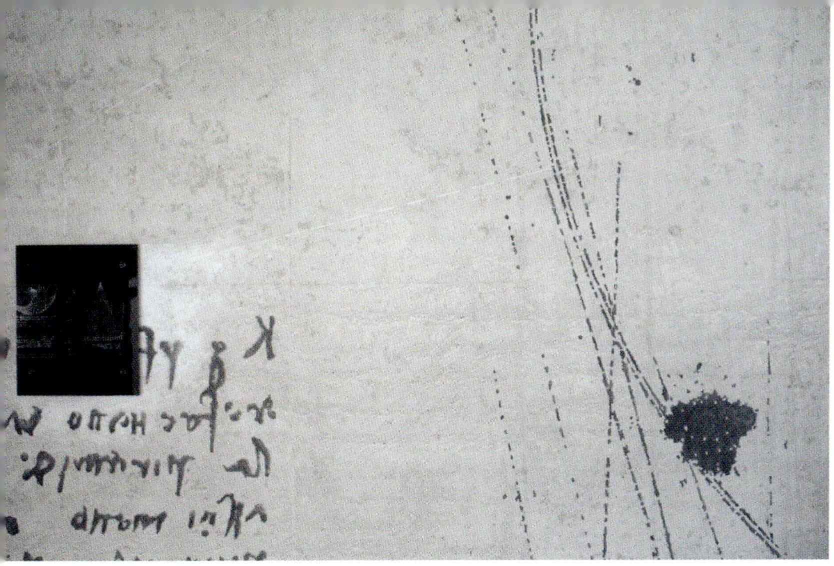

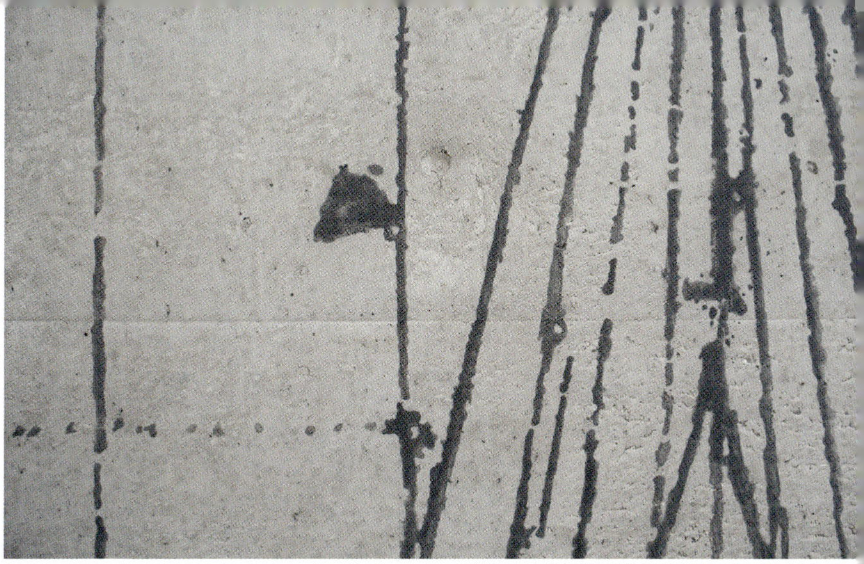

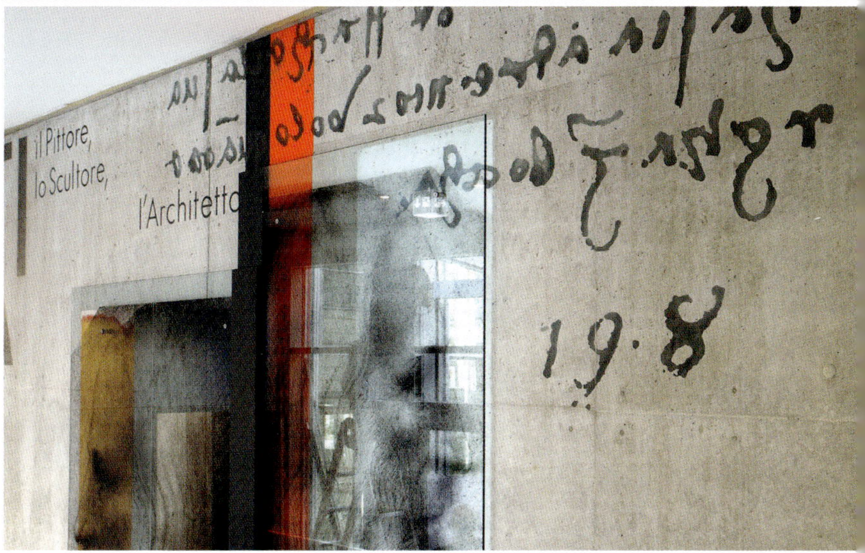

il Pittore,
lo Scultore,
l'Architetto

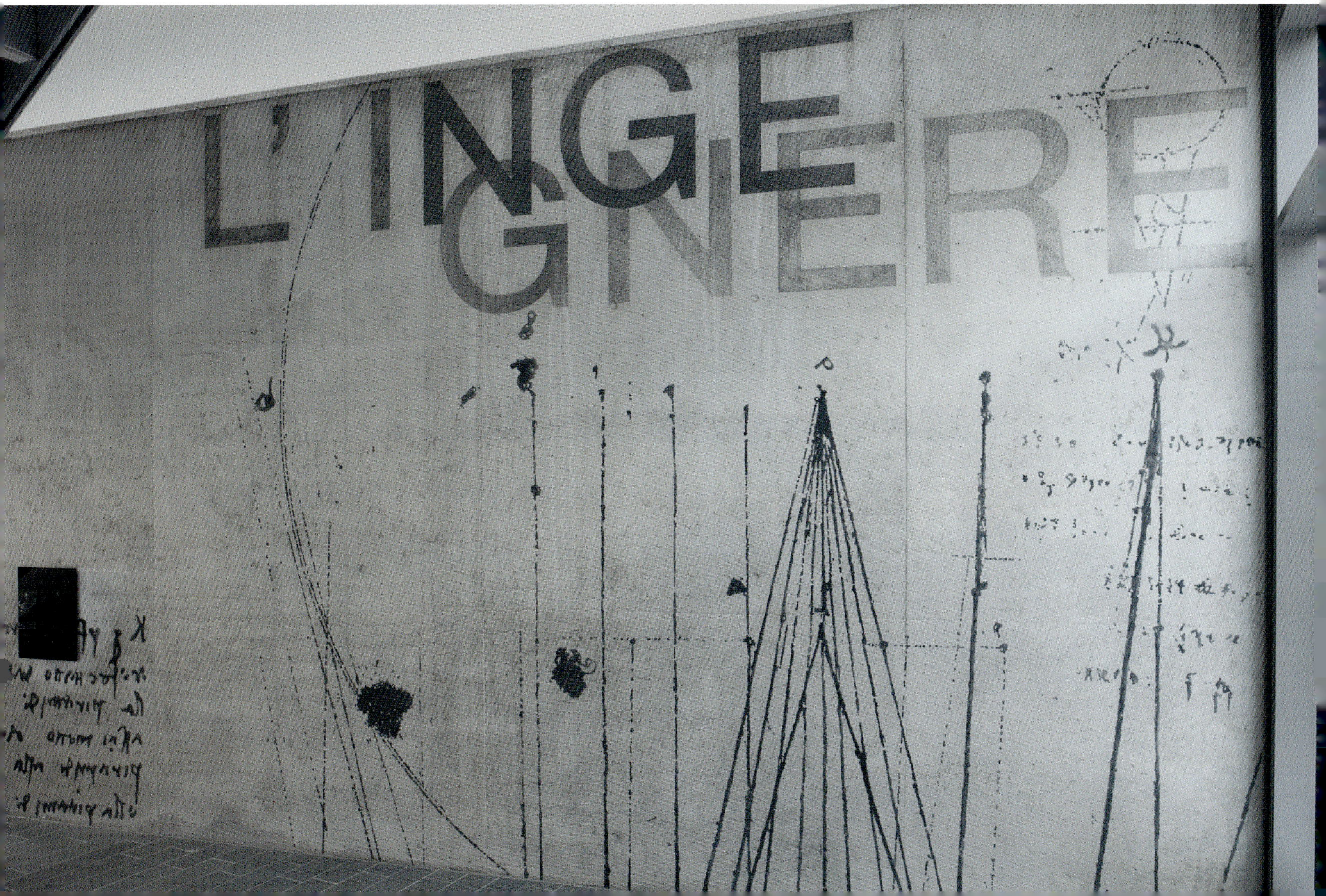

L'INGE
GNERE

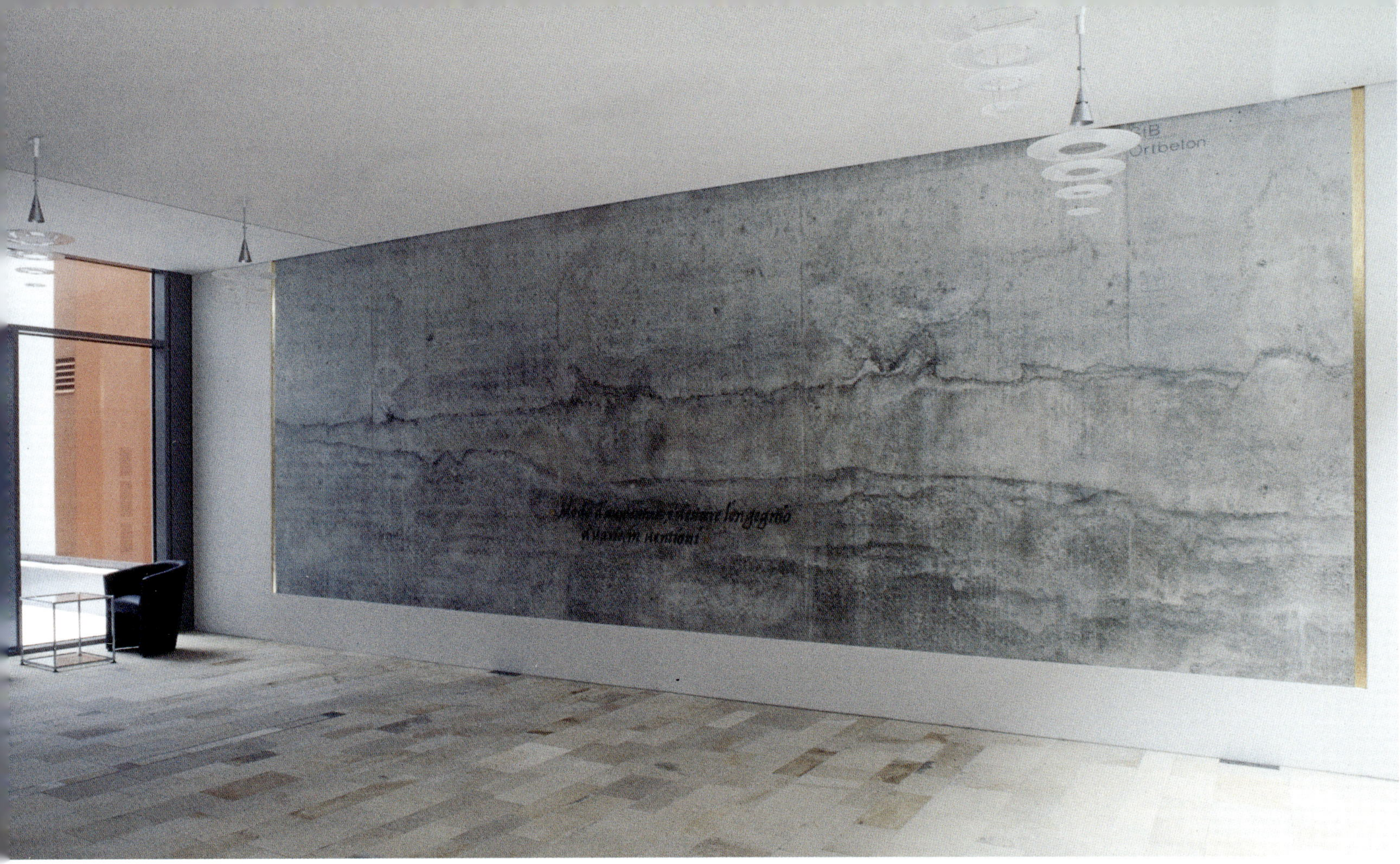

„Sichtbeton – ein zufälliges Wandbild"
„Modo d'aumentare e destare ligegnio a varie, inventioni." –
Trattato della Pittura – Leonardo da Vinci (1452–1519)
Graphit und Blattgold auf Sichtbetonwand Nord, 345/975 cm

Eingrenzung eines Wandbildes durch ein flach aufgeputztes Passepartout auf der Sichtbetonwand, die mit ihren Flecken, Formen und Linien, ihren partiellen Zeichnungen und Hell-Dunkel-Schattierungen die Erinnerung an Leonardo da Vincis berühmten Text über „die Flecken auf den Mauern" wachruft und uns durch intensives Sehen die Fantasiewelt der „Zufallsbilder" erschließt, um zu neuen Assoziationen und Ideen zu gelangen.
Der Titel des Zitats aus „dem Traktat über die Malerei" läuft als Doppelzeile (Graphit) durch die untere Bildebene, ein schmales, vertikales, vergoldetes Band grenzt beidseitig das Bildformat ein.

"Exposed Concrete – a Chance Mural Image"
"Modo d'aumentare e destare ligegnio a varie, inventioni." –
Trattato della Pittura – Leonardo da Vinci (1452–1519)
Graphite and gold leaf on north-facing exposed-concrete wall, 345 x 975 cm

The demarcation of the mural image is achieved by means of a flat plaster passepartout applied to the exposed-concrete wall. With its patches and forms and lines, with its fragmentary drawings and light and dark areas, the work recalls Leonardo da Vinci's famous words about "the patches on a wall". Through a process of intense perception, it opens up to us a fantasy world of "chance images" that conjure new associations and ideas.
The title of the work, taken from the "Treatise on Painting" by Leonardo, runs through the lower part of the picture as a two-line quotation (in graphite). The picture is flanked on both sides by a narrow, vertical gilded strip.

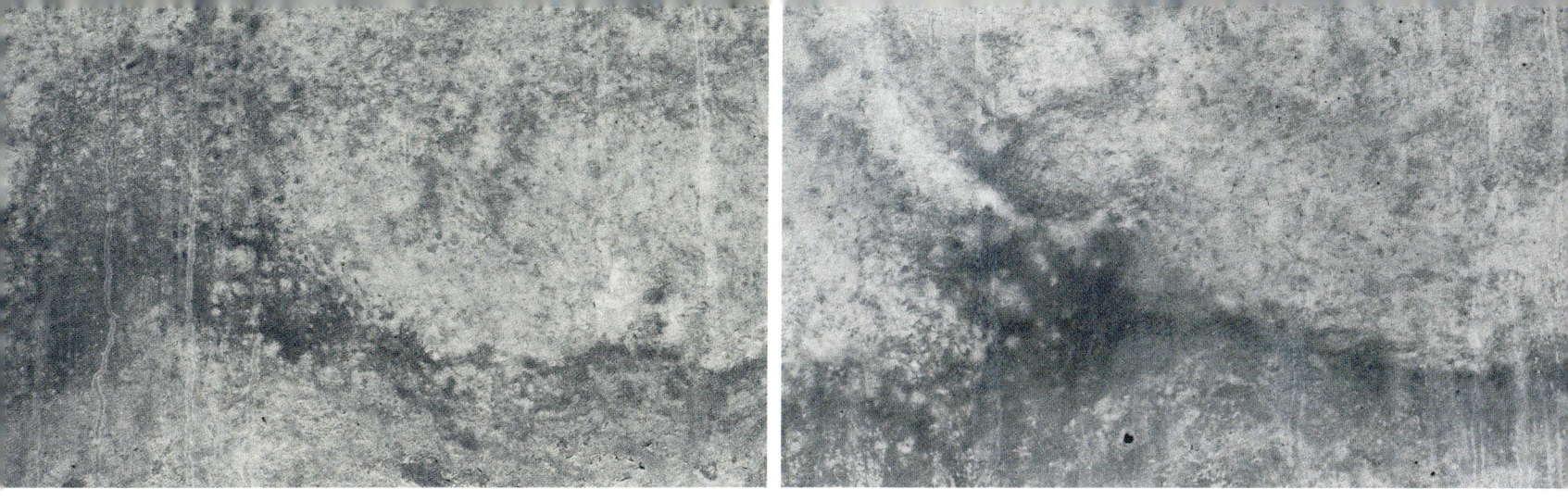

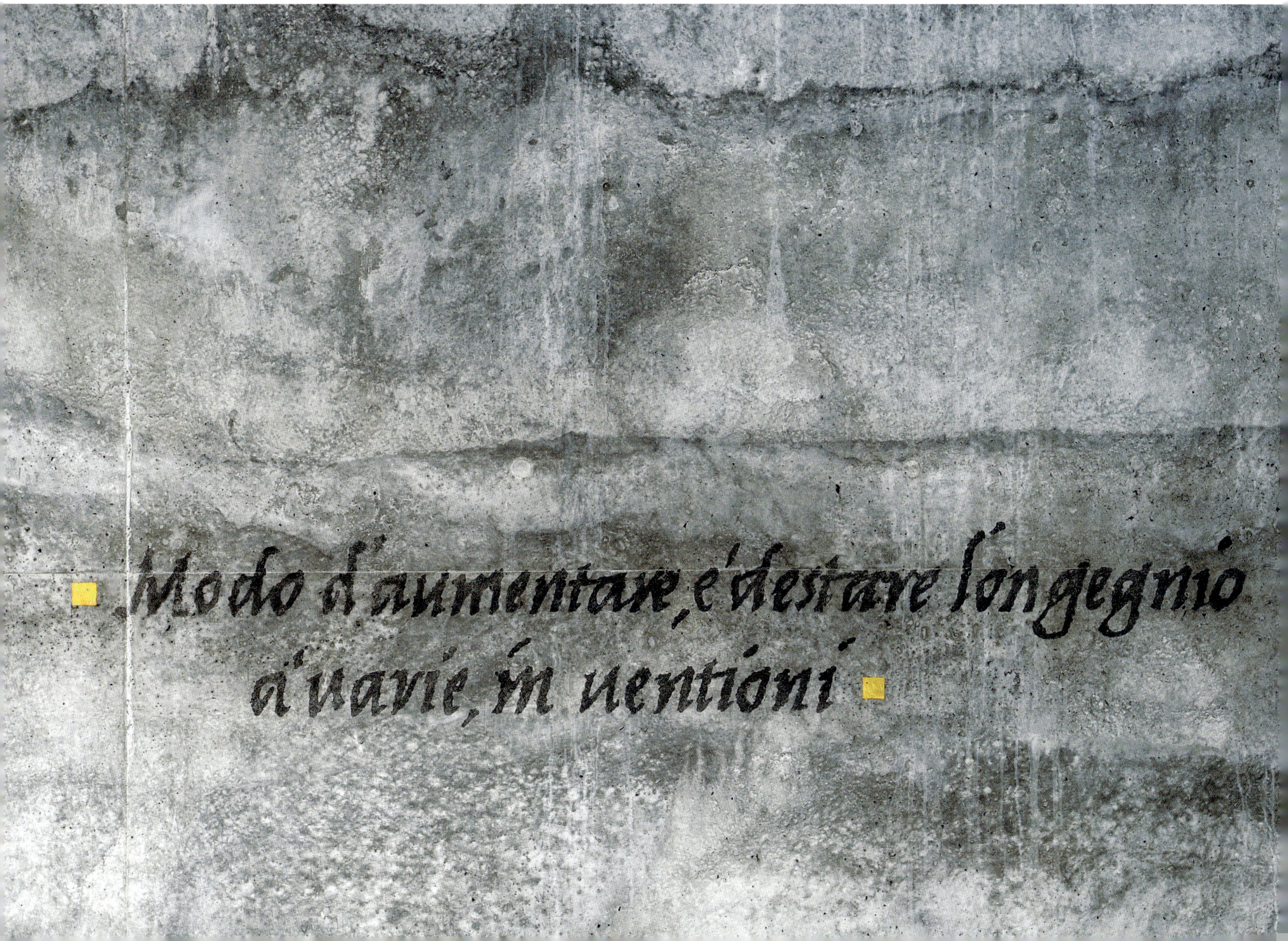

Projektdaten

- Traufhöhe ca. 22 m, maximale Firsthöhe ca. 28 m
- Grundstücksfläche 1.286 m²
- BGF Bruttogeschossfläche 7.541 m²
- BRI Bruttorauminhalt 25.229 m³
- 56 Studentenzimmer mit vorgelagerten Gemeinschaftsräumen (Küche-Wohnen-Arbeiten)
- 7 größere Wohnungen für Gastwissenschaftler 1. OG – 4.OG
- Einzelappartement für Kurzaufenthalt (z.B. Vortragende)
- Veranstaltungs- und Ausstellungsbereich im EG (100–150 Personen)
- Veranstaltung 7. OG mit Dachterrasse (60–75 Personen)
- Clubraum und Bibliothek (20–30 Personen)
- Bistro im EG (25–30 Personen)
- 20 anmietbare Kombiparker-Stellplätze PKW im 1. UG
- Dachflächen begrünt
- Türen zu den Treppenhäusern T30 Qualität
- Thermische Solarkollektoren auf dem Dach des Südgebäudes
- Primärenergiebedarf: 137kWh/(m²a)

Wärmetechnik
- Gesamtwärmeleistung des Gebäudes 400 kW
- Wärmeerzeugung über Fernwärme 81 % und Solarthermie 19 %
- Wärmeverteilung im Gebäude über Flächenheizungssysteme und RLT-Anlagen

Kältetechnik
- Gesamtkälteleistung des Gebäudes 150 kW
- Maximale Gesamtkälteleistung 160 kW
- Kälteerzeugung über „Freie Kühlung mittels Kühlturm 69 %, Solar Cooling 16 % und Kompressionskälte 15 %
- Kälteverteilung des Gebäudes über Flächenkühlungssysteme und RLT-Anlagen

Raumlufttechnik RLT-Anlagen
- Mit Wärmerückgewinnungseinrichtung mit Befeuchtungseinrichtung für die Wohnbereiche (ca. 4.400 m³/h)
- Mit Luftqualitätssteuerung für den Hallenbereich (ca. 4.500 m³/h)
- Mit Luftqualitätssteuerung für den Bistrobereich (ca. 2.700 m³/h)
- Mit Luftqualitätssteuerung für die Nebenraumbereiche (ca. 4.500 m³/h)
- RLT-Anlagen zur Entrauchung (ca. 27.000 m³/h)
- RLT-Anlage zur Garagenentlüftung (ca. 4.600 m³/h)
- Optional mit außentemperaturabhängiger Zuluft-Sollwertschiebung 19 bis 21°C)
- Konstante Zuluftfeuchte (Absolutfeuchteregelung) im Winter bei ca. 6g/kg

Sanitärtechnik
- Legionellenprophylaxe durch Protectolyse
- Zentrale Kalkschutzanlage

Sprinklertechnik
- Hochdruckwassernebel-Sprinkleranlage für die Bereiche Halle und OG-Flure
- Einstufung der Brandgefahrenklasse für EG und OG 2–6:OH 1
- Wasserbeaufschlagung:1,5–2,0l/min/m²
- Ansatz für die Auslegung der Wasserbevorratung: 6 Sprinkler
- Betriebszeit: 40 Minuten
- Hochdruckpumpenaggregat mit 3 Pumpen
- Löschwasservorrat im PE-Behälter ca. 9,0 m³
- Die Hochdruck-Wassernebel-Löschanlage arbeitet mit Pumpendrücken bis zu 180 bar und Drücken am Sprinkler von 80 bis 120 bar

Zu- und Abluftvolumen
Südbau – Wohnbereiche + 7. OG: 3.990 m³/h
Luftmenge pro Zimmer (60 Zimmer): 20 m³/h/30 m³/h (ZU/AB)
Zuluftmengen: 1.990 m³/h (ZU)
Luftmenge für das 7. Obergeschoss: 2.000 m³/h

Westbau: 660 m³/h
Luftmenge pro für EG bis 1.OG:480 m³/h
Luftmenge für 2. OG bis 3. OG:180 m³/h

Ostbau: 480 m³/h
Luftmenge pro Dozentenappartement: 60 m³/h (ZU/AB)

Halle EG/Südbau: 4.500 m³/h
Luftmenge pro Person (max. 225 Personen): 20 m³/h

(Bistro) EG Ostbau: 2.700 m³/h
Luftmenge pro Person (max. 60 Personen): 45 m³/h

Lager- und Technikbereiche UG: 2.850 m³/h/2.650 m³/h
Tiefgaragen: 5.400 m³/h
Müllraum: 500 m³/h
Batterieraum: 200 m³/h

Entrauchung
Tiefgarage: 23.700 m³/h
2. Untergeschoss: 4.700 m³/h

Project data

- eaves height: ca 22m; maximum ridge height: ca 28m
- site area: 1,286 m²
- gross storey area: 7,541 m²
- gross volume: 25,229 m³
- 56 student rooms with adjoining group spaces (kitchen, living, working areas)
- 7 larger dwellings for visiting scientists (1st–4th floors)
- single apartment for short stays (e.g lecturers)
- space for exhibitions and other events on ground floor (100–150 persons)
- events space on 7th floor with roof terrace (60–75 persons)
- clubroom and library (20–30 persons)
- bistro on ground floor (25–30 persons)
- 20 rentable combination car-parking units on first basement level
- planted roof areas
- solar thermal collectors on roof of south tract
- staircase doors (30-min. fire resistance)
- primary energy needs: 137 kWh/(m²a)

Heating technology
- overall heating capacity of building: 400 kW
- heat generation: district heating – 81 %; solar energy – 19 %
- heat distribution in building via radiant panel-heating systems and air-conditioning plant

Cooling technology
- overall cooling capacity of building: 150 kW
- generation of cooling energy: free cooling from cooling tower – 69 %; solar cooling – 16 %; compression cooling – 15 %
- cooling-energy distribution in building by means of surface cooling systems and air-conditioning plant

Maximum overall cooling-energy capacity: 160 kW

Air-conditioning plant
- with heat-recovery system and humidifying plant for living areas (ca 4,400 m³/h)
- with air-quality control for hall (ca 4,500 m³/h)
- with air-quality control for bisto (ca 2,700 m³/h)
- with air-quality control for ancillary spaces (ca 4,500 m³/h)
- air-conditioning plant for smoke removal (ca 27,000 m³/h)
- air-conditioning plant for air extract from garage (ca 4,600 m³/h)
- option for adjustment of air-supply nominal value from 19 to 21 °C, depending on external temperature
- constant humidity of air supply (absolute moisture control) in winter at ca 6g/kg

Sanitary technology
- legionella prophylaxis by means of Protectolysis- process
- central limescale protection plant

Sprinkler system
- high-pressure water-mist sprinkler plant for hall and student corridor areas
- classification of fire risk for ground floor and 2nd–6th floors: OH1
- water discharge: 1.5–2.0 l/min./m²
- basis for dimensioning water reserve: 6 sprinklers
- operating time: 40 mins.
- high-pressure pump system with three pumps
- water supply for firefighting in polythene container: ca 9.0 m³
- the high-pressure water-mist extinguishing plant functions with pump pressures of up to 180 bar and sprinkler pressures of 80–120 bar

Air-supply/air-extract volumes

South tract – living areas + 7th floor: 3,990 m³/h
volume of air per room (60 rooms): 20–30 m³/h (supply/extract)
air-supply volume: 1,990 m³/h (supply)
volume of air for 7th floor: 2,000 m³/h

West tract: 660 m³/h
volume of air for ground and 1st floors: 480 m³/h
volume of air for 2nd and 3rd floors: 180 m³/h

East tract: 480 m³/h
volume of air per lecturer's apartment: 60 m³/h (supply/extract)

ground floor hall/south tract: 4,500 m³/h
volume of air per person (max. 225 persons): 20 m³/h

Ground floor bistro/east tract: 2,700 m³/h
volume of air per person (max. 60 persons): 45 m³/h

Basement store and mechanical services areas: 2,850 m³/h and 2,650 m³/h
basement garage: 5,400 m³/h
refuse space: 500 m³/h
battery space: 200 m³/h

Smoke extract
basement garage: 23,700 m³/h
second basement level: 4,700 m³/h

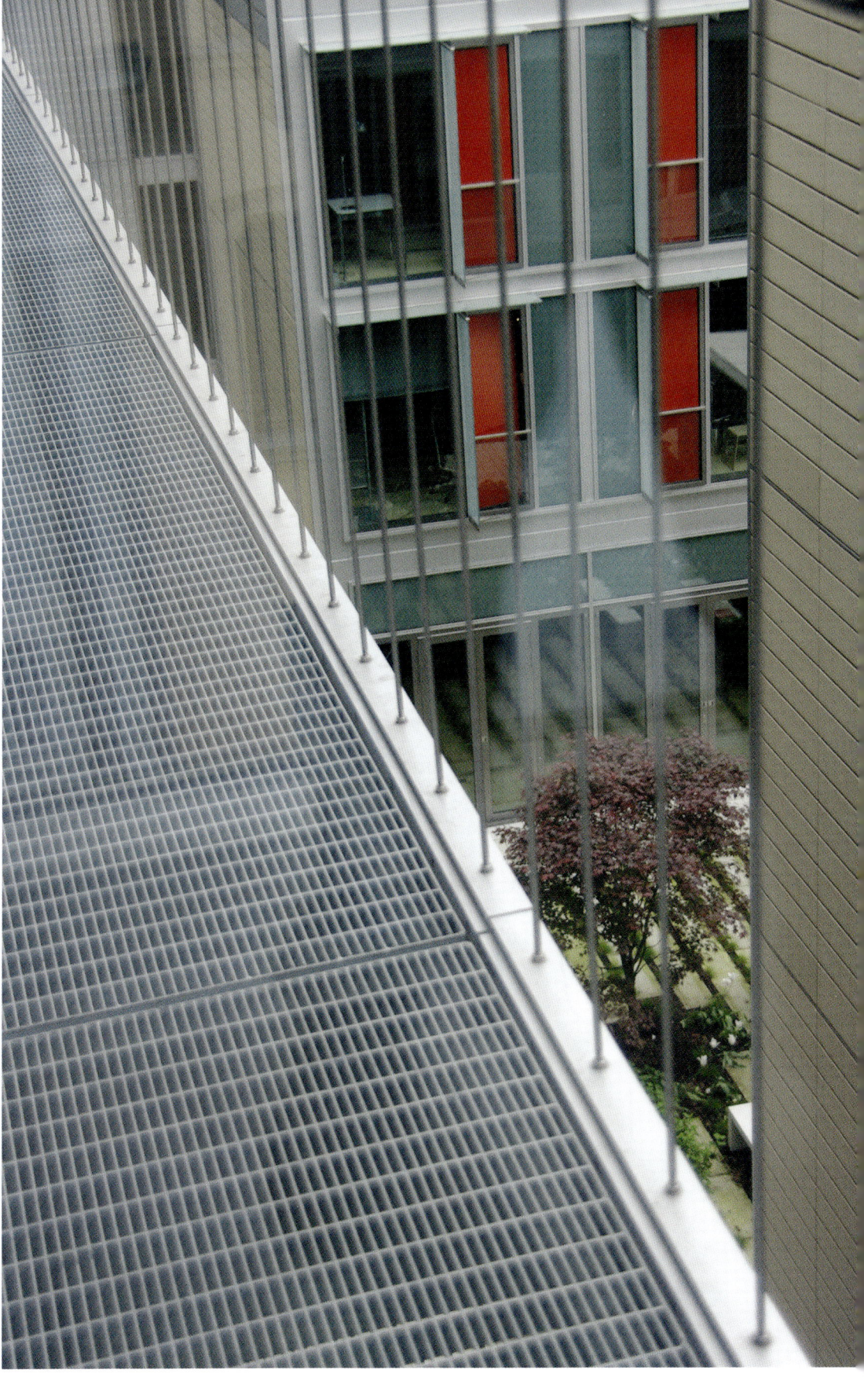

Projektbeteiligte Planer / Credits Planners

Bauherr / Client
Gemeinnützige Urlaubskasse des Bayerischen Baugewerbes e.V., München,
www.urlaubskasse-bayern.de

Vorstand / chairman:
Hans Beer
Robert Feiger
Otto Frischeisen
Senator E. h. Gerhard Hess

Bauherrenvertreter / Client's agent
Inhuber Krusche Rechtsanwälte, München,
www.inkrura.de
Dr. Christopher Krusche

Planer / Planning and design

Architekt / Architects
Herzog + Partner, Architekten BDA GbR,
München,
www.herzog-und-partner.de
Prof. Thomas Herzog, Hanns Jörg Schrade
Projektleiter / Project architect: Roland Schneider
Project team: Yann Friedl, Martin Schumacher, Tina Bayerl, Patrick Bröll, Kirsten Braun

Projektsteuerung / Project management
Drees & Sommer GmbH, Stuttgart,
www.dreso.com
Thomas Berner

Ausschreibung und Objektüberwachung für H+P / supervision for H+P
Dieter Zinner Ingenieure GbR, Büro für Baudurchführung, Krailling, info@ib-zinner.de

Sicherheits- und Gesundheitsschutzkoordination / Coordination of safety and health protection
Dieter Benthaus, München,
dieterbenthaus@t-online.de

Freianlagen / Landscape planning
Valentien + Valentien, Landschaftsarchitekten und Stadtplaner, SRL, Weßling,
www.valentien.de
Prof. Christoph Valentien

Ausschreibung und Objektüberwachung für Valentien + Valentien / supervision for V + V
Christoph Bücheler Landschaftsarchitekt,
www.cbuecheler.de

Tragwerksplanung / Structural engineering
Sailer, Stepan and Partner GmbH, München,
www.ssp-muc.com
Dr.-Ing. Kurt Stepan,
Projektleiter / Project engineer
Thomas Winkler

Baugrund-Gutachten / Soil mechanics
Lehrstuhl und Prüfamt für Grundbau, Boden- und Felsmechanik und Tunnelbau, München,
www.gb.bv.tum.de/main-zg.htm
Prof. Dr.-Ing. Norbert Vogt, TU München

Heizung, Lüftung, Sanitär, Kühlung / Heating, ventilation, sanitary, cooling installations
Climaplan GmbH, München,
www.climaplan.de
Christian Dotzauer

Elektro-, Licht- und Netzwerkplanung / Electrical, lighting and network planning
Hross & Partner GmbH,
A-Ödt-Traun,
www.hross-partner.at
Peter Hross

Mess-, Steuer-Technik / Instrumentation and control
Ingenieurbüro Rösener, München,
werner.roesener@t-online.de
Werner Rösener

Voruntersuchungen zum Energiekonzept / Pre-investigations for the energy concept
DS-Plan GmbH, Stuttgart,
www.ds-plan.com
Prof.Dr.-Ing. Michael Bauer
Dr.-Ing. Andreas Niewienda

Strömungssimulation / Airflow simulation
I.F.I. Institut für Industrieaerodynamik GmbH,
Fachhochschule Aachen
Rolf-Dieter Lieb
www.ifi-aachen.de

Wärmeschutz, Raumakustik und Schallschutz / Thermal insulation, spatial acoustics and sound insulation
Müller-BBM Gruppe, München,
www.muellerbbm.de
Gerhard Hilz

Küchenplanung / Kitchen planning
HPM Consult
www.hpm-consult.de
Hans-Peter Mühlethaler, André Tillich

Baulicher Brandschutz / Constructional fire protection
Kersken + Kirchner GmbH, München,
www.kk-fire.com
Dr.- Ing.Marita Kersken-Bradley; Christian Leis

Sachverständiger für den vorbeugenden Brandschutz / Consultant for fire prevention and protection
Rassek & Partner – Brandschutzingenieure,
Wuppertal, www.brandschutzbuero.de

Vermessung / Surveying
Karner Ingenieure GmbH, München,
www.entwurfs-vermessung.de

Bausubstanzuntersuchung / Soil investigations and geotechnics
Kraft + Dohmann, Geotechnik + Umwelttechnik GmbH
Institut für Erd- und Grundbau, München,
www.kdgeo.de

Beweissicherung / Preservation of evidence
Lange & Blaschke, München,
www.lange-blaschke.de

Infoleitsystem für H+P / Information Guiding System
HERZOGDESIGN, München
Cassian Herzog MSc

Bildende Kunst / Visual Arts
Sabine Kammerl,
Neuburg an der Donau
Prof. Nikolaus Lang, Murnau
Prof. Rainer Wittenborn, München

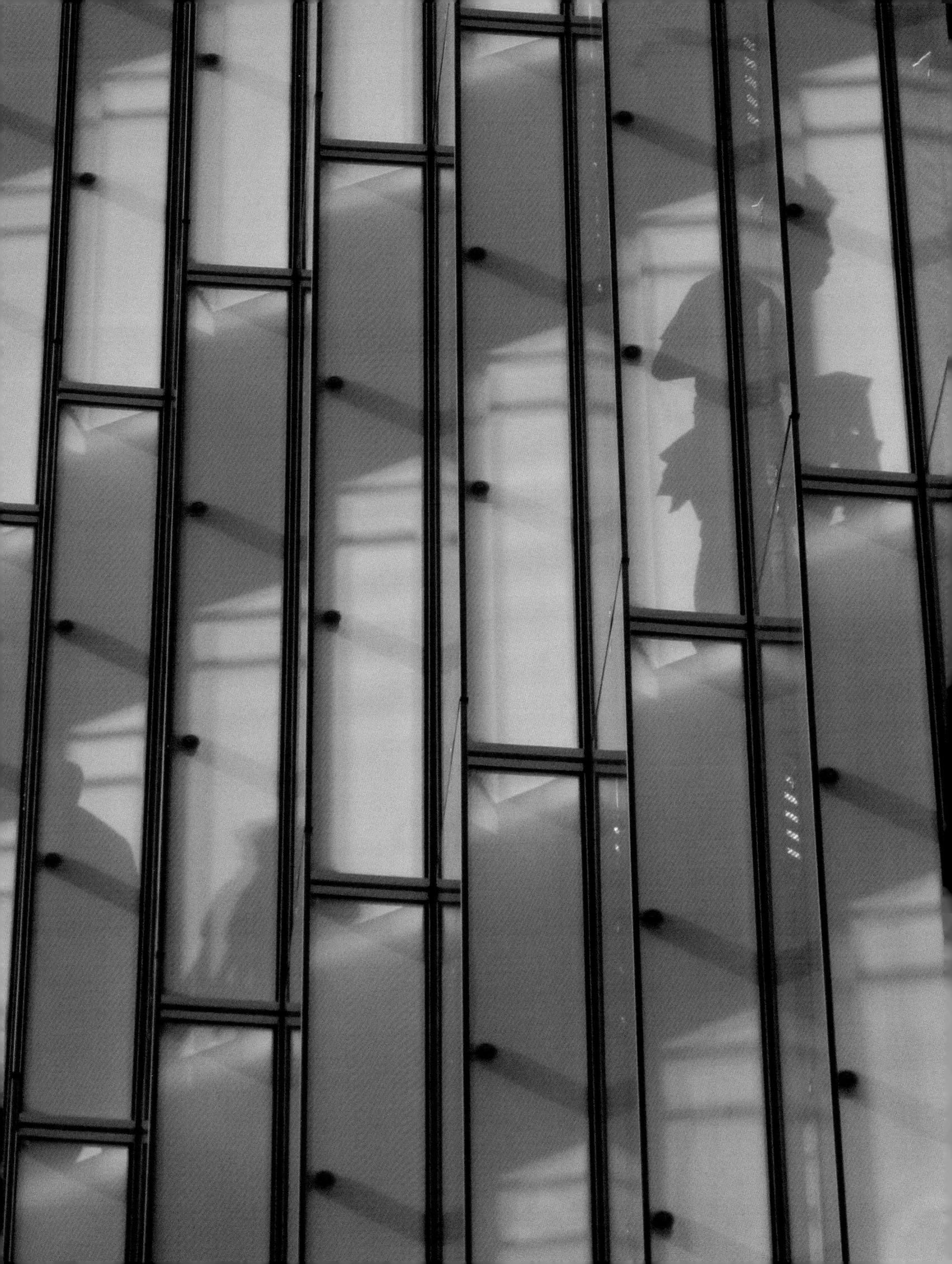

**Projektbeteiligte Firmen /
Credits Firms**

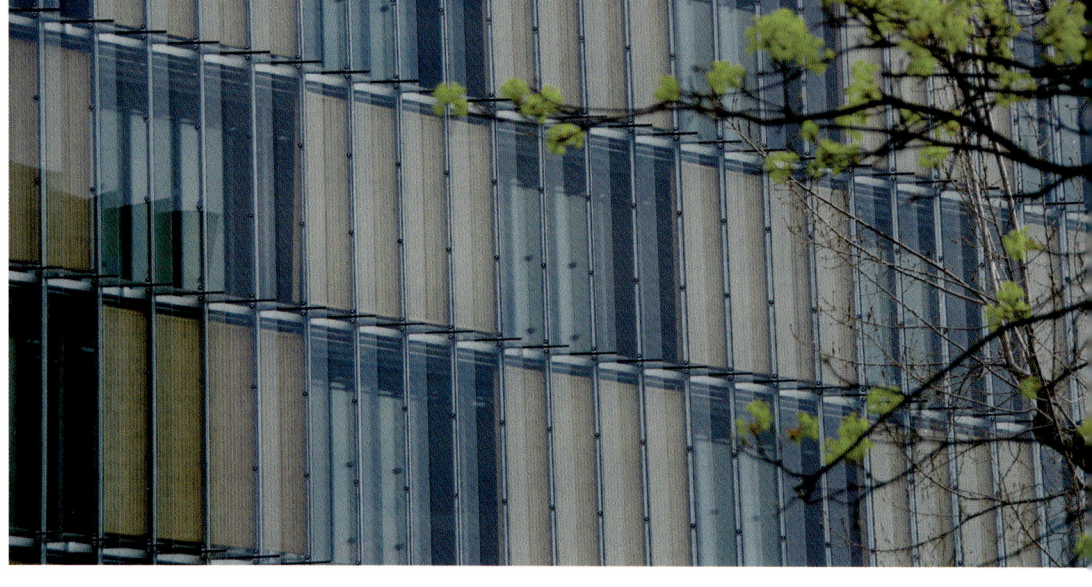

Abbrucharbeiten / Demolition work
Johann Ettengruber GmbH, Dachau, www.ettengruber.de

Baugrubenverbau / Shoring
Kassecker GmbH, Waldsassen,
www.kassecker.de

Baustrom / Site power supply
J. Baumgartner, Baustrom-Anlagen,
München, www.baumgartner-baustrom.de

Fußgängertunnel und Bauzaun /
pedestrian tunnel and site fence
Wilhelm Heinrich GmbH, München,
heinrich-zimmerei@t-online.de

Rohbau / Structural works
Max Bögl Bauunternehmung GmbH & Co. KG,
www.max-boegl.de

Gerüstbauarbeiten / Scaffolding
Michael Fritsch, Gerüstbau GmbH, München,
www.fritschgeruestbau.de

Dachdichtungsarbeiten / Roof seal
Flachdachbau Fuss GmbH, Mainleus, www.flachdachbau-fuss.de

Aufzugsanlage / Lift installation
Butz & Neumair, Aufzugbau GmbH,
Bergkirchen / Priel,
www.butz-neumair.de

Autoparksysteme / Car-parking systems
Otto Wöhr GmbH, Auto-Parksysteme,
Friolzheim, www.woehr.de

Estricharbeiten / Screeds
Knöller Fußbodentechnik GmbH, Nürnberg,
www.knoeller-fussbodentechnik.de

Naturstein- und Fliesenarbeiten /
Stonework and tiling
Abel GmbH, Fliesen – Marmor, Otzing,
fliesen-abel@t-online.de

Fassadenarbeiten / Facade construction
FKN Fassaden GmbH + Co. KG, Neuenstein,
www.fkn-gruppe.de

Glaselemente Ostfassade /
Glas elements east facade
OKALUX, www.okalux.de

Keramikfassadensystem /
ceramic facade system LONGOTON®
GIMA GmbH, Marklkofen,
www.gima-ziegel.de

Heizung, Lüftung, Sanitär, Kühlung /
Sanitary installation
Stingl GmbH, Heizung-Kälte-Sanitär-Kanal,
München, www.stingl-online.de

Elektroarbeiten / Electrical installation
Elektro Schöffmann GmbH & Co. KG,
Weilheim, www.elektro-schoeffmann.de

Medientechnik / Media technology
Kraftwerk Living Technologies GmbH,
A-Wels, www.kraftwerk.at

MSR Technik / Measurement, regulation
and control technology
Neuberger Gebäudeautomation GmbH &
Co. KG, www.neuberger.net

Trockenbauarbeiten /
Dry construction systems
A.S.T. Sommer GmbH, Kirchdorf am Inn,
www.ast-sommer.de

Metallbau: Türen und Tore /
Metalwork: doors and gates
Siegfried Wölz Stahl- und Metallbau GmbH &
Co. KG, Gundelfingen, www.woelz.de

Metallbau- und Schlosserarbeiten, Faltwände
der Halle / Metalwork and fittings: folding
partitions in hall
Glasl Stahl- u. Metallbau GmbH, Geretsried,
www.glaslstahl.gemeindeausstellung.de

Membrankonstruktion Faltwände /
Membrane construction: folding partitions
Aeronautec GmbH, Seeon,
www.aeronautec.de

Außenanlagen / External works
May Landschaftsbau GmbH & Co. KG,
Feldkirchen bei München,
www.may-landschaftsbau.de

Malerarbeiten / Painting works
Martin Faßnacht GmbH, Martinsried,
www.fassnacht-gmbh.de

Innenausbau Bäder /
Internal furnishings and fittings bathrooms
Koch Möbelwerkstätten GmbH, Karlskron,
www.koch-moebel.de

Küchentechnik / Kitchen fittings
Edgar Fuchs GmbH, Aschaffenburg,
www.edgarfuchs.com

Einrichtung Bistro und Halle /
Bistro furnishings and fittings
Innenausbau Kiem, I-Villnöß,
www.innenausbaukiem.com

Infoleitsystem / Information Guiding System
Vornehm Mediengestaltung, München,
www.vornehm.org
Stadler Siebdruck, München,
mail@stadler-siebdruck.de

Film / film
Hasso Bräuer

Bildnachweis / Photo Credits

Christoph Rehbach, Fuchstal,
atelier.hohenwart@t-online.de
11, 15/1, 16, 20/1, 21/2, 24,
27, 29/1/2/3, 32, 35/3, 36, 37,
40/2/3, 42/1, 43, 55, 56, 58, 59,
76, 77/2/3, 78, 79, 80, 81/1,
83/1, 84/2, 85/3, 87/3, 94, 95, 96
Climaplan
52
Cassian Herzog
14/1, 17, 18, 69/2, 71, 94/9
Verena Herzog-Loibl
Cover, 3, 4, 8, 19, 22/1 , 26, 28,
29/5, 31, 34/2, 35/1/2, 39/2, 41,
51, 57, 60, 61, 67, 69/1, 75,
77/1, 81/2, 84/1, 89, 91, 92, 93
Herzog + Partner
2, 6, 12, 13, 14/2, 15/2, 20/2,
21/1/3, 23/1, 29/4, 30, 45, 53,
54, 63, 73
Tanja Huber
95/12
Jörg Koopmann, München,
www.latebutgreat.com
82, 83/2, 85/1/2/4, 86/2
Rolf-Dieter Lieb
46, 47, 48, 49
LONGOTON® Moeding
22/2
Sailer, Stepan and Partner GmbH
38, 39/1, 40/1, 42/2/3
Roland Schneider
23/2, 65
Valentien + Valentien
34
Rainer Wittenborn
86/1, 87/1/2

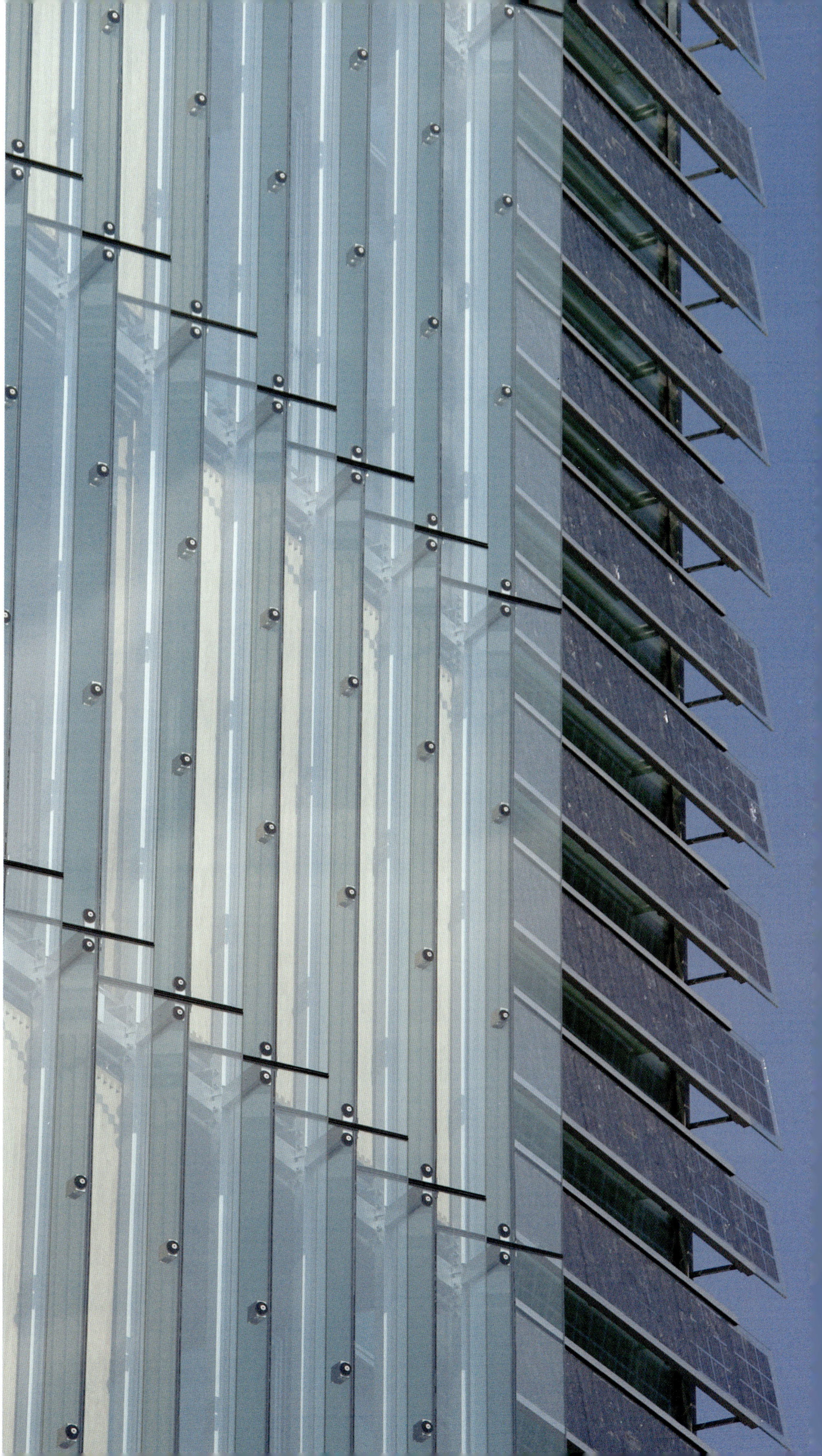

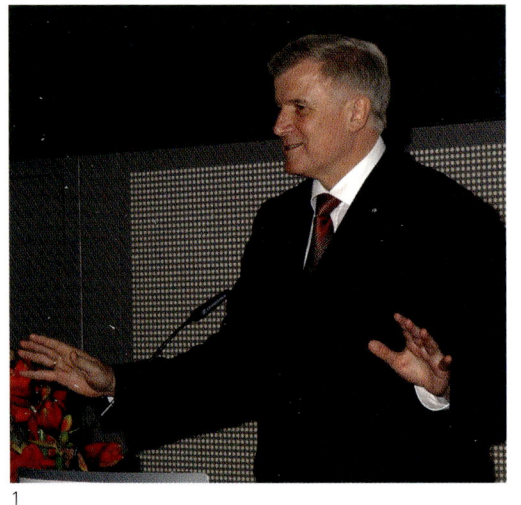
1

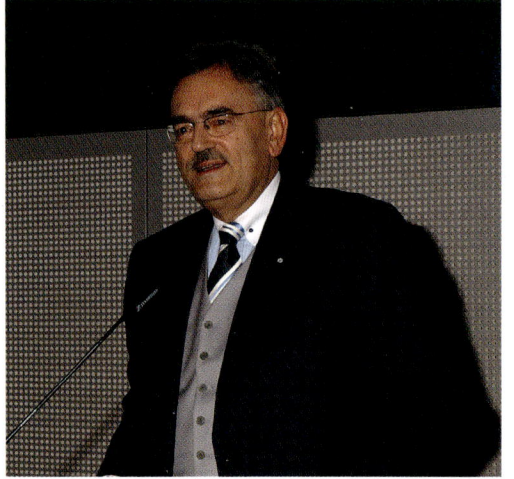
2

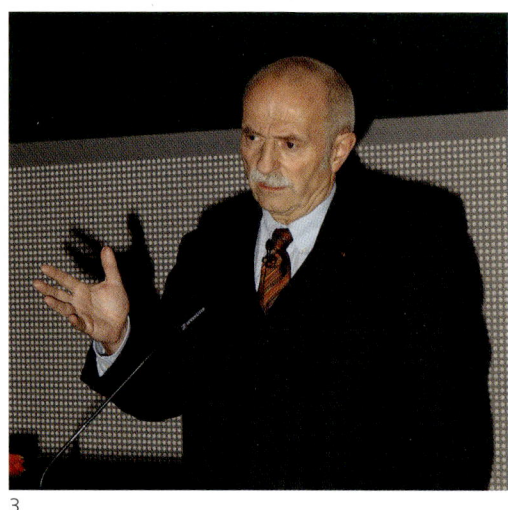
3

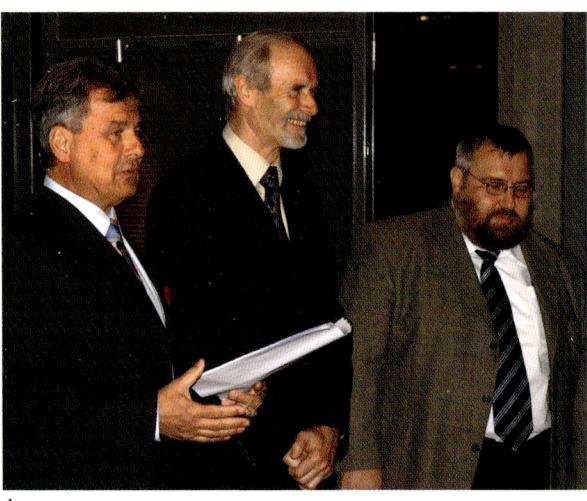
4

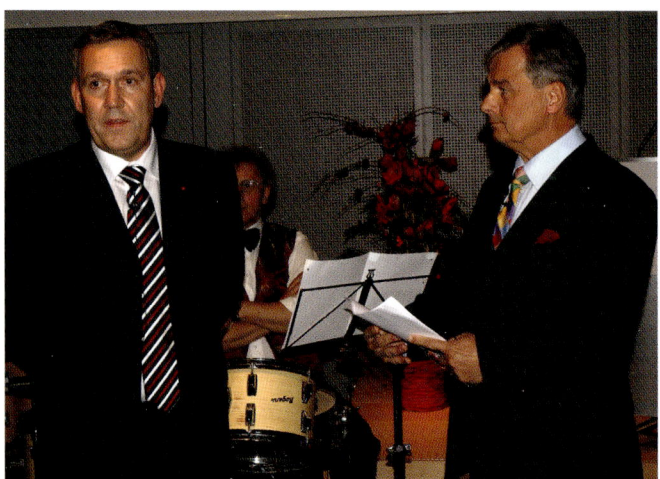
5

1 Horst Seehofer
2 Wolfgang A. Herrmann
3 Thomas Herzog
4 Gerhard Hess,
　Robert Frischeisen,
　Hans Beer
5 Gerhard Hess,
　Robert Feiger
6 Thomas Bauer,
　Horst Seehofer,
　Klaus Wiesehügel
7 Thomas Herzog,
　Robert Feiger
8 Klaus Wiesehügel
9 Christopher Krusche
10 Ernst Treitz
11 Christoph Valentien
12 Studierende aus dem Haus /
　 Students from the house
13 Segnung des Hauses /
　 Benediction of the building
14 Sabine Kammerl
15 Nikolaus Lang
16 Rainer Wittenborn,
　 Winfried Nerdinger
17 Dieter Zinner,
　 Thomas Berner
18 Kurt Stepan
19 Yann Friedl,
　 Roland Schneider
20 Hanns Jörg Schrade,
　 Peter Hross
21 Gerhard Hess,
　 Christine Thalgott
22 Horst Seehofer,
　 Verena Herzog-Loibl

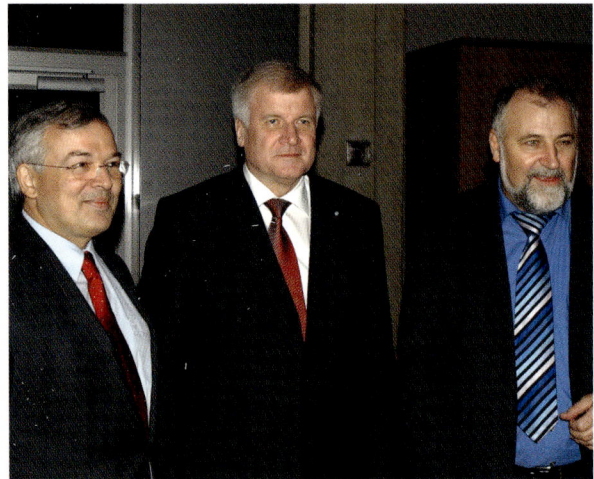
6

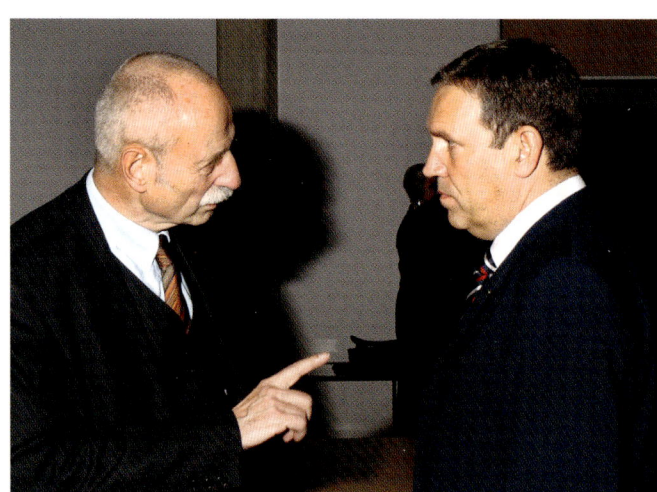
7

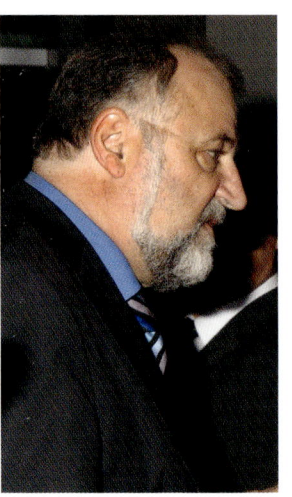
8

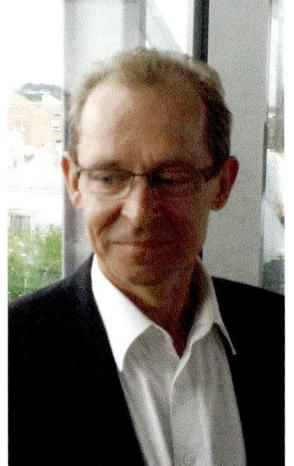
9

Bilder von der Einweihung und einige aus der Zeit davor

Images from the opening ceremony and before

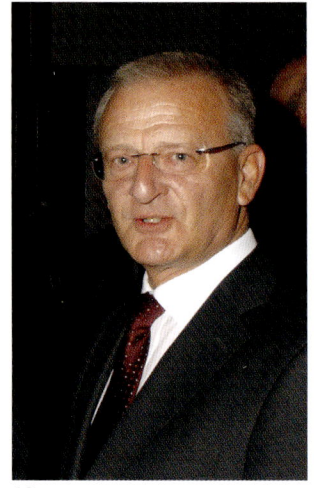
10

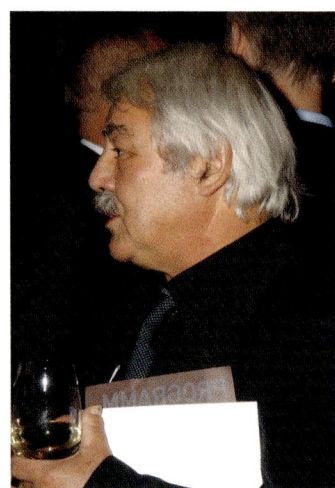
11

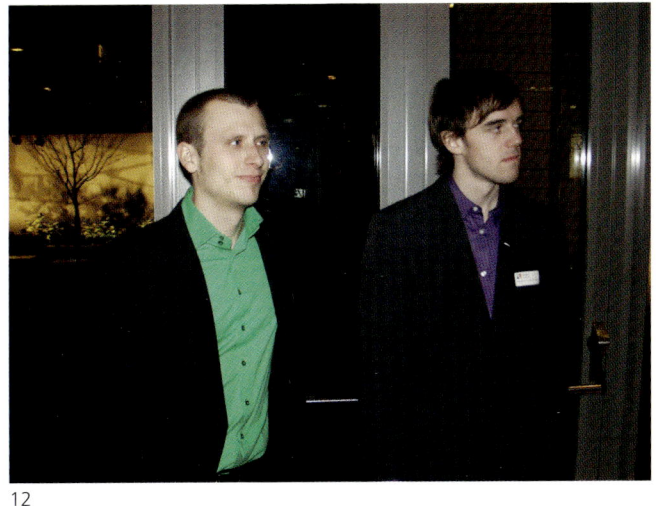

12

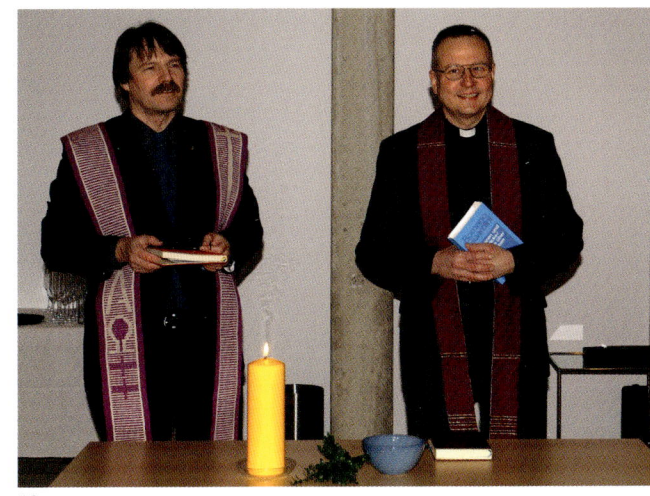

13

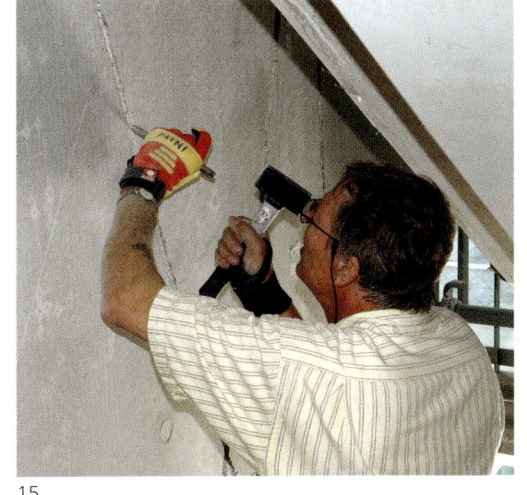

14

15

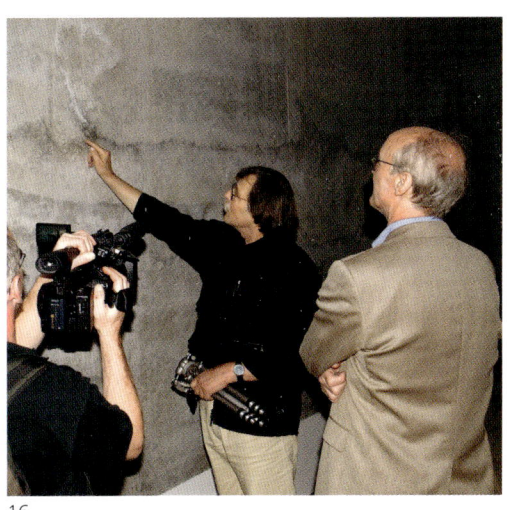

16

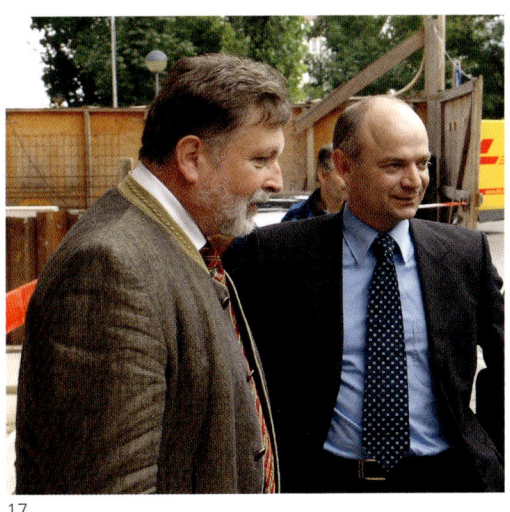

17

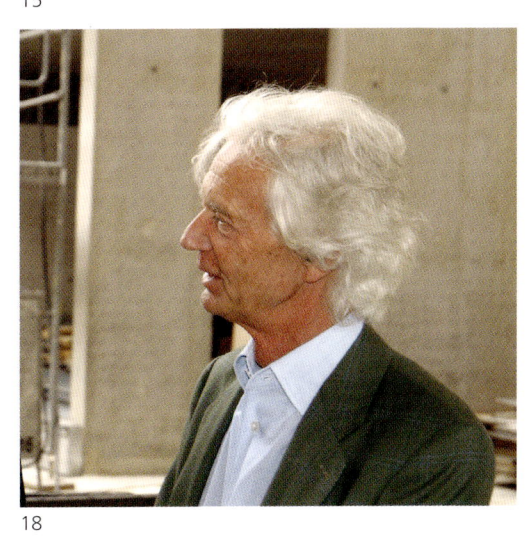

18

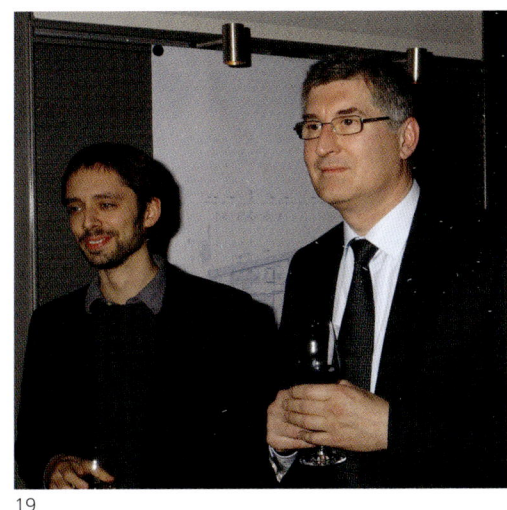

19

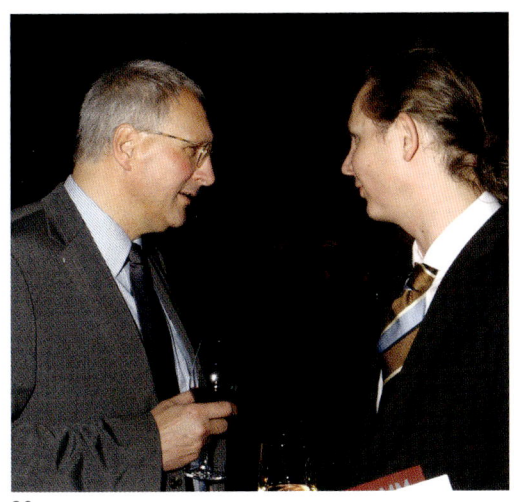

20

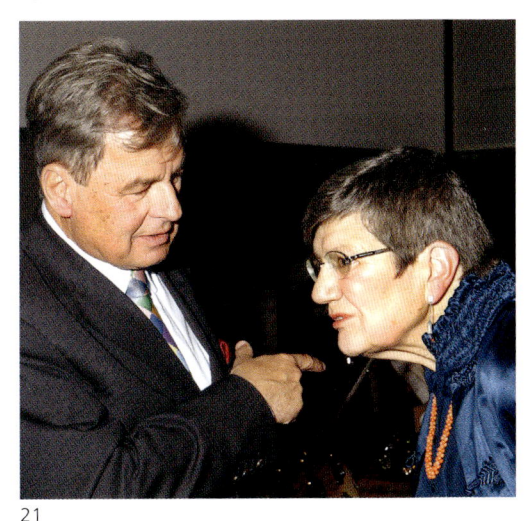

21

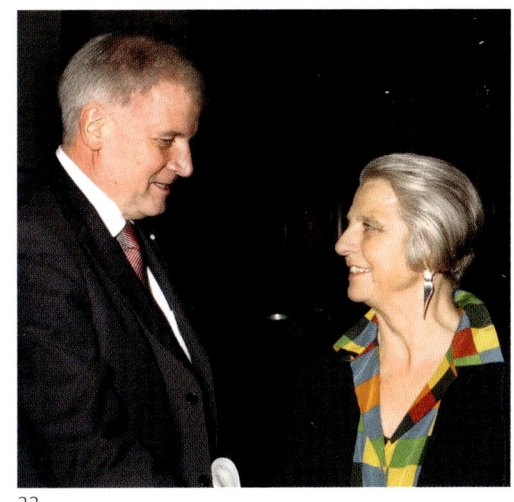

22

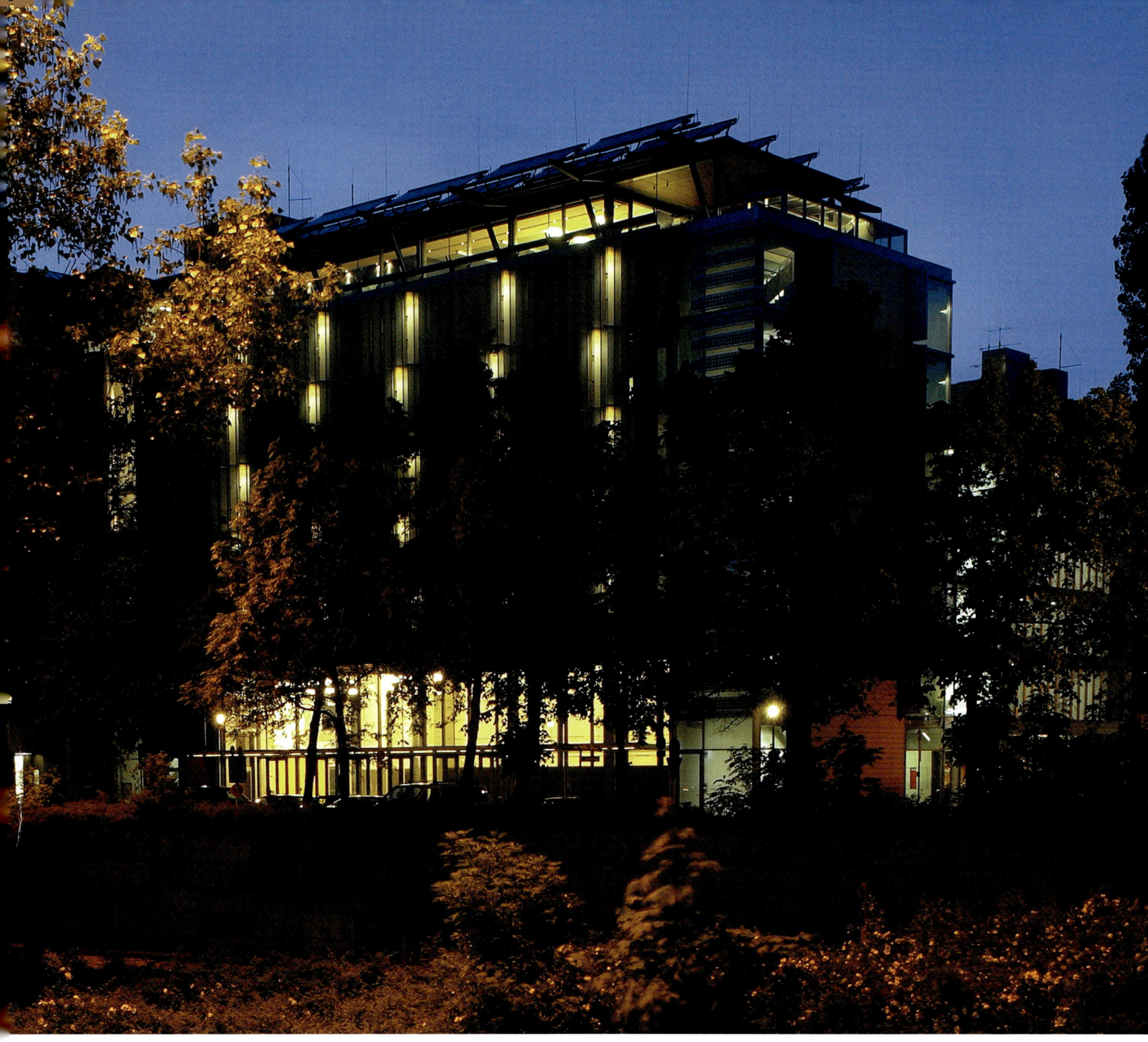

Bibliographische Informationen der Deutschen Nationalbibliothek:

Die Deutsche Nationalbibliothek verzeichnet diese Publikation in der Deutschen Nationalbibliographie; detaillierte bibliographische Daten sind im Internet über http://dnb.d-nb.de abrufbar.

© 2010 by Thomas Herzog und Hirmer Verlag GmbH, München

Design, layout, implementation, coordination
Cassian Herzog Communication Consulting

Beratung / Consultant
Verena Herzog-Loibl

Satz und Repro / Typesetting and Reprography
Vornehm Mediengestaltung GmbH, München

Übersetzung / Translations
Peter Green, München

Korrektorat / Proof-reading
Stefanie Adam, München, Jane Michael, München
Herstellung / Production
Gunnar Musan, Hirmer Verlag
Druck und Bindung / Printing and binding:
Printer Trento s. r. L, Trento

ISBN 978-3-7774-2921-2
Printed and bound in Italy

www.hirmerverlag.de